Alias "Paine"

Alias "Paine"

Lewis Thornton Powell, the Mystery Man of the Lincoln Conspiracy

Second edition

BETTY J. OWNSBEY

McFarland & Company, Inc., Publishers
Jefferson, North Carolina

When Lewis Thornton Powell crossed Union lines at Fairfax Court House, Virginia, on January 13, 1865, he gave his name to the provost marshal as Lewis *Paine*. He used this same name on the Oath of Allegiance he took in Baltimore on March 14, 1865. After his arrest on April 17, there was much speculation about his actual name. Some thought he was one of the notorious Payne brothers of Kentucky. This name stuck. He was charged as Payne, tried as Payne, and hanged as Payne. Where the name "Payne" appears in documents used in this book, this name has not been changed to Powell.

Frontispiece: Lewis Thornton Powell (Library of Congress).

LIBRARY OF CONGRESS CATALOGUING-IN-PUBLICATION DATA

Ownsbey, Betty J., 1953–
Alias "Paine" : Lewis Thornton Powell, the mystery man of the Lincoln conspiracy / Betty J. Ownsbey. — 2d ed.
    p.   cm.
Includes bibliographical references and index.

ISBN 978-0-7864-7623-7 (softcover : acid free paper) ∞
ISBN 978-1-4766-1437-3 (ebook)

1. Lincoln, Abraham, 1809–1865—Assassination.   2. Payne, Lewis, 1845–1865.   3. Booth, John Wilkes, 1838–1865—Friends and associates.   4. Soldiers—Confederate States of America—Biography.   I. Title.

E457.5.O96 2015   973.7092—dc23   2014049586

BRITISH LIBRARY CATALOGUING DATA ARE AVAILABLE

© 2015 Betty J. Ownsbey. All rights reserved

No part of this book may be reproduced or transmitted in any form or by any means, electronic or mechanical, including photocopying or recording, or by any information storage and retrieval system, without permission in writing from the publisher.

On the cover: Powell in irons aboard the monitor USS *Saugus* (Library of Congress); restrictive shackles, commonly called "lily irons," worn by Powell (Dr. John Lattimer Collection); Lewis Powell's Bowie knife inscribed with the words, "Rio Grande Camp Knife" (courtesy Huntington Library)

Printed in the United States of America

McFarland & Company, Inc., Publishers
Box 611, Jefferson, North Carolina 28640
www.mcfarlandpub.com

For the Surratt Society—
without whom this book would not
have come to pass

Acknowledgments

A book may have only one author, but the research is the combined work of many talented people.

No one anywhere could ever top the historical detective work and accuracy of the late Mr. James O. Hall of McLean, Virginia. His dedication to his craft had been unsurpassed for over forty years. To him I owe an immeasurable debt. He is greatly missed.

Three other "godparents" of this work were the late John C. Brennan, whose sharp-eyed grammatical accuracy, research "grapevine" and encouraging suggestions were invaluable; good friend and assassination scholar Michael W. Kauffman, whose pertinent historical data is so well versed in John Wilkes Booth and the assassination that one wonders if he wasn't actually there; and the late Dr. John K. Lattimer, who provided immense historical and medical data, including rare photographs and vast encouragement and interest which bolstered me during many rough times.

At the top of the "cheering section" among those who pushed and prodded me to write this book was the late Shyrl Littleton, fourth cousin of Lewis Thornton Powell, with whom I corresponded on a regular basis. Ms. Littleton was deeply interested in the project and provided much data which would otherwise have remained unknown. Although we never met, through our correspondence and telephone calls, we shared our research freely. Likewise, the late Jewell Powell Fillmon, grand-niece of Lewis Thornton Powell, was been equally helpful, particularly regarding information on Powell's boyhood and home life: many a late-night call lasted into the wee hours. Helen Alderman and Sharon Tate Powell, great-grand nieces of Lewis Powell, have also been wonderfully helpful as well as delightful friends. Richard Sloan generously offered encouragement and help as did the late Monsignor Rev. Robert Keesler with suggestions and help regarding photos.

There were others whose encouragement and interest formed a permanent bond of friendship: Dr. William Hanchett, professor of history at San Diego State University; William Tidwell; Frank Hebblethwaite; Ed Steers; Dr. William Coyle; Dr. Terry Alford, professor of history at Northern Virginia Community College; the late Arthur F. Loux; Arthur Candenquist; Dr. Richard Adicks, University of Central Florida; the late Dr. Constance Head; Nancy Scott, archivist, Gettysburg College; Joan Chaconas, former president of the Lincoln Group of the District of Columbia as well as a dear friend; Laurie Verge, site manager and historian of the historic Mary Surratt House and Tavern and another close friend; Nancy Griffith, past president and librarian of the Surratt Society and "undying Confederate" as well as comrade-in-arms; Vallianne Trusler, possessed of expertise in photographic matters; John Elliott and Barry Cauchon, who are familiar with just about *all* information on the conspirators' incarceration on board the monitors as well as at the Old Arsenal; Dr. Kate Larsen, for assistance with research and encouragement; Dr. Blaine

Houmes for medical expertise; Wesley Harris, weapons expert; Erik Jendresen; Roger Norton, whose wonderful online "Lincoln Discussion Symposium" has united friends and historians nationwide; Linda Anderson, Seward family expert, researcher and historian; Rich Smyth and Jim Garrett; William Richter, the *ultimate* professor; Rick Smith; Lindsey Horn; David Taylor; Madeleine Mitchell; N. Westervelt; Angela Smythe; Kari Peppers; the wonderful staff at the Seward Museum in Auburn, New York; Mary Kline, archivist for the Episcopal Diocese of Maryland for all of her help regarding St. Barnabas Episcopal Church; Larry Paarlberg, director of the General Lew Wallace Study and Museum; Susan Sutton, archivist, Indiana Historical Society; Susan Lempke, librarian at Fort Leslie J. McNair; Diana Speck; and all others whose interest has held for so long. Without these fine folk, I would have been lost.

And finally, to my family, who have patiently endured my absorption with the Civil War and Lewis Powell—to each and every one: a heartfelt and resounding "Thank you!"

Contents

Acknowledgments vii
Preface 1

1. Youth and Family: The Pieces of the Puzzle 3
2. In the Beginning: War 10
3. Captured: The Turning Point 14
4. Part-Time Partisan 19
5. The Baltimore Connection 30
6. Scandal and Skullduggery 37
7. "The Nest That Hatched the Egg" 43
8. The Road to Ruin 49
9. Countdown to Tragedy 54
10. April 14, 1865 58
11. Blood on the Moon 63
12. "How the Game Was Bagged" 73
13. In the Belly of the Whale 82
14. Blind Justice 89
15. "Hero Villainy": A Field Day for the Media 97
16. In the Shadow of Death 104
17. The Last Mile 111
18. Afterword 122

Appendices 127
Chapter Notes 193
Bibliography 202
Index 205

Preface

The Lincoln assassination continues to fascinate, as much today as it did in the previous century. A vast amount of literature has been devoted to the subject and a rousing argument can still arise over the facts surrounding those who were implicated.

In researching the life of Lewis Thornton Powell, I have consulted several primary sources, among them the three transcripts of the 1865 conspiracy trial. These include the "official" record compiled by Ben Pitman, the T. B. Peterson version, and the Ben Perley Poore edition. Of these three, the Peterson transcript covers the trial with the most clarity. Unfortunately, the official Pitman version had been extensively edited before publication and therefore lost a lot of the data covering the trial from a day to day basis. The 1867 John H. Surratt trial transcript published by the Government Printing Office contained information not disclosed during the 1865 trial.

Pertinent documents in the Lincoln Assassination Suspects' File, National Archives, were also consulted, as well as the various news releases and reports of the day. It is interesting to read the eyewitness accounts concerning Powell's demeanor while on trial. These give wonderful insight into his character. I have used, as much as possible, first-hand accounts from those associated with Powell in one way or another. Many of these were in the form of letters and journals, and most were written after the subsequent trial and executions.

Several newspaper articles were published more than thirty years later, in the 1880s, 1890s and at the turn of the century covering Powell's military career. The question still arises, was Powell recruited from Mosby's Rangers for secret actions directed at Lincoln and his cabinet?

Although there is no *concrete* evidence, there are enough accounts written after the conflict to substantiate this allegation. Both Gen. Bradley C. Johnson in 1869 and Lewis Edmonds Payne in 1882 confirmed that Powell was one of five men dispatched from Col. John Singleton Mosby's command for such an enterprise. Powell's later affiliations with John Surratt, Jr., and D. Preston Parr also give credence to the idea.

In an article written in 1892 by the son of the Rev. Dr. Abram Dunn Gillette, Powell's spiritual advisor in the death cell and on the gallows, Powell admitted to the minister that "for months previous while in the *Secret Service of the Confederacy* [author's italics], he had journeyed back and forth from Richmond to Washington and Baltimore in conference with prominent men in the latter city." He did not name the men. According to Gillette, these men kept him in funds and encouraged him with dreams of glory and the lasting gratitude of the Southern people.

Relatives of Powell have provided a wealth of family information. Both they and I hope this compilation will enhance study of the assassination by providing a multifaceted portrait of one of its most intriguing personalities.

1. Youth and Family: The Pieces of the Puzzle

The Arsenal reverberated with sounds: the tread of heavy boots on the cobbled floors, the clink of swords and spurs, shouted orders, the hollow thud of heavy iron doors.

On this particular morning, there was more bustle than usual. The air was heavy with tension. The stark skeleton of a gallows tree was being hastily constructed in the prison yard, its raw green wood gilded by the sharp rays of a July sun.

Four prisoners were to die this day of July 7, 1865, one of them a woman. Their crime, complicity in the assassination of President Abraham Lincoln.

In a small cramped cell on the first floor, the youngest of the four prayed with his spiritual advisor while waiting for the final hour. Young Lewis Thornton Powell sat manacled hand and foot on a lumpy mattress spread on the stone floor of his cell in company with the Rev. Dr. Abram D. Gillette of Washington's First Baptist Church.

This young man had shocked a nation by his one-man strike-force attack on United States Secretary of State William H. Seward and his household, an act coinciding with John Wilkes Booth's murder of the president on the night of April 14, 1865.

All during the sensational six-week trial which followed, Powell had shown a stoicism that defied all explanation. Even his death warrant was received by him without emotion, and he would walk to his premature death with a Spartan display that awed a nation.

The "Mystery Man" was what they called him. "Payne the Mysterious." (The correct spelling of the alias was "Paine," as it appeared on the confirmation copy of his Oath of Allegiance, dated March 14, 1865. The court records and newspaper reports of this time spelled the name "Payne.") He continues to be one of the most intriguing and controversial figures involved in the Lincoln assassination.

Almost everyone is familiar with the role played by John Wilkes Booth in the murder of President Lincoln, but there were other principals involved, one of whom was the twenty-year-old Confederate stalwart, Lewis Thornton Powell, at that time using the alias of Lewis Paine. Powell participated with a group of other like-minded young Southern sympathizers in an organized plot to abduct President Lincoln and hold him captive in exchange for Confederate prisoners of war confined in Northern prison camps—a scheme that abruptly turned to murder and then to Powell's own death on the gallows at age twenty-one, three months after his attempt to assassinate Secretary of State Seward.

Powell's name has been buried in obscure passages and paragraphs. Although history is splashed with blood and thunder adjectives used to describe him, a vastly different fellow existed from that which the press of 1865 painted; an extremely likeable and personable young man, a portrait which surprised many considering the heinous crime with which he was charged.

To get beneath the cloak of mystery which so completely shrouded Powell, one must delve into his origin. Col. William E. Doster, a former Washington provost marshal, who represented Powell during the conspiracy trial, valiantly tried this approach. His final argument before the court gave a brief but error-laden biography which laid the foundation for future historians. Since 1865 Doster's biography of Powell has been taken as gospel. That Powell did reveal *some* truths about himself is apparent. However, most of Doster's story is melodramatic fiction told in the best Victorian tradition in an attempt to sway the court's sympathy for a good boy gone wrong.

Using the correct information in Doster's background sketch in conjunction with important archival papers and documents which are available today, we can better understand our subject and perhaps broaden our perspective of this puzzling young man and his equally puzzling crime. As much a mystery as Powell himself is the unveiling of his family tree.

Initially, one might suspect that Powell's parents were related inasmuch as his mother's maiden name, as well as his father's surname, was Powell. The family asserts that they were second cousins. Although the genealogy of his mother's line has been worked out, little is known of his father's ancestry aside from the fact that he was descended from the Powell family of Virginia.

The maternal side of Powell's family can be traced as far back as 1600 in Bristol, England, and records show that the first progenitors on American soil probably sprang from one Richard Powell and his brothers, William and John, who settled in Norfolk County, Virginia, in 1663–64. Over the ensuing years, the family became scattered throughout the Carolinas, Virginia, and ultimately migrated into Georgia.[1]

Patience Caroline Powell, mother of Lewis, and her sister, Miranda B. Powell, were the daughters of William Powell and Mary (Polly) Cox Powell, of Jones County, Georgia. According to the Powell family Bible, Patience Caroline was born April 23, 1811. Her sister was born two years later. Very little is known of their early years, other than the fact that their father died shortly after Miranda's birth in 1813, apparently from wounds received in the War of 1812. The surviving daughters received a land grant dated January 16, 1835, for their father's wartime services.[2] Their widowed mother married William Rushin in 1817 and eventually moved to Alabama. Outliving her grandson Lewis, by three years, she died in 1868.

On March 23, 1830, Patience Caroline Powell married George Cader Powell.[3] The wedding took place in Talbot County, Georgia, and was performed by Patience's uncle by marriage, the Rev. Zachariah Gordon. Gordon's wife was a sister of Patience's mother, Mary Cox Powell. Zachariah and his wife, Melinda, were the parents of John Brown Gordon, a Confederate major general who subsequently became governor of the State of Georgia and a United States senator—giving him the distinction of being the first Southerner to serve in the Senate after the war and reconstruction. The illustrious General Gordon was a second cousin of Lewis Thornton Powell. Other highly esteemed family members were Lewis' great-great uncle Ichabod Cox, founder of Cox College, of College Park, Georgia. Chappel Cox, a distant cousin, had served in the legislature of Talbot County, Georgia, in the 1830s.

The records of Lewis's own birth are confused. Records from the Powell family Bible list Lewis' day of birth as April 23, 1844. Powell's father, in a letter to William Doster, gave the date as April 22, 1844. Doster himself, in his delivery to the court during the conspiracy trial proceedings, went one better and changed the year of birth to 1845, thus adding further

1. Youth and Family 5

to the confusion! Perhaps the infant was born sometime between the night and the early morning hours, hence the conflict of the exact date.

Since Lewis' military records show the birthdate of April 22, it would be reasonable to conclude that our subject was born on April 22, 1844.

By 1840, Mr. and Mrs. Powell with their five children, had moved from Georgia to Alabama. It was there, in Randolph County, that Lewis, the sixth surviving child out of eight, was born into a family that would total ten children by 1852—five girls and five boys, with Lewis being the youngest of the three surviving sons. The youngest boy, William L., died at ten months of age in 1852.[4]

It would be difficult to sustain the charge that Lewis' early life in some way contributed to his tragic end. Although details of Lewis' boyhood are sketchy at best, we shall see that he was raised in a moral and religious environment.

In 1844, George C. Powell was the assistant tax collector and later tax assessor for Randolph County, Alabama, a job he assumed apparently in addition to his regular task of farming. It wasn't until 1847 that George C. Powell was called to the ministry, and Lewis was three years old before he received his middle name.[5]

The versatile Mr. Powell received the "calling" at Liberty Baptist Church in Russell County, Alabama. So thrilled was he by his new religious convictions that he gave his youngest son, Lewis, the middle name of "Thornton," in honor of Powell's mentor and associate, Dr. Reuben Thornton, a Presbyterian clergyman of Charleston, South Carolina, who had served on his board of ordination. In deference to his new vocation, the Rev. Mr. Powell gave up his employment as tax assessor and settled down into the life of a rural clergyman and farmer while operating a small smithy as an additional source of income.

John Brown Gordon, second cousin of Lewis Thornton Powell (Library of Congress).

The Powell children were probably educated by their parents at home. Patience Caroline had exceptional educational advantages in an era when most young girls received only enough schooling to enable them to write their names and record a few scriptural passages on needlework samplers. In her youth, Patience had the good fortune to attend a school for young ladies in Jones County, Georgia.[6]

The Rev. Mr. Powell was well educated, widely read, and able to write a beautiful hand, as is verified by his letters now in the Manuscript Room of the Library of Congress. His qualifications enabled him to serve as schoolmaster at various times in the small rural school of the area.

This provides an incongruous backdrop to Doster's allegations that Lewis Powell was "rough and illiterate," a misstatement that continues to this very day in history books. The Rev. Dr. Abram Dunn Gillette, Powell's spiritual advisor in the death cell and on the gallows, was impressed with the boy's intelligence and stated that he was "of cultivated mind."[7] Various press releases of 1865 affirmed that "his manner is that of refinement, his speech, both in respect to grammar and pronunciation, gives evidence that he has had educational advantages."[8] Certainly such conscientious parents, with more than a rudimentary education, would not permit their children to grow up illiterate.

One may assume that rural life in the pioneer settings of the 1840s and 1850s consisted of more than a fair amount of manual labor, and the senior Powell was undoubtedly earning his bread by hard work. Young Lewis would, of course, be required to pitch in and help his father and brothers about their small farm.

Prior to the 1850s George Powell owned a few slaves, but a check of the 1850 census shows no listing for him in the slave schedules. He did have hired domestic help, however, possibly ex-slaves. The 1850 marriage of Lewis's oldest sister, Mary Ann Caroline, to James O. Newman, brought yet another hand to help about the farm. There is no support for Doster's allegations at the conspiracy trial that Lewis was given the responsibility to supervise his father's "slaves" after the war broke out in 1861. He had no slaves then.

However, according to the *Church Record Minutes of Fort Early Baptist Church* (now Warwick First Baptist Church, Warwick, Worth County, Georgia) 1837–1865, a listing for 1859 has one "Nelson, Jr., property of Patience C. Powell." Apparently this Nelson was the son of another slave, Nelson Sr., who is listed as the "Property of" G.W. Bryant, an apparent Powell neighbor.[9]

When Lewis was four years old, the family moved to Georgia to settle in Stewart County. The Powells would remain in Georgia for the next eleven years until, according to the reminiscences of Lewis's younger sister, Angeline; George was forced to sell his farm when a friend for whom he endorsed a note refused to meet his obligation. The good Reverend Powell therefore packed his family and their belongings into a wagon pulled by four mules and headed to Florida, settling in Belleville, Hamilton County.[10]

Recently located records indicate that in the early to mid–

Copy of daguerreotype of Lewis Powell, at approximately two years of age, and his mother, Patience Caroline Powell (courtesy Sharon Powell Tate and the late Jewell Powell Fillmon, grandniece of Lewis Thornton Powell).

1850s the family was living in the community of Green Hill, though that may also be the name of the farm itself. Research shows that Green Hill was the name of a community post office in the uppermost region of Steward County, Georgia.[11] Reverend Powell had accepted a pastorate at Beulah Baptist Church, a sizeable fellowship of 138 members, 41 of which Reverend Powell baptized in 1851.[12]

By the mid–1850s, Reverend Powell was pastor at Fort Early Baptist Church in Worth County, Georgia. Minutes from the church give a good indication of what went on within the congregation, and Entry No. 153, dated July 10–11, 1858, states: "Opened the Door of the Church and received Brother G C Powell, Sister Patience Powell, Sister Lydia Powell, Brothers Oliver H Powell and Lewis T Powell ... all by letter." This apparently means that young Powell joined his father's church at this time. Likewise, Entry No. 163, September 10–11, 1859, clarifies that "Brother George C Powell application for Brother H Vines for letter of dismission for himself and Family and the same was granted."[13] This is about the time that the Powell family prepared to move to Florida.

Copy of daguerreotype of the Reverend George C. Powell, father of Lewis Thornton Powell (courtesy Sharon Powell Tate and the late Jewell Powell Fillman, grandniece of Lewis Thornton Powell).

The oldest son, Benjamin, had married on January 1, 1855, and subsequently moved to Florida with his bride, Sarah Ann Hooper. This may have further influenced his father to settle there with the rest of the family after the financial difficulty suffered in 1859. Benjamin died shortly afterwards on June 9, 1859.[14]

Having been brought up under a strong religious influence, Lewis Powell was sensitive, intense, and thoughtfully reserved in nature, very much an introvert. He had learned to whittle at an early age and was highly proficient at carving various whistles and toys out of wood. An animal lover, he was always bringing strays home and caring for the injured ones about the farm, earning him the nickname of "Doc" from his sisters. The nickname stuck.

Lewis had a pet mule which he had raised and which followed him around like a dog. One morning, when Lewis was about twelve years old, he was playing outside by the back door and was attempting to do something with the animal when it kicked him. The injury was severe; resulting in a broken left jaw and a lost molar, and quite possibly a broken nose into the bargain. The unconscious child was quickly packed into the family wagon and driven to the nearest doctor. His mother was understandably upset and wanted his father to sell the mule. The Rev. Powell demurred, saying that to sell the animal would break Lewis' heart. The boy loved his pet, and inasmuch as he had raised and cared for him, Lewis should be allowed to keep him. It seems Lewis had been tickling the animal with a straw, while he and his sister Angeline giggled at watching its skin quiver. The mule tired of the play and thus kicked Lewis, prompting his father to remark that it was a "dumb thing to do."

The boy had acquired various pets, including dogs and kittens, as well as chickens, guinea hens, and a goat in addition to the mule. Lewis also had a tiny orphaned puppy which he had found and brought home to nurse, making a sugar tit out of a rag for the baby animal to suckle.[15]

Lewis' sisters remembered him as being a "sweet, lovable, kind young boy" who was "pious, tender-hearted," and much devoted to Sunday school, prayer meetings and other religious activities.[16] His father reminisced, "When he was 14 or 15 years of age, he would hold prayer meetings and could speak with ease and force. He was very popular with all and seemed to be a great favorite with the ladies."[17] Young Lewis was so proud of his first teaching engagement in church that his parents took him into town afterwards and had his photograph taken. A handsome youngster, he gazes confidently into the camera, proudly sporting a large watch guard chain across his vest front. Lewis took immense pride in his watch, a gift from his parents. He had seen the watch in a store window and coveted it, saving his pocket money in hopes of making the purchase. Upon the occasion of his twelfth birthday and subsequent baptism by his father, Lewis' parents realized that the boy still did not have enough money to make the purchase, and putting up the balance, bought the watch for him."[18] Reverend Powell remembered a streak of stubbornness threaded throughout his youngest son's character and recalled that he was marked by determination in all of his undertakings.[19] Dan McAlpin, editor of a Florida newspaper, remembered young Powell as possessing a fierce temper and stated that the whole family was "hot-headed."[20]

Young Lewis, in keeping with a great many rural youths of the day, loved to pursue his favorite sport of fishing. He would always hurry and finish his chores so that he could grab up his pole and head for the river. Joshua Hoyet Frier, a neighboring boy, recalled how "Doc" Powell's fondness for the sport lured him away one Sabbath morning to play "hooky" from Sunday school. "He [Powell] told me he had slipped off one Sunday morning with tackle for some sport and caught 'the Devil.' He had a terrible fight to land him and when he finally succeeded, he came near biting off one of his fingers and walked right back into the water." An old black man explained what Lewis had caught that day. From the descrip-

Tintype of Lewis Thornton Powell, age twelve (courtesy Rufus Yent, great-grandnephew of Lewis Powell).

tion he gave of it, Frier concluded that Lewis caught an alligator ("snapping") turtle.[21] This episode accomplished a reform. Lewis quit fishing on Sunday.

Like most children, Lewis loved to climb trees. He had a tree-house which he called "The Perch." One evening, after calling for him repeatedly, his mother could not find him. As dusk and suppertime approached, his father and brothers went looking for him, and going into the woods, found him curled up asleep in a tree, beneath which stood his pet mule.

When Lewis was about 8 or 9 years of age, he and his younger sister, Angeline ("Annie") went against their mother's warnings and decided to go skinny-dipping in a pond on their father's property. The children stripped down and, folding their clothing on the bank, splashed about in the water. When they emerged from their swim, they found a large black snake curled up on their clothing. Rather than disturb the reptile, the children ran naked down the road, much to the amusement of a passing neighbor. When they reached home, Lewis and his sister were admonished by their mother and told they would have to do additional chores for the next two weeks which would entail slopping the hogs and milking. Lewis made a deal with his sister, telling her he would slop hogs if she would milk, and Lewis even offered to carry the milk pails for her. When time came to slop hogs, Lewis fulfilled his part of the deal, but went into a sulk and climbing up into the Perch, refused to come down, leaving Annie to carry the heavy milk pails.

Lewis' mother scolded him, telling him that "good boys do not try and deceive their sisters but strive to help them." The repentant little boy thereafter offered to do both the milking as well as slopping the hogs for the following two weeks.[22]

Upon his baptism, Lewis expressed a desire to be a minister and to follow in the footsteps of his father as well as his namesake, Dr. Thornton. When the family would gather in the evenings in the parlor, Lewis would sing his favorite hymn, "The Convert's Farewell," to the family.[23] Lewis possessed a "fine voice" and liked to sing. His sisters remembered hearing him singing to himself when going about his work or playing with his pets. His mother probably had cause to dote on him. She was a loving, attentive woman who seemingly lived for her children and took good care of them. Lewis loved his mother immensely, and perhaps he was a bit spoiled, being the youngest boy in a family made up largely of women. Patience Caroline must have taken a little extra pride in her youngest son. After all, he was the one who wanted to be like his father, and it did seem as if Lewis was destined to follow him into the ministry.[24]

Fate, in the guise of war, would find a way to direct Lewis away from this path and into the Civil War.

2. In the Beginning: War

A dark cloud was settling over the land, a land torn by states' rights and abolitionism. With John Brown's raid in 1859, the South saw the portents of bloodshed and war. The Northern Republicans were sympathetic and openly supportive of the abolitionists' activities, a slap in the face to the South. One by one, the Southern states dropped out of the Union to form their own independent Confederacy. The portents of war extended down into Florida, casting a gloom over the small turpentine village of Live Oak in Suwannee County, and the population waited for the inevitable conflict to begin.

Sometime during 1860, George C. Powell and family had moved from Hamilton County to the outskirts of the small settlement of Live Oak on the railroad between Jacksonville and Tallahassee. The Rev. Powell had established a church in Apopka, Florida, in the same year, so this may have occasioned the move from Belleville. At any rate, the family was living a half mile from Live Oak Station at the outbreak of the rebellion. Another move sometime during the war would find the family six miles further down the railroad.

With his thick, dark brown hair and large, penetrating blue-gray eyes, Lewis was growing into a strikingly handsome youth whose dimpled smile and easy-going, affable ways made him many friends. Over six feet one and one-half inches tall at seventeen years of age, long and lean in build, he made quite an impressive picture, combining in his makeup his father's stoic reserve, height, and finely proportioned frame. Heavily muscled and broad-shouldered, he was more than likely strengthened by the work in his father's smithy and seemed much older than his seventeen years.

He had good reason to want to appear more a man than a teenager. The military fever was spreading hot and fast, extending even into the deep backwoods of sparsely settled Florida. It caught and fired the imagination of Reverend Powell's impressionable young son. When Florida voted to secede on January 10, 1861, thereby becoming the third state to sever ties with the Union, Lewis was but sixteen years old, certainly too young for enlistment. But enlist he would!

By the time his seventeenth birthday had rolled around on April 22, 1861, Lewis, along with a friend, Samuel A. Mitchell, had managed to join the Jasper (Hamilton) Blues. Lewis gave his age upon enlistment as nineteen.[1] Located in Hamilton County, this outfit would subsequently become Company I of the Second Florida Infantry. (See Appendix B.)

Lewis was the first of the three Powell boys to answer the call to arms. His enlistment date is given in his military records as May 30, 1861, with the muster-in date of July 13, 1861.[2] The older brothers did not enlist until much later, neither of them serving in the same regiment. Oliver Powell enlisted on September 5, 1861, in Company C, Fourth Florida Infantry, and George, on May 12, 1862, Company B, Tenth Florida Infantry.[3]

Apparently the Rev. Powell at first had mixed emotions about his youngest son going into the military. During the conspiracy trial proceedings, Lewis told his attorney, William E. Doster, that he had enlisted over his parents' protests by persuading the authorities to believe that he was nineteen years of age. His muscular development being well advanced for his age, he was accepted into service, and the admonitions that awaited him at home can only be imagined.

Eventually, the Rev. Powell decided to go along with his youngest son's enlistment. After all, the boy *had* volunteered. If the thought of revealing his son's true age to the authorities ever occurred to him, the father must have rejected the idea of opposing his son's service to the Confederacy and to a seemingly "righteous" cause. Other parents were making the same sacrifice. Like the father of the prodigal son, he would give the boy his blessing and await his return. The conflict wasn't scheduled to last long anyway—perhaps a few months or a year at the most. If he couldn't stop Lewis from enlisting, he would do what he could to see that his son enlisted *properly!*

An article which appeared in the *Washington Star* for December 3, 1887, recounted

Lewis T. Powell at age sixteen, one year previous to joining the Confederate army (courtesy Rufus Yent, great-grandnephew of Lewis Powell).

among other things that "Reverend Powell ... was very careful in *selecting a captain* for his son, Lewis, then scarcely grown ... to enlist under. He went into his former county and placed [Lewis] under one of the best in the Confederate Army ... Judge H. J. Stewart, of Hamilton County, who would exert a sort of parental control ... along with the military." If this account is to be believed, Lewis thus left home with his parents' somewhat reluctant consent. Another account tells of young Lewis coming home to proudly report his enlistment to his parents. Enraged, his father hustled the boy into the family wagon and drove him back to town, demanding that the mortified youth divulge his true age to the enlisting officer. Somehow, young Lewis was then able to persuade his father to allow him to enlist by giving parental consent.

Allowed to enlist, Lewis was "kitted up" at home by his mother. Patience Caroline apparently made sure that her youngest son had the proper apparel and means. Mrs. Powell was said to have a special talent with a needle and thread and always kept her sewing basket near. Among Lewis' most cherished possessions that he would take away from home was a "fine little embroidered pin cushion"; part of his soldier's "housewife" sewing kit. Young Powell would keep this pincushion with him until the very end.[4] (See Appendix L.)

Regardless of his means of enlistment, and in spite of his enthusiasm for a military life, it would appear that at first, army life did not suit young Powell. He became extremely ill with the measles and was confined in a military hospital in Jacksonville missing his company's departure for Richmond in July of 1861.

Lewis was so ill that his mother received a letter from his commander indicating that the boy appeared to be dying.[5] Upon his recovery three months later, Lewis was reunited with his unit in Richmond.

The following year, from June 30 to November 5, 1862, Private Powell would again be hospitalized, this time admitted to the Florida Hospital (also known as the Globe Hospital or General Hospital number eleven) in Richmond.

Having finally adapted to the life of a foot soldier, Powell re-enlisted for the duration of the war on June 23, 1862, and received his fifty-dollar bounty. It wasn't long before he was in the thick of rough army life, and the gentle, pious youth soon found himself caught up in its temptations. Everyday camp life hardened him, and he became like his companions, full of pranks and boyish spirits—good natured and ready for devilish fun. Gradually he fell away from his strict upbringing, although occasionally homesick, he would write his parents wanting to know about his pets, and stated that he "never really appreciated his home until after he had joined the army."[6]

A Lakeland, Florida, resident remembered that

> army life caused him [Powell] to fall away from his piety; but he did not become a prey to drink, that arch enemy to many soldiers. He did become rather fond of cards ... his captain once had him sentenced to mark time between bayonets several days for gross neglect of his rifle. The next day in crossing the camp, [the captain] suddenly came upon the execution of his punishment. The culprit was stepping away hard and the perspiration was running down his face in streams, but instead of "sulking," he smiled so good naturedly at his captain that this officer had the sentence remitted. He had become warmly attached to his captain.[7]

The same source also related that "he was not a surly, but a happy boy, full of fun and frolic." His frolicsome disposition is evident in the following incidents:

> Once, while enjoying a short soldier's leave of absence in one of the Virginia towns, he took down a pair of pantaloons in front of a store and folded them and walked in and sold them to the owner. At another time, he sent a shop-keeper in hot chase down the street after an innocent person when he and his comrade helped themselves to what they wanted.
>
> Powell was good at foraging and whatever he got was freely shared with his mess or company. He was endowed with high health and athletic strength.[8]

No doubt, his soldierly qualities and massive strength would stand him in good stead later on when he became a part of J. Wilkes Booth's conspiracies. Lewis had considerable spunk, and his army record is good. He participated in most of the major campaigns, and he was inured to battle by the time he was twenty. Baptized by fire at the siege of Yorktown in the spring of 1862, Private Powell later savored the taste of battle at Williamsburg, Seven Pines, Gaines Mill, Beaver Dam Creek, and Frayser's Farm. Incarcerated in the Florida military hospital in Richmond for most of the summer and fall of 1862, he rejoined his unit in late November of that year and although present, was held in reserve at the Battle of Fredericksburg. With the opening of the Spring Campaign of 1863, he saw action at Chancellorsville.

It was after the first of the year of 1863 that Lewis was advised of the death of one of his elder brothers, Oliver. A private of Company C, Fourth Florida Infantry, the twenty-three-year-old Oliver saw his last battle at Murfreesboro during the Stone River Campaign.

A member of Preston's Brigade, First Division of J. C. Breckenridge under William J. Hardee's Third Corps, Oliver had fallen mortally wounded under heavy fire. The battle of Murfreesboro lasted from December 31, 1862, until January 5, 1863. Oliver died one day after the conflict ended, on January 6, 1863.[9]

George W. would be the sole survivor of the four Powell boys. Although seriously wounded in the siege of Petersburg near the end of the war and maimed for life, he would return home to his family. Service records do not state the extent of his wounds, but family accounts describe him as a cripple who walked with a cane for the rest of his life, having been shot in the thigh, leaving one leg shorter than the other.[10]

Although young Lewis was aware of Oliver's death, he seems to have assumed that George was also slain.[11] His reaction remains unrecorded. Just how much these personal tragedies affected Lewis may be evident in the tragedy of April 14, 1865.

3. Captured: The Turning Point

The early summer of 1863 found Lewis' regiment of the Second Florida Infantry a part of the Army of Northern Virginia. Under the command of General A. P. Hill, the army moved into the hazy foothills of Pennsylvania, each step bringing them closer to a little town called Gettysburg and a massive battle that would mark the beginning of the end for the Confederacy as well as the beginning of a new phase of Lewis Powell's brief military career. During this, his final campaign, Powell was fighting as a member of Perry's Brigade in Maj. Gen. R. H. Anderson's Division, a part of A. P. Hill's Third Corps.

Powell would tell Doster that he participated in Pickett's charge on July 3, 1863, but this was more than likely just braggadocio. His military records clearly state that he was wounded on the day before the famous assault on the Federal center, and it was on July 2 that he took a gunshot wound in his right wrist. Captured the following day, he was admitted to the Twelfth Army Corps Field Hospital, Army of the Potomac, on July 4. Two days later, Powell was a patient at Pennsylvania College, then in use as a makeshift hospital. Confederate army records would now carry him as a prisoner of war to the end of hostilities in April 1865. Although records do not state the seriousness of his particular injury, a gunshot through the wrist could not have been too incapacitating a wound, because Powell was soon serving as a male nurse at the hospital. Apparently his right arm was broken as a result of the wound, because he was described as having his arm in a splinted sling. Broken bones aside, the surgeons would be understandably relieved to have the helping hand of this strong and capable youngster, who was characterized as being "good at the work and kind to the sick and wounded."[1] Apparently Powell went about his duties ungrudgingly. After all, if he had to be a POW, being a hospital steward was preferable to being consigned to the living hell of a prison camp.

About mid–July, a very attractive diversion, in the form of starched petticoats and aprons, arrived from Baltimore. Miss Margaret Branson left her mother's boarding house, at 16 North Eutaw Street in Baltimore and in accompaniment of her older cousin, Mrs. A. Dubois Egerton, and other Baltimore ladies, traveled the fifty-four miles to Gettysburg to offer her services as a nurse. Later described as an avid secessionist, she went to the hospital determined to care for the Confederate wounded.[2]

To let Maggie Branson speak for herself: "I have sent provisions, etc., to [Confederate] prisoners at Forts McHenry and Johnson's Island ... I have never taken the Oath of Allegiance."[3]

Powell was evidently playing the role of male nurse to the hilt, as Margaret would remember that he went by the name of *Doctor* Powell. Recuperating at an amazing rate, Powell was up and about, dressed in his regimental sky blue pants, a white shirt and a slouch hat, assisting the Baltimore lady on her medical rounds. An intimacy of some kind soon

Wests Buildings Hospital, Baltimore, Maryland—The Federal Infirmary from which Powell escaped in September 1863, possibly aided by Margaret Branson (courtesy the late Reverend Robert Kessler).

developed between the teenage Confederate soldier and the young spinster. According to Assistant Secretary of War Maj. Thomas T. Eckert, Powell related that he had fallen in love with his nurse at Gettysburg.[4] Or was it just that this woman, so ardently pro–Confederate, reminded the boy of his own sisters back home? After three years of coarse masculine company in the army, Lewis was probably delighted with this female companionship. No matter that Maggie was thirty years old to Lewis' callow age of nineteen.

All throughout July and August of 1863, Doctor Powell continued his nursing duties in the Gettysburg hospital, and by the end of the summer seems to have found himself a well established prisoner of another sort. In addition to being a POW of the United States Government, he now found himself held captive by feminine charms.

On September 1, Lewis was turned over to the provost marshal, who decided that he could continue his usefulness to the U.S. Government serving as a nurse in the Wests Buildings Hospital in Baltimore.

A North Carolina soldier, Henry E. Shepherd, wounded in the knee at Gettysburg and like young Powell, captured on the third day of the battle, had some horrid recollections of the hell hole which was West Buildings Hospital:

> On the 14th of August I was taken to Baltimore. Upon arriving, I was forced to march with a number of fellow prisoners from Camden Station to the office of the Provost Marshal, then situated at the Gilmor House, directly facing the Battle Monument. The weather was intensely hot, and my limb was bleeding from the still unhealed wound. After an exhausting delay, I was finally removed in an ambulance to the "West Hospital" at the end of Concord Street, looking out upon Union Dock and the wharves at that time occupied by the Old Bay Line or Baltimore Steam Packet Company.
> The West Building was originally a warehouse intended for the storage of cotton, now

transformed into a hospital by the Federal government. It had not a single element of adaptation for the purpose to which it was applied.

The immense structure was dark, gloomy, without adequate ventilation, devoid of sanitary, hygienic appliances or conveniences, and pervaded at all times by the pestilential exhalations which arose from the neighboring docks. During the seven weeks of my sojourn here, I rarely tasted a glass of cold water, but drank, in the broiling heat of the dog days, the warm, impure draught that flowed from the hydrant adjoining the ward in which I lay. My food was mush and molasses with hard bread, served three times a day.

When I reached the West Building, I was almost destitute of clothing, for such as I had worn was nearly reduced to fragments, the surgeons having mutilated it seriously while treating my wound received at Gettysburg. My friends made every effort to furnish me with a fresh supply but without avail. The articles of wearing apparel designed for me were appropriated by the authorities in charge, and the letter which accompanied them was taken unread from my hands. Moreover, my friends and relatives, of whom I had not a few in Baltimore, were rigorously denied all access to me; if they endeavored to communicate with me, their letters were intercepted; and if they strove to minister to my relief in any form, their supplies were turned back at the gate of the hospital, or confiscated to the use of the wardens and nurses.

On one occasion a party of Baltimore ladies who were anxious to contribute to the well being of the Confederate prisoners in the West Building, were driven from the sidewalk by a volley of decayed eggs hurled at them by the hospital guards. I was present when this incident occurred, and hearing the uproar, limped from my bunk to the window, just in time to see the group of ladies assailed by the eggs retreating up Concord Street in order to escape these missiles. They were soon out of range, and their visit to the hospital was never repeated, at least during my sojourn within its walls.

I remained in West Hospital until September 29th, 1863.... A word in reference to the methods of treatment, medical and surgical, which prevailed in West Hospital, may serve to illustrate the immense advance in those spheres of science, since the period I have in contemplation—1863–64. Lister had only recently promulgated his beneficent and far reaching discovery, *aseptics*; and even the use of anesthetics, which had been known to the world for nearly fifteen years, was awkward, crude and imperfect. The surgeons of that time seemed to be timorous in the application of their own agency, and the carnival of horrors which was revealed on more than one occasion in the operating room, might have engaged the loftiest power of tragic portrayal displayed by the author of "The Inferno." The gangrene was cut from my wound, as a butcher would cut a chop or a steak in the Lexington market; it may have been providential that I was delivered from the anesthetic blundering then in vogue, and "recovered in spite of my physician." Consideration originating in sensibility, or even in humanity, found no place in West Hospital. To illustrate concretely, a soldier, severely wounded, was brought into the overcrowded ward in which I lay. There was no bunk or resting place at his disposal, but one of the stewards recognizing the exigency, soon found a ghastly remedy. "Why," he said, pointing to a dying man in his cot, "that old fellow over there will soon be dead and as soon as he is gone, we'll put this man in his bed." And so the living soldier was at once consigned to the uncleansed berth of his predecessor.[5]

Described as a virtual pestilence hole, the notorious West Buildings with its inhumane conditions and crowded throngs of wounded was described as such a horror that one did not have to die to go to hell.

When Powell was transferred to the Pratt Street Baltimore West Hospital on September 2, Margaret followed—a much more convenient "close to home" arrangement for the lady— especially in view of what occurred next.

There are few, if any, accounts of how Lewis managed to escape from the hospital a few days after his arrival on September 7, but most writers agree that Powell's escape had something of a "woman's touch" involved in it.

In a letter to Colonel H. L. Burnett, judge advocate of the 1865 conspiracy proceedings,

Samuel S. Bond, a hospital steward of the surgeon general's office, recites the following in reference to Miss Branson and her activities at the Gettysburg Hospital and Hospital West buildings:

> Surgeon General Off.
> Washington City, D. C.
> June 3rd, 1865
>
> Colonel,
> I perceive by reading the Proceedings of the trial on Saturday the 3rd inst. that a Margaret Branson was a witness for the defense.
> Desiring that all evidence adduced shall tend to conviction of the guilty, and acquittal of the innocent, I feel it my duty to inform you as one of the prosecuting officers in the trial that Miss Branson while a female nurse in the General Hospital in Gettysburg together with several others was always considered as a strong sympathizer with the rebellion, coming to the Hospital for the purpose of caring for the wants of the rebel wounded therein;—about the time of her departure from the Hospital, or a day or two previous, a first Sergt. of the Rebel Army who was nearly recovered from his wounds, a man of unusual intelligence and one of the most unyielding of all the rebels we had, in company with some eight or nine others made their escape from the Hospital and were never heard from afterwards; it was the general belief that they were assisted in their escape by this Miss Branson and another of the same stripe, who left about, or at the same time; this lady was always considered as devoted to the interest and success of the rebel cause, and associated only with those of the same proclivities; the loyal lady nurses refusing to associate with them; there are some others now in this city who will bear me out in these statements I have no doubt, they having been on duty in the Hospital at the time.
> I was the Chief Steward of the Hospital referred to.
> I have the honor to be very Respectfully Yours,
> Samuel S. Bond
> Hospital Steward, U.S. Army Surgeon Generals Office[6]

One particular passage in the preceding letter seems to hit the nail right on the head: "a first sergeant of the Rebel Army, nearly recovered from his wounds, *a man of unusual intelligence and one of the most unyielding of all the rebels."*

This in itself sounds like a minute characterization of Lewis Powell—not at all unlike the journalists' "pencil sketches" which appeared in the various newspapers across the country during the conspiracy trial. Powell was a shrewd fellow and as his bearing during the trial would testify, was "most unyielding."

Perhaps a masquerade as a first sergeant would help distinguish him from Private Powell, whose reputation as a male nurse was well known to the authorities about the hospital. If this assumption is correct, then this was just the beginning of Lewis' long line of aliases.

Apparently Margaret was quite adept at carrying off this charade, but she gave herself away when giving a statement to Lt. H. B. Smith in March of 1865: "if he [Powell] wore a blue uniform when he came from Gettysburg, it was worn to aid him in getting south; it was not worn to act as a spy."[7]

More than likely, so close to home, Miss Branson found it no trouble in Baltimore to obtain a Union uniform and money to arrange Lewis' escape.

An unidentified source states: "a young lady's sympathy was so aroused for him that she managed to convey to him a Federal uniform and money which enabled him to leave the prison. According to this version, two of his fellow soldiers saw him leave in such a uniform. One watching saw him halted by the sentinel, when he parlayed a little, handed him something, supposed to be a bribe and passed out [of the hospital]."[8]

Young Samuel Mitchell, Lewis's comrade and crony, had been one of those who watched him leave. Mitchell had been wounded at Gettysburg also, although his wound was more serious, requiring the attention of a nurse. Lewis tended his friend's needs until "a young lady visitor [Maggie Branson?] brought him a cloak to aid his disguise, and a large cake in which was concealed a ten dollar bill. With this money, he bribed the guards on duty and wrapped in his cloak, he made his escape."[9]

It seems a short "lay-over" was in store for Lewis at the Bransons' boarding house. One evening in 1863, Lewis called at 16 North Eutaw Street to see Miss Maggie Branson. Dressed in a "blue Federal uniform," he spent a quiet two hours in the parlor and was subsequently introduced to Maggie's sister, Mary, thirty-two years old and also deeply pro–Southern in feeling. He was known to Mary as *Powell* on this first visit and apparently told her he was going south.[10]

Here was all he needed—a "way station" of sorts in Baltimore with two attractive, spunky young spinsters who would apparently do all they could to aid the Cause and a handsome, escaped POW.

Although he may have been tempted to linger for a while longer, the Confederacy beckoned him back to the south.

4. Part-Time Partisan

> It was in the month of September 1863, that my uncle, John Scott Payne, who lived at *Granville Tract*, an old-fashioned Virginia homestead, some four miles from Warrenton on the Waterloo Turnpike, came home from the Confederate Army on furlough.... While sitting on the porch with my uncle one evening, talking about the prospects of the Confederacy, a very young looking man, wearing the gray uniform came sauntering across the lawn. This was the first that any of us had ever seen of him. I remember distinctly that the man wore no beard and I wondered what such a boy was doing in the army anyhow. His arm was in a sling, bound about with bandages and splints, as if it had been broken. His uniform was pretty well worn out. It was of regulation Confederate gray and bore the stripes upon the collar which indicated his rank to be that of a first or second lieutenant. He was tall and well built, being particularly broad and robust about the chest and shoulders. He had one of those peculiar dark southern complexions, blue eyes, dark hair, and an imperfection in one of his front teeth ... the stranger's name was Lewis Powell.[1]

Thus was Lewis described by a Northern Virginia resident at whose home the soldier remained for a short period of time. Apparently fresh from his escapades at the West Buildings Hospital in Baltimore and newly arrived in Northern Virginia, the youngster was feeling his way about, seeking to get a hold on the bearings of his latest predicament.

Obviously, the gray Confederate uniform was not what he wore when squeezing past the guards at the Baltimore West Buildings Hospital.

Somehow, he had managed to procure a Confederate uniform after he crossed the lines. Not at all particular, any uniform would do, no matter how tattered or what the insignia, provided that butternut-gray was the overall color.

It would appear that Lewis was on the lookout for his own company, or so he related to the gentleman at whose home he was staying.[2] After all, Longstreet's Corps, of which Powell's Second Florida outfit was a part, had retreated from Gettysburg by way of Hagerstown, Maryland, and through Waynesboro, Virginia.

It must have been a footsore and weary Lewis who stumbled up to the Granville Tract homestead that September evening. What was he to do now? It seemed trouble had a way of riding on his coattails. To continue to hound the trail of his regiment might take weeks, even months. As he recuperated at Granville Tract, the young foot soldier probably heard much of a man named Mosby and his Partisan Rangers.

Guerrilla warfare was not new to the Confederacy. As early as March and April of 1862, the Confederate Congress had passed a Partisan Ranger Act, giving authorization to organize individual guerrilla companies for the express purpose of irregular warfare.[3] Virginia was no stranger to such units.

Col. John Singleton Mosby and his Forty-third Battalion were held in high esteem by Gen. J. E. B. Stuart who gave free rein to the Partisan Rangers, thus enabling them to control much of northern Virginia—an area aptly called "Mosby's Confederacy."

The cavalrymen boarded at various homes scattered across the countryside and, like the minutemen of old, would ride to arms at the first sign of alarm, meeting at a prearranged place to quickly discuss and then carry out their hit-and-run tactics.

Lewis soon came under the intoxicating spell of this irregular type of partisan patriotism. Just exactly how or when he joined the guerrillas is lost to record.

However, Mosby himself, who it is said "hand-picked" his elite members, apparently met the young convalescent foot soldier, and, impressed with his physique and keen intellect, decided he would make a good prospective member for his group. Mosby didn't dilly-dally. Shrewd, abrupt and cool in nature, the "Gray Ghost" was a good judge of men's characters. One had to have the right qualifications for this unit, whose members were enviously regarded as "spoiled darlings" and "feather-bed soldiers" by infantry outfits. Deserters and seedy, half-witted roustabouts had no place with Mosby.

When considering Powell's family connections with Brig. Gen. John Brown Gordon, one wonders if perhaps this kinsmanship could have had a direct bearing on Powell's admittance into Mosby's battalion.

A Private Powell (no first name) is listed on Company B muster rolls dated January 22, 1864, for the period of October 1, 1863, to December 31, 1863. Having enlisted in Fauquier County, Virginia, by a Captain Smith for "war," he was never paid although marked "present." On a clothing receipt for the fourth quarter of 1864, *Private L. T. Powell* is listed for Company B as having received two shirts and two pairs of drawers. The awkward, boyish scrawl is easily discernible as written by the same hand which signed the Oath of Allegiance in March 1865 as *L. Paine,* of which we shall read in a later chapter. (See Appendix E.)

Mary Branson contributed to the tantalizing speculation about Powell's service with the report that he had ridden briefly with the notorious Marylander Harry S. Gilmore and his raiders. A run-in with a group of innocent Jewish peddlers during which they were robbed and

Colonel John Singleton Mosby, commander of the Forty-third Battalion Virginia Cavalry (Library of Congress).

treated most harshly by Gilmore's men offended Powell in some way and provoked his comment that he deserted because "they were such a rough class of men that they did not suit him."[4] It apparently inflated Powell's ego to think of himself as a gentleman who was above such thievery, and he would tell Mary Branson that he never approved of robbery.

It wasn't long before Lewis had proved himself a very apt Ranger, described by John W. Munson, one of Mosby's foremost men, as a youngster who was "always keyed up for any new sensation ... a first class fighting man, always ready for any duty, and game."[5] The spirited part-time partisan way of life apparently suited Powell's idea of soldiering.

Lewis Edmonds Payne, son of Dr. Albin S. Payne, a prominent Warrenton physician, was a lad of eleven years when he watched Powell amble across the lawn of his uncle's home, *Granville Tract*.

Years after Powell had met his end on the gallows, Lewis E. Payne, former United States attorney from Wyoming, "whose name the assassin assumed," wrote in June 1882 a lengthy and highly romanticized article about Powell and his exploits. Although most of L. E. Payne's recollections appear a bit swashbuckling, some particulars are intriguing, especially when backed up by other information. (See Appendices C and D.)

To quote Mr. Payne:

> Powell was a good horseman and he knew all the byways and highways and shortcuts across the fields and through the woods, and he used to say he could travel from Warrenton to Winchester or from Fairfax Court House to Front Royal in a third of the time by his own routes than it would take to travel the roads ... Powell was with Mosby's men all during the raiding in the rear of General [David] Hunter's army in June of 1864, when the celebrated "burning order" was being put in operation.

While working the valley with three separate detachments, one of Mosby's men killed a young Federal picket during a slight skirmish. The slain soldier's commanding officer, none other than the flamboyant George Armstrong Custer, ordered the homes of five innocent families in the area burned to avenge the picket's death.

In retaliation for these atrocities, a group of Mosby's men clashed with a detail of Federals and caught them in the process of burning a house. The resulting fray culminated in the death of eighteen Union soldiers. More than likely, Powell was one of the vengeful Rangers.

One particular incident confirmed by both Mr. Payne and John W. Munson, related Powell's reckless daring:

> Lieutenant Edward Thompson, a member of Mosby's command ... had charge of sixty men on the grade near Salem, in Fauquier County, Virginia. A small body of Federal cavalry was in the town with pickets on all the roads leading to and from the place. Thompson had concealed his men in the woods and was waiting to capture the Federals at night, but fearing they would get information of his designs, he determined to change his plans. He therefore called for two men who were willing to ride upon the picket line of the enemy and firing upon them, to retreat a certain distance down the road, so that he could attack the pursuers in the rear with his sixty men. Powell, (and a soldier named Tom Benton Shipley of Baltimore) volunteered for the special duty of drawing the enemy into the trap. Thompson says his orders were executed to the letter. Powell and Shipley galloped up the road in full view of the enemy, discharged their revolvers almost in their very faces, and turning their horses, sped down the road, followed by a volley of balls. The pursuit was almost instantaneous and when the rear of the charging column of the enemy had passed on in pursuit of Powell and Shipley, Thompson wheeled his men into the road and with a terrible "yell" and a storm of bullets, rushed

Granville Tract—The Fauquier County country home of the Payne-Meredith family with whom Powell boarded while serving with Colonel John Singleton Mosby's Forty-third Battalion, Company B (author's collection).

upon the enemy. In the meantime, Powell and Shipley turned in the road and charged the enemy from the front. The result was the capture by Thompson of almost the entire command of the enemy, who of course, thought they were entirely surrounded.

Dr. Albin S. Payne and wife Naomi (courtesy Nancy Beardon).

Even life in the Forty-third Battalion wasn't all excitement. While off duty, Powell probably made himself useful about the farms where he boarded. Mr. L. E. Payne recalled one instance in his boyhood in which he saw Powell "dismount from his horse, shoulder five newly-split chestnut rails, remount with the rails on his shoulder and ride a mile to my uncle's house and deposit the rails in the wood yard."

Powell boarded with various members of the Payne family throughout northern Virginia. In addition to making his home with the Paynes of Granville Tract, Lewis also boarded with the family of Dr. Alban S. Payne on his farm, The Willows, at the upper end of Fauquier County in the little village of Paris, and also found lodging at the old manor house, Nalley, located near Paris, Virginia.[6]

Confederate Gen. William H. Payne also had a few vivid recollections of young Powell, recalling him as a "chivalrous, generous, gallant fellow, particularly fond of children." General Payne remembered how "he rarely visited Warrenton that he did not bring them some little thing." Often, Lewis would be seen in the streets of Warrenton with one of the Payne youngsters perched up on the saddle in front of him on his horse.[7] (See Appendix D.)

Life with the Rangers also gave Powell ample time to mix swords and roses. According to the Payne family, the handsome Ranger was interested in one of their cousins, Miss Bettie D. Meredith, the eighteen-year-old daughter of a well-to-do Prince William County farmer.[8]

In his recollections, Mr. Payne covers Miss Meredith's identity with a false name and a fancifully conceived story of how they met. However, portions of the romantic episode have a ring of truth when put back-to-back with the account of General Payne.

Apparently, Powell possessed tender feelings for the young lady—enough to give her his photograph to remember him by. He also purportedly left his diary in her care as a keepsake. Miss Meredith is remembered as being an "accomplished and very attractive young lady who had many suitors."[9]

Mr. Payne relates a pretty story in which Miss Meredith claimed that Powell promised, upon his leaving the service of Mosby and Northern Virginia in January of 1865, to return for her in a few months. Needless to say, Miss Meredith never saw her gallant Ranger again after he met and fell in with John Wilkes Booth.

Unfortunately, an attempt to trace these enticing articles—diary and photograph—through the Payne and Meredith descendants has failed, although Mr. Payne *did* remember one "specimen of Powell's composition," a surprising bit of prose which reveals an academic air to say the least:

> In battle, in the fullness of pride and strength, little recks the soldier whether the hissing bullet sings his sudden requiem or the cords of life are severed by the sharp steel.
> L. Powell

Taken from *An Appeal on the Behalf of Ireland*, an 1847 address of one S. S. Prentiss, a Mississippi Whig Orator, the fact that Powell was aware of this oratory leaves little dispute

The Willows—Home of the Payne family in Paris, Virginia (author's collection).

that the young man was somewhat educated above the average and was most certainly *not* the illiterate booby he has been made out to be.

In mid–November of 1864 perhaps came Powell's most important venture with the Rangers. "A hardened Indian fighter," Federal Captain Richard Blazer was given a crack command of one hundred selected soldiers to "wipe out Mosby." The summer-long raids of Mosby and his Forty-third Battalion culminating in an attempt to capture Sheridan himself in August, prompted the exasperated commander of the Army of the Shenandoah to approve Blazer's command for just such a purpose. Armed with Spencer carbines, Blazer and his men roved over the valley for weeks at a time without even a glimpse of the Gray Ghost or his command.

On November 15, the day Mosby received word that Blazer and his men had ambushed a small party of Rangers and killed two, companies A and B of the Forty-third Battalion were ordered by Mosby to "wipe him out." Under the command of Capt. Adolphus Richards, Blazer was traced to Kabletown, Virginia. In true Ranger fashion, one company was concealed with another feigning retreat when the Federals rushed into the trap. The retreating group then wheeled and charged their pursuers while those concealed clashed from the rear.

Amid the resulting confusion, many of Blazer's scouts were knocked from their saddles under the fire of the Rangers' Colts. Those remaining broke and fled. With Blazer himself racing toward Rippon, four Rangers pounded hot on his trail: Syd Ferguson, Sam Alexander, Cab Maddox and Lewis Powell.

Ferguson's fleet mount managed to overtake Blazer, and leaning from the saddle, Ferguson clubbed the captain over the head with his pistol butt. Blazer crumpled from his horse. Under Ferguson's direction, Alexander, Maddox, and Powell bandaged up the head of the dazed captain with a handkerchief and proudly conducted their charge to Captain Richards.[10] Various sources give reference to Powell's participation in this capture.

Powell is mentioned as being one of the four in Scott's history of Mosby's battalion, just as he is also mentioned in Virgil Carrington Jones's scholarly work on Mosby. Lewis Edmonds Payne likewise leaves the impression that Powell participated in the Blazer affair. However, in going over Blazer's own version, the story develops some interesting twists and turns. To begin, Blazer seems to have remembered Powell by the specific name *Paine*—the precise alias by which he signed his Oath of Allegiance in March of 1865.

One A. H. Windsor, an army chaplain, wrote from Winchester, Virginia, on April 24, 1865, to Seward's youngest son, Brig. General W. H. Seward that

> Captain Dick Blazer of the Blazer Scouts was captured last summer and taken to Richmond by one Payne, belonging to Mosby's gang. He thinks from the description, it is the same Payne arrested with the Surratt family and supposed to be the assassin who attempted the life of your honored father, the Secretary of State. Capt. Blazer is well acquainted with the man and would recognize him at once if he were the same. He has made inquiries of Mosby's men as to this Payne and they say he went away some time ago but where they could not tell. I send you this note thinking that the testimony of Captain Blazer might throw further light upon the history of this man. Captain Blazer belongs to the 91st OVC 1st Brig. 4th Prov. Div. Army of the Shenandoah. I am sir, very Respect. Your obt. Servant, A. H. Windsor, Chaplain, 91st O. V. C.[11]

So far as is known, Powell was using his *own* name during his service with the Forty-third. The records state as much. Furthermore, the Payne family—including L. E. Payne and Gen. William H. Payne—remembered Powell as *Powell*. For what reason would he use the name *Paine*? Of course, Blazer's description of this Paine was written at the time of the conspiracy trial when all the world wanted to know just who "Lewis Payne" (or Paine) was. The letter was written to enlighten authorities as to Payne's identity which could perhaps account for the inconsistency of the names.

At any rate, the same four Rangers who participated in the capture were supposedly given the assignment of escorting Blazer to imprisonment in Richmond's Libby Prison.

Likewise, according to the *New York Daily Courier* for May 20, 1865, one "Lieutenant Colonel Hutchins, who was present in court, [during Powell's trial], felt confident that Payne had visited Libby Prison while he was there, but was unwilling to swear to his identity."

Late in the year of 1864, there was a new development in military assignments for the feckless Powell. Could he have also been sent to Richmond for *other* reasons than to escort a prisoner? On the eve of his death, young Powell would tell Reverend Dr. Abram D. Gillette that he had worked "for *months* before the assassination" in the secret service of the Confederacy and had journeyed back and forth from Richmond to Washington and Baltimore in conference with prominent men ... men who would forever remain unknown. (See Appendix I.)

Was service with the Rangers becoming stale to Powell? Always a restless youngster, was he looking for a new outlet? Or did Colonel John S. Mosby see bigger possibilities for his husky Ranger? New blood was quickly needed for the Confederacy.

Recently discovered sources hint at rash dealings by top officials in the Confederate hierarchy. An account written by Maryland's Brig. Gen. Bradley T. Johnson, CSA, tells of a plan in late 1864 to raid the soldiers' home area outside Washington and, with two hundred carefully picked horses and men, take President Abraham Lincoln captive and send him back into Virginia with an escort of five men. This plan had the express consent of Gen. Jubal A. Early. Another source, Maj. W. W. Goldsborough, had confirmed the existence of Johnson's plans as early as 1869.[12]

Johnson's scheme was in accord with John Wilkes Booth's initial plot to abduct President Lincoln—a plan that also had to be aborted. Booth's plan has been dismissed by some as being the result of a frenzied brain. But was it? "The similarity of this Confederate proposal with the abduction plan actually attempted by Booth and his *five* assistants, Messrs. Surratt, Atzerodt, Arnold, O'Laughlen and Paine [Powell] a short time after General Johnson's preparations had to be aborted because of military developments, is quite marked."[13]

Knowing the elite quality of the Gray Ghost's courageous men, could Mosby have been detailed to handpick five men for this kidnapping enterprise under orders from superiors? Although sheer speculation, the idea does seem feasible. Most histories claim Powell "deserted" Mosby's command. This is a ludicrous contention in the light of Powell's subsequent subversive activities against the Federal government.

According to an article in the *Richmond Dispatch* for December 11, 1902, Powell as a member of Captain R. S. Walker's squad sent for fellow soldier and comrade W. Ben Palmer

> to tell him goodbye. The latter found the young man dressed in a badly fitting suit of citizen's clothes and with a black slouch hat pulled down over his eyes. He was in high spirits and talked of his plans. He said that they intended to kidnap Lincoln and bring him South. No mention was made of killing anyone.... Powell left later that night.... Mr. Palmer was staying at the home of Mrs. Coollidge. A newspaper came to the house with a picture of the man who had tried to assassinate Seward. Under the name of Payne, Mrs. Collidge did not recognize the former Mosby soldier. But Mr. Palmer said:

"Don't you remember that fellow? That's certainly Powell, the man who had his feet so badly frost-bitten some time ago that when he stopped at this house we had to cut his boots off."

To assume that Powell was a "hired gun" for the part he played against Secretary of State Seward is also absurd. The reward seemed to have been much more than monetary gain. According to Dr. Gillette, Lewis was encouraged "with dreams of glory and the lasting gratitude of the Southern people." Powell claimed that he expected a "promotion" for his subversive activities.[14] For what reason would a deserter want a promotion? There is, however, the belief that some men in the Confederate Secret Service were labeled as deserters as a blind for their underground affairs.

At any rate, Lewis E. Payne seemed to feel that Powell went to Richmond and returned under mysterious circumstances:

> Powell went to Richmond as a guard to some prisoners.... Leaving Richmond, Powell returned to the Piedmont section a changed man. He seemed to be more grave and thoughtful than ever. He often spoke of his visit to Richmond and his intention soon to go to Baltimore to *meet friends he had met in Richmond* ... after his return from Richmond, he never went on any raid, but was continually talking about a visit or a raid into Maryland and he and other soldiers would go off to the stables or woods and have long talks and seem to be particularly anxious that no one should know what they were talking about.... Powell soon began to sell off his horses and dispose of his effects, saying he would be gone for several months on his Maryland expedition. Among those who were to accompany him were William H. Sowers, John H. Coxe, and others of Norfolk, but when the time came to depart, all of them backed down except Powell. Whether these men knew anything as to the nature of the expedition, I will not pretend to say. I do know they were intimates with Powell and I saw and overhead them talking about their Maryland expedition just before Powell left the Piedmont section. Powell left Fauquier sometime in January 1865.

Who were the "Baltimore friends" Powell met in Richmond? Was one of them John Wilkes Booth? This is doubtful as Powell did not yet know Booth, or so it would seem. Doster would state that Powell met Wilkes Booth in Richmond in 1861, when Lewis was a raw young recruit. This is equally silly when we find John Wilkes Booth was not in Richmond in 1861. His stage engagements in Richmond ended prior to the war, after May 1860. As of mid-to-late November 1864, John Wilkes Booth was in New York where he appeared on November 25 with his two brothers at the Winter Garden Theater in *Julius Caesar*. Powell would have cause to emphasize later that he first met Booth in 1863. We shall hear more of this later.

Powell would later relate to Dr. Gillette that "the head of the house where he was staying in Baltimore was in on the abduction plot.[15]

This would have been Captain Joseph Branson, father of Mary and Margaret Branson.

Quite naturally, Powell could have met the esteemed Captain Branson *if* he (Powell) was in Richmond to gain insight on the abduction plot, provided Branson was also a conspirator. Subsequently, right after leaving Northern Virginia, Powell headed straight to Baltimore and to the Branson boarding house.

Before taking leave of the Rangers, however, an incident of especial interest occurred. Mr. L. E. Payne contradicted himself when he wrote that Powell took no part in any raids after his return from Richmond. Very shortly after his return, Lewis and a comrade, according to General Payne,

> captured six of [Torbet's] men near Warrenton. [Powell] left them in charge of somebody in the town while he rode up to greet some of his friends.

The men that he had captured were stragglers from Torbet's command, who had been guilty of some gross and infamous brutality to Isham Keith ... and his family. They sacked the house, piled the furniture and beds in the yard and burned them. They insulted his old mother and his wife. Isham at the time was concealed in the woods. As soon as they left, he came to his ruined home and heard the story. Mounting his horse, he started in pursuit. Upon reaching Warrenton, he found these men prisoners. He killed four of them. When the news was brought to Powell, with weapon in hand, he galloped to the place where he heard the pistol shots, stopped the massacre and was with difficulty prevented from killing Keith. He claimed the prisoners as his and announced his intentions of saving their lives at the risk of his own. This scene was witnessed by several citizens.

Sufficient evidence at the conspiracy trial upheld the truth of this incident:

MRS. LUCY ANN GRANT

A witness called for the accused, Lewis Payne, being duly sworn, testified as follows:
(Examined) By Mr. Doster:
Q. State where you live.
A. In Warrenton, Virginia, on the Waterloo Pike.
Q. Look at the prisoners at the bar, and see whether you recognize any of them.
A. I recognize the gentleman that they said was Mr. Powell.
Q. Which is that?
A. That one, with the gray shirt (pointing to the accused, Lewis Payne).
Q. Where did you see him before?
A. In front of our house in the road.
Q. Was he not at that time in charge of soldiers; prisoners?
A. Three Union prisoners.
Q. Did or did not, somebody attempt to kill these prisoners?
A. Yes, sir.
Q. Who tried to kill the prisoners?
A. I do not know who it was.
Q. Were they citizens or soldiers?
A. They were said to be soldiers. They had on soldiers' uniforms.
Q. Where did these prisoners belong? Do you know what command they had been captured from?
A. I do not know.
Q. What time was this? Was there or not a raid at the time?
A. It was after General Torbert passed through Warrenton; about Christmas. I do not recall the day; but it was about Christmas time.
Q. Did or did not these soldiers try to kill those Union soldiers?
A. Yes, sir; they did, and the gentleman whom they called Powell tried to prevent it.
Q. What did he say on the occasion?
A. I saw him in his saddle-stirrups; and he told them that whilst he was a gentleman, and wished to be treated as one, though he could not defend all, if they killed or captured the one he had in his charge, they would do it at the peril of their lives, as well as I recollect the words. That was the meaning anyhow.
Q. What time of the year was that?
A. It was about last Christmas. I reckon you all recollect the raid of General Torbert; and on his return, he passed through Warrenton.
Q. Did he succeed in getting the prisoner away?
A. They left our house, I do not know what became of them afterwards. They left the road.
Q. Was one of those men killed by the soldiers?
A. Yes, sir; one was killed. I did not see him fall off the horse; but one of the Confederate soldiers rapped at my door and wanted to bring him into my house. My husband was not home, and I was scared nearly to death; there was nobody there but me and my small children.

Q. The man who was called Powell, you say, saved the lives of the two?
A. Yes, sir; they left there. I do not know what become of them. Those prisoners ought to be here to answer for themselves, I should think.
(Examined) By the Judge Advocate:
Q. What name do you say he bore when there?
A. I know nothing about his name—I never heard of him, nor saw him before or since, that I know of.
Q. You did not hear his name?
A. No, sir; I was speaking of his trying to save those Union soldiers to a citizen; and he said his name was Powell; that is all I know of him.
Q. You feel certain that is the same person?
A. That is the same person; I would know him anywhere, I think.
Q. You had never seen him before?
A. Never that I know of.
Q. Was he dressed as a Confederate soldier?
A. Yes, sir.
(Examined) By the Court:
Q. Did he seem to be a Confederate officer?
A. Some of them called him "lieutenant," I think; but I did not know anything about it.
Q. How was he dressed?
A. In a dark-gray Confederate uniform.
Q. Had he any marks of an officer?
A. None at all. He looked rather more genteel than the common soldier.

JOHN GRANT

A witness called for the accused, Lewis Payne, being duly sworn, testified as follows:
(Examined) By Mr. Doster:
Q. Are you the husband of Mrs. Grant, who has just left the stand?
A. I am.
Q. Were you, or not, present at a certain affray that occurred in front of your house last Christmas?
A. I happened there a few minutes after it occurred. I was not at home at the time, but got up a very few minutes afterwards. I was three hundred yards from my house, I suppose, when the pistol firing commenced; and I rushed home as quick as I could.
Q. Could you see the firing?
A. I could at that time.
Q. Do you know whether or not the prisoner at the bar saved the lives of two Union soldiers?
A. That is what was said there when I got to the house.
Q. What name did the prisoner go by?
A. I understood his name was Powell.
Q. Was he an officer, do you know?
A. Not that I am aware of.
Q. When was it?
A. On the first day of January last.[16]

One of the soldiers captured by Powell was Private Augustus Lockner of the 21st New York Calvary. Lockner would survive the war and in 1903 write about this affair with the soon to be Seward Assassin. (See Appendix F.)

Powell's term with Mosby was quickly drawing to a close. Bidding farewell to his sweetheart, Miss Meredith, and promising to return in a few months, the ex–Ranger rode to Fairfax Court House where he exchanged his uniform for a suit of civilian clothes, sold his horse, and was conveyed to Alexandria where he took the Oath of Allegiance to the United

States government. The document carried the name "Lewis *Paine*" and gave his description as having black hair, blue eyes, of dark complexion, height six foot one and a half inches. This oath was issued on January 13, 1865.[17]

Mr. Lewis E. Payne gave a good explanation as to why Powell used his name:

> His reasons for assuming the name of Payne can only be accounted for upon the two-fold hypothesis; first, that he wanted to hail from a section of the country with the people and geography of which he was familiar, and to select a name identified with that section of the country ... second, he probably desired to take a name easily remembered and one with the connection and relationship of which he was familiar. The information acquired during his brief stay with my uncle gave him this advantage.... In short, in case of arrest or surprise, it is reasonable to suppose Powell wanted to give a name easily remembered and one identified with the section of the country from which he claimed to be a refugee, with the history of which and its people he was so familiar that he could not be liable to be caught by sharp questioning.

According to an old, undated clipping from the *Washington Republican:* "Payne (Powell) explains that he assumed that name as he did not wish his parents to know—if he perished in the attempt—that he had died in such a way; he hoped they would think he had fallen on the battlefield."

This is Powell's first *known* indication of having an alias, a name by which he would be tried, executed, and projected into history; his own name practically lost.

The fatal chapter was now beginning to open in Powell's life. John Wilkes Booth, and eventually the gallows, awaited him.

5. The Baltimore Connection

On a raw January day in 1865, a tall, husky young man in a black overcoat rapped at the door of Mrs. Branson's fashionable, brick three-story Federal style townhouse at 16 North Eutaw Street.

Powell hadn't forgotten his Baltimore lady friends, the Branson sisters, and undoubtedly hoped they hadn't forgotten him, either. According to Mary, "He called as soon as he came to the city." Apparently eager to renew the acquaintance, Lewis wasn't wasting any time. Or was his visit based on an *invitation?* If Powell had met the ladies' father Joseph Branson in Richmond during a secret service briefing, could he have been urged to visit on the basis of "business?" This is, of course, conjecture, as subsequent developments give the impression that Powell was paying a social call to the ladies and saw no one else. Or did he?

Powell and the Misses Branson spent a pleasant evening, according to Mary, who said Lewis talked on a variety of subjects, ranging from his brother's death to his own exploits in the army. She claimed that he spoke a great deal of Mosby, but for the most part, "his talk was principally of the ladies—he complained of his poor education."[1] Apparently, Lewis liked to play the role of gallant and could be quite conversational and charming when he so chose.

Inquiring about vacancies at the boarding house, Powell was told regretfully that he could not be accommodated at that particular time. Not one to be put off, Powell, who was rooming then at Miller's Hotel, respectfully asked if he could call again and being answered in the affirmative, decided he would pursue a change of address in the near future. Meanwhile, he would nevertheless continue to pursue his relationship with the Branson ladies.

Several social calls and ten days later, Powell established his residence at the Branson boarding house.

Seemingly from the start, Powell was connected in shady dealings with the Branson girls, who introduced him to the other boarders as Mr. Payne from *Frederick County, Maryland*.[2] Yet another source has him listed as a "Mr. Ferguson."[3] Why the cover? What sort of secret dealings rated such anonymity? Certainly Federal officials in the provost marshal's office were not *still* looking for a Confederate POW who had escaped over a year before. From all appearances, the Branson house was just as subversive a place as the Surratt boarding establishment in Washington. Mysterious patrons seemed to make the Branson house their headquarters. One visitor was Mr. Charles G. Heim, whose father had "business" of some sort in Richmond. Another gentleman, one Mr. E. W. Blair, was also a frequent guest, and the Misses Branson were themselves, so Maj. H. B. Smith stated, "notorious rebels."[4]

Apparently people with underground connections in Confederate espionage were using the boarding house as a "front." A tally of paying guests or boarders in April 1865 reveals fourteen men and five women. According to Major Smith, who interrogated the household after the president's murder, only four of the fourteen men could be designated as "loyal" although there may have been more.[5]

One Isabel Branson Williams of Ohio wrote Secretary of War Stanton regarding the Branson household and its affinity for housing "Rebel Spies." Apparently this Mrs. Williams *nee* Branson was a family member who wanted nothing to do with her Baltimore kinsmen.

ISABELL WILLIAMS (3:39–40)
"W" 372 (JAO) 1865
Isabel Williams
Greensburg, Ohio

Sec. Stanton

Sir, I see by one of the Baltimore papers the arrest of Mrs. Branson and daughters concerning Payne, the alleged assassin of our beloved President. I feel it to be my duty to my husband as he has served his two years and eight months and cam home a cripple for life & also duty to my country to give some information that probably lead to his capture. Mrs. Branson has been a southern rendezvous ever since the war commenced and have harbored more than one southern spy and have removed them from one place to another as suspicion would lead for a search. Now have John P. Egerton house searched. Thomas Dukehart is on McCullough St. Mr. Polock, he keeps store on Baltimore St. near Holiday St. and Mr. Green's house of Washington as he would hide everyone that had sympathy for the South. Very likely he is in Baltimore as he, I am pretty sure boarded with Branson before last March and they have supplied the southern army with clothes and medicine for the last four years. The rebels in Baltimore were watched so close and Branson's had never been searched, so the money was sent to Mary and Margaret and they would get the things and send them off by the Alms House wagon. I can't say the keeper knew of the driver carrying those things but it is more than likely he did or they would hardly trust a town pauper with so much. His name I can't remember but you can find out at the Mayor's office in Baltimore 1862 & 63 was the time he was in & and I don't know if he is still in office or not. I have been living in Ohio for the last year & I know that President Lincoln had no where more bitter enemies than the Branson's & I am sure no other family has done more against the government than they have in Baltimore; that I am confident of.

I hope this may be of some service to the government as I would feel happy if the villain was only caught and no mercy shown to any of them.

Isabel Williams
Greensburg, Summit County, Ohio
Formerly Isabel Branson at Baltimore[6]

If indeed, as Powell hinted to Dr. Gillette, Joseph Branson *was* in on the abduction plot, then Powell had landed right in the middle of the doings, so to speak. Here was intrigue, adventure and skullduggery, all rolled into one, with two attractive spinsters thrown in for good measure.

Lewis, held in high esteem by his fellow boarders, blended into the household. Affectionately known as "Longfellow" due to his height, he played chess with the ladies and gentlemen boarders and read the medical books in the family library.[7] To all appearances, he was a proper young gentleman boarder. And then there were the Branson ladies themselves, especially Mary, the younger sister. Twenty-year-old Lewis seemed to have taken a particular shine to the thirty-four-year-old Mary. They went out often together, according to Mary, *very* often. Maj. H. B. Smith wrote that "the intimacy between Miss Branson and Payne would be remarked under ordinary circumstances."[8]

In addition to such gentlemanly duties as escorting the ladies to church and taking Mary for leisurely walks, Lewis was courting intrigue as well as Miss Branson. A recently discovered article states that although there was about a 14 year age difference, the result of this whirlwind romance was that the twenty-year-old Powell was engaged to be married to the thirty-four-year-old Mary; a fact which was not widely known at the time.[9]

Without any apparent livelihood, young Powell made ends meet somehow. Doster recounts in Dickensian detail how poor Powell sat in his room at the Branson house and watched helplessly while "the little money he got for the sale of his horse melted away," he being too proud, as a Southern gentleman, to seek manual labor.[10]

Perhaps Lewis did live on money obtained from the sale of his horse, but more credible would be that he used funds paid him by the Confederate secret service. Powell was no doubt an agent in training awaiting further orders with nothing better to do than squire the ladies about and take his ease while better acquainting himself with others in the underground service.

Mary Branson recounted how some social calls seemingly mixed "business" with pleasure:

> I called with him [Powell] on Mrs. Heim on Paca Street. I might have called several times with him. We took tea there once. At other times, only made short calls. At no time when we called was there any visitors there ... Mr. Heim was in business in Richmond ... Mrs. Heim knew Payne was from Virginia, but I don't know that she knew he was in the Rebel Army. I don't think Charles G. Heim was home at any time when we called.[11]

The intriguing punch line to this little anecdote is the reference to Mr. Heim's "business" in Richmond. What sort of business would he have conducted in the war-torn and beleaguered Confederate capital? And Mrs. Heim was also aware that Powell "was from Virginia," a fact which Miss Branson had taken care to conceal from others. Mary wasn't sure if the other woman knew that Lewis was in the Rebel army. Noting the use of the word "was" in the foregoing statement, one could easily come to the conclusion that perhaps Powell was *still* at that very time in the Confederate service. If so, then perhaps we can assume that she was referring to Powell's secret service activities and not his so-called desertion from the Rebel armed forces. Of course, Mrs. Heim would most probably not be in the dark as to her husband's "business" in Richmond or blind to the names of colleagues in the same business.

A search of the 1860 city directory for Baltimore lists a Jacob B. Heim, who resided at 79 North Paca Street. Mr. Heim was a partner of H. Nichodeamus and Company, Importers and Dealers in Foreign and Domestic Liquors, located at 383 West Baltimore Street. Of what need would Richmonders have for "fine foreign and domestic liquors" when in late 1864 things were so bad that they could barely afford adequate food?

Sister Margaret also accompanied Powell on "social" calls to the Heim residence and confirmed visits to the Branson house made by Heim's oldest son, Charles. Charles was also acquainted with Lewis and according to Maggie, "called to see Mr. Payne."

Margaret enlightens us further: "Mr. E. W. Blair called on us very often. He used to meet Mr. Payne at our house. On one occasion, he took him to the theater." The theater. Here is an interesting angle, perhaps not so innocent as it appeared on the surface.

As far as is known, John Wilkes Booth never visited the Branson household. Neither did a Confederate courier, one John H. Surratt, Jr. Surratt, aged twenty, had been involved in Confederate espionage activities since 1863 and had done quite a bit of traveling. His underground routes carried him back and forth between Richmond, New York and Montreal,

5. The Baltimore Connection

Canada, by way of Washington and Baltimore. Being the only unmarried man on his circuit, he was given most of the hard riding to do. Surratt seems to have considered himself unusually clever at deceiving the Federals. With all the flamboyancy of youth, he devised ingenious ways to hide his dispatches, once in the heel of his boot, another time under the floor-boards of a buggy. Hailing from Prince Georges County, Maryland, where his widowed mother owned the local tavern at Surrattsville, Surratt knew all the underground routes through southern Maryland. He also knew a popular young thespian, John Wilkes Booth.

Early in 1864, Booth, 26, of the famous Booth family of players, had decided to let his activities as Confederate secret service agent take precedence over his acting engagements. Long known as a Southern man, Booth had loudly voiced his opinions about the conflict, much to the dismay of his Unionist family.

There are many speculations as to why John Wilkes Booth so ardently proclaimed his sympathies for the South.

History makes much of the fact that Booth, during his early years of treading the boards was well received below the Mason-Dixon line, while more sophisticated Northern critics frowned upon his "gymnastic" and boisterous style of acting. Booth was an actor made, not born, and this fact, combined with the glowing successes of his older brother Edwin, stung him deeply. He thirsted for fame.

Always preferring the flamboyant "blood and thunder" style of melodrama, the chivalrous South lauded this classically handsome young Jove. Impressive with his beauty, his courtly manners and elegant dress, he was wined and dined in grand style by his Southern hosts. Almost overnight he had become a sensation in 1858 Richmond. Donning a borrowed uniform of the Richmond Grays, Booth was a temporary member of that elite company present in Charles Town to witness the 1859 execution of old fire-eating John Brown. Booth's sentiments were sealed in fashionable parlors and salons where he played Romeo to Richmond's Juliets.

Imbibing brandy and Southern politics by the pint, Booth, for all his fiery outbursts appeared to be just another zealot full of braggadocio who could spout secessionist euphemisms for hours on end. In reality, John Wilkes Booth was an agent serving the Confederate secret service, a service whose underground connections went deep, extending across the lines into the North and reaching far into Canada.

Booth revealed his activities to his sister Asia: smuggling quinine and morphine in horse collars through the Union lines for the use of Lee's ragged soldiers.[12] He had a pass signed by Gen. Ulysses S. Grant to allow his passage back and forth through the lines at will for the express purpose of meeting his theatrical engagements.[13] A resourceful operative could have no better disguise than that of a popular actor.

In late 1864, John Wilkes Booth was introduced to John H. Surratt, Confederate courier, by Dr. Samuel A. Mudd. Booth was obsessed with a scheme to abduct President Lincoln, and Surratt, rash and reckless, gave consideration to joining in the attempt. Such an undertaking would require extensive planning.

Confederate underground routes were threaded all through Washington and Baltimore, that hot-bed of rebellion and divided loyalties. Many were the upstanding citizens of Baltimore who were involved in the kidnapping plan. Take, for instance, David Preston Parr, china merchant. Under the prestigious name of "Mr. Parr's China Halls," Parr operated a glass and china shop at 210 Baltimore Street. Apparently catering to an upper-class clientele,

Parr's China Halls to all appearances constituted a most respectable business. The very essence of a Victorian shop proprietor, Parr on the surface was courteous and helpful, the embodiment of a well-to-do citizen content with his station in life. Behind a glittering facade of fine china, delicate teacups and japanned ware was the other side of the man who used his affluent and flourishing business as a front.

David Preston Parr was involved in Confederate espionage work. How deeply is anyone's guess. Very little survives him other than a few statements taken down during his brief imprisonment after the president's murder, which was due to his connections with young John Surratt and subsequently Lewis Powell, as will be seen later. It was Parr who arranged for Surratt and Powell to meet. The fact that Parr had a son in Confederate service didn't help matters any either.

In the natural consequence of things, it wasn't long before Parr made the acquaintance of John H. Surratt, Jr. A police deposition taken by Colonel Foster on April 26, 1865, tells us what little we know of Parr's connections with Surratt: "I accidentally met him about two years ago while I was 'drumming' in my business just below Washington and we came up together in the stage, when I made his acquaintance. I stated to him my business, at the place where we were examined by the military and gave him my business card."[14]

One wonders just how "accidental" the meeting really was. Soon afterwards, Surratt was a regular caller at Mr. Parr's China Halls; not that he was interested in glassware. Parr's establishment was a Confederate mail drop, a clandestine meeting place for people seemingly interested in fine china, but actually members of the underground organization.

It is known that in late 1864, Parr began to send and receive telegram messages from John H. Surratt.[15] This is where Powell comes into the hazy picture. A reading of Parr's statement gives the impression that Surratt and Powell knew each other, as well they did. As of March 1865, Lewis Powell and John Surratt were using D. Preston Parr's china shop as a clandestine meeting place. Testimony at the 1867 Surratt trial established that as early as January 21, 1865, John H. Surratt, accompanied by Louis Weichmann made an evening trip to Baltimore, where they registered at the Maltby House, occupying room 127.

This was more than a pleasure excursion as subsequent trial testimony would reveal. Surratt had business to attend to the following morning, business which he did not want to divulge the nature of to the inquisitive Weichmann. Claiming to have three hundred dollars in his possession, Surratt hired a carriage and stated his intentions to see "some gentlemen" on private matters. One of the gentlemen was probably Powell, as established by the prosecution at the Surratt trial.[16] Powell, at this time, had just changed his residence from Miller's Hotel in Baltimore to that of the Branson boarding house.

It is undeniable that both Mary and Maggie Branson knew perfectly well what their handsome new boarder was up to. Powell's trips to the theater, to Mr. Heim's residence (with Mary in tow) and to Parr's china shop soon pointed Powell's feet in the direction of Washington, D.C., and to the city residence of Surratt's mother.

From the beginning of Powell's stay at the Branson house until his abrupt departure in March 1865, Maggie Branson claimed to remember but one time during which Powell remained away all night. This occurred during February 1865. Lost to record are the reasons why Lewis sought out John Surratt in Washington that night. However, it can be determined that whatever the reason, it most probably had to do with the proposed abduction plot.

5. The Baltimore Connection

The time was late evening, after the supper hour. Clad in a shabby black overcoat, Powell rang the doorbell of 541 H Street, a tall three-story brick boarding house under the proprietorship of the widowed Mrs. Mary E. Surratt. Answering the summons was Louis Weichmann, War Department clerk and college chum of John Surratt. Rotund, bookish and irritatingly inquisitive, Mr. Weichmann had boarded with the Surratt family since its move to the city the preceding November. His presence in the household had resulted in a sort of foster-son status. He performed menial and odd jobs for the landlady while casting an attentive eye on Anna Surratt, John's older sister.

Weichmann had also been lending an attentive ear to what was happening at the boarding house and to the various people coming and going. During the Civil War, Washington was virtually a city of boarding residences, flats and lodgings, all full of transients and folk on the move. Weichmann, however, suspected something strange happening at his place. He knew the sort of courier work young Surratt dealt in, and he knew what sort of people frequented Surratt's company.

Powell stood on the door stoop, hunched against the evening chill, his hands jammed in his overcoat pockets. Looking Weichmann full in the face and giving his name as "Mr. Wood," he asked if this was the Surratt residence and if Mr. Surratt was at home. Apparently Powell had by this time fallen into the habit of acquiring a string of aliases. Upon being told

The Surratt Boarding House—"The Nest That Hatched the Egg." Here Powell boarded for three days in March of 1865 and here he was captured on the night of April 17, 1865. The house was a known rendezvous for Confederate sympathizers (courtesy Surratt House Museum).

that John Surratt was not in, Powell expressed a desire to see Mrs. Surratt and was promptly ushered into the hallway to await proper introduction to the lady of the house.

Mrs. Surratt, daughter Anna and a couple of lady boarders were assembled in the front parlor for an enjoyable social hour after supper, and the landlady requested Mr. Weichmann to bring Mr. Wood into the parlor and introduce him.

The social courtesies completed, Powell approached Mrs. Surratt and spoke with her in a low tone of voice. Meddlesome Mr. Weichmann testified later, "I do not know what was the purport of his remarks, but in a few moments, the mistress came to me and remarked, 'The gentleman would like to have some supper, and inasmuch as the dining room is disarranged, I will be very much obliged to you if you will take the meal to him in your own room.'"[17]

How much did Mrs. Surratt know? That she was unaware of her son John's secret service activities seems a bit ludicrous, likewise the fact of strange young men coming and going unnoticed and unheeded through her house at odd hours. Subsequent developments would indicate that the widow, for all her piety, was not left in the dark concerning her son or his friends. As far as is known, Mrs. Mary E. Surratt had never met Lewis Powell before this occasion. She apparently just assumed that he was another youngster working for "The Cause" along with her son. Was there any crime in that? Many women had sons and husbands in gray uniform and were proud of it.

Weichmann politely did as he was told, taking Powell's supper on a tray up to his third-story bedroom. He just couldn't resist an opportunity to question his uninvited guest. Powell shed his overcoat, sat down and commenced to eat his supper while Weichmann kept an eye on him, noticing that Powell "ate voraciously as if very hungry."

"Where are you from, Mr. Wood?"

"Baltimore," was the laconic reply.

"What are you doing there?"

"I'm a clerk in the china store of a Mr. Parr."[18]

That much Powell admitted. Apparently, he was using a supposed clerkship with Mr. Parr's establishment as a front for his livelihood. Powell showed an apparent dislike for the prying nature of the little man and coolly concentrated on his supper rather than any conversational conviviality. Retiring right after finishing his meal, Powell was given a room in the back attic. Early the next morning, he would take the first train back to Baltimore.

Weichmann, intrigued by the enigmatic "Mr. Wood," but defeated in any attempts to meddle, retreated back down to the parlor. He was never in his life to forget "Mr. Wood."

6. Scandal and Skullduggery

Mr. Parr's China Halls was bustling with activity in March of 1865, that much is certain, and not all of it was legitimate business either. Powell continued to use Parr's business establishment as a clandestine meeting place where he and John Surratt would drop telegrams. According to a statement by Parr taken shortly after the assassination, a lady accompanied Lewis to his china shop on at least one occasion.[1] How much were the elusive Branson ladies implicated, if at all? Possibly Mary was involved just because Lewis was. That they were enamored of each other is certain. Did Mary know what Lewis knew?

The fact that Powell was meeting Surratt accompanied by a lady does seem to indicate that perhaps Mary knew something was afoot. Surratt also had a lady on his arm at this meeting, a lady whose identity cannot now be established. Cornered and questioned, Parr gave elusive particulars concerning Surratt and ladyfriend meeting Powell and ladyfriend sometime in early March:

> At the same time, he [Surratt] met a girl at the store and a party [another woman] called on me afterwards and asked me if I knew that man. I said I had some knowledge of him and that his name was Surratt. She asked me about his meeting this girl .. there were two or three of them met there together.... If my memory serves me, the lady was rather tall—I could not say how old—should suppose she was in her 20's—something in that neighborhood. As near as I can remember, she was rather slight. I am unable to say whether she was fair or dark complected. Could not tell how she was dressed; I should *not* think she was dressed as a strictly fine lady ... do not recall the name he called her by. One lady and this man were there. I don't know who the man was.[2]

Of course, Parr *knew* who this particular man was: Powell! Prodded further, Mr. Parr stated that Surratt met the man (Powell) at the door and that they appeared to be about their own business: "The man with him was tall, rather rough looking. Rather think he had no whiskers. I am uncertain what kind of hair he had. Did not have his hat off. I cannot tell what kind of a hat he wore. I suppose the man would weigh about 170 pounds."

This word portrait could easily be of Powell.

> Did not see this man at all afterwards. Am quite sure I have not seen Surratt since. When they came there and were talking together, I left them talking together as I considered it not a matter of my own. The woman asked me if I knew where he [Surratt] lived and I told her in Washington. She asked me something in reference to the [other] lady and I told her I did not know anything about her ... I think he [Surratt] left with the ladies and the gentleman.

If John Wilkes Booth was also present at the occasional gatherings at Parr's china shop, the proprietor never mentioned it. Booth may have gotten his men together at the Capitol on the occasion of Lincoln's second inaugural, on March 4. That Booth himself *did* attend the ceremonies is certain.

The evening before Booth had spent in the Surratt parlor engaged in lively conversation with John Surratt. Together with Louis Weichmann, the three men had gone up to the Capitol to witness the adjournment of Congress.

The morning of the inauguration dawned in a dreary downpour that turned Pennsylvania Avenue into a river of sloppy mud. Thick gluey muck oozed up even on the slippery plank sidewalks, and a persistent drizzle pelted the gathering crowds. None seemed to pay attention to the mirey bog that was Pennsylvania Avenue. Even ladies in their voluminous skirts paid no heed as they dragged their hems through the mud. There was a carnival atmosphere everywhere that the mud and rain failed to dampen.

John Wilkes Booth had been paying special court to a Miss Lucy Hale, daughter of Senator John P. Hale of New Hampshire. The Hale family resided at the National Hotel. Naturally, Mr. Booth was not long in taking note of the two eligible daughters, Lucy and Lizzie, and he was soon seen squiring them about town. Rumor was to the effect that he was secretly engaged to Lucy. A love match? Surely not! But the plump Miss Lucy *could* be useful in gaining him admission into higher social circles.

Inauguration day found John Wilkes Booth provided with a ticket to the ceremony and a seat not far from Lincoln, courtesy of his "fiancée," Miss Lucy Hale.

"What an excellent chance I had to kill the President if I wished, on inauguration day," Wilkes Booth ruefully moaned to a fellow actor, Samuel Knapp Chester. Had Booth decided at this early time to change the plans from kidnap to kill? Were others in his group present to back him up? Lewis Powell? John Surratt?

Photographic evidence *may* supply proof. Alexander Gardner took four photographs of the inauguration. Someone closely resembling Booth is seen above the speaker's stand, while below the platform, directly under the podium, stand four men whose features bear some resemblance to certain individuals supposed to be the conspirators. There has been great dispute over the identity of those in the photographs over the years. Surprisingly enough, the figure directly below the speaker's stand does bear a startling resemblance to Lewis Powell when thoroughly examined.[3] However, logical evidence is not there to support this contention whatsoever. Furthermore, on the 4th of March, Lewis Powell was incarcerated in the Provost Marshall's headquarters in Baltimore after his altercation with the Bransons' maid, Annie Ward.

Although it is doubtful Miss Hale knew what was brewing, certain questions do rise to mind. How much were the Branson sisters involved, if at all? Just how intimate was the relationship between Lewis Powell and Mary Branson? (See Appendix K.)

The next (and last) major incident which occurred during Powell's stay at the Branson house makes one wonder. To quote Powell himself: "I whipped a colored woman at that house on Monday last because she insulted me."[4]

In early March 1865, Powell was involved in a fracas at the Branson house. Something had erupted which caused the quiet, gentlemanly boarder to lose his self-control.

Margaret Kaighn, a servant employed at the Branson house, testified at the conspiracy trial and gave quite a graphic description of the disturbance at the boarding house:

> I am a servant at Mrs. Branson's. I have seen the prisoner Payne at Mrs. Branson's boarding house; he came there last January or February and remained till the middle of March. I remember he asked a Negro servant to clean up his room, and she gave him some impudence and said she would not do it. She called him some names, and then he struck her; threw her

on the ground and stomped on her body, struck her on the forehead, and said he would kill her, and the girl afterward sent to have him arrested.[5]

Powell's response was a pretty rash reaction to a simple housekeeping matter. Or was there more to the argument? Details better left untold? Surely such brutal treatment was not just the result of a mere insult.

In his examination of Maggie Branson for Lewis Powell's defense at the conspiracy trial, William Doster was rudely interrupted by Judge Advocate John H. Bingham:

> Doster: Do you know how the prisoner happened to leave your home?
> Branson: We had a Negro servant who was exceedingly impudent to him.
> Bingham: You need not state what passed between that girl and that man.[6]

Why not? Could there have been deeper implications—of a seamy or sordid sort? The maid, Annie Ward (and one notices the word *Colored* in parentheses beside the name), was subpoenaed for testimony during the trial but was never called as a witness.[7] One wonders why. Likewise, she never appeared before Provost Marshal H. B. Smith in Baltimore either. Could Annie the maid, whom Margaret Branson described as being "exceedingly impudent," have known of an intimacy between Lewis and Mary that went far beyond that which was considered proper in a repressed and rigid era? Could such an affair have been the subject of caustic and sneering remarks?

The following year, 1866, Oscar D. Ladley, a former Union soldier, boarded at the Branson house because it was close to his business, "a very nice place and ... cheap." His room was across the hall from the one Powell occupied. Ladley talked to Margaret Kaighn, "one of the dining room girls," who told him that she "knew more than she told the Commission" in 1865. "The daughter [Mary?] of Mrs. Branson the landlady, used to get up and give Payne his meals at midnight and pay all kinds of attention to him."[8] Again, we are reminded of H. B. Smith's comments on Powell's "remarkable intimacy" with Miss Branson.

Speculation concerning the presence of sexual overtones may seem somewhat out of place in a historical perspective, but the existence of such an affair is a thought-provoking possibility. More than likely though, the maid was cognizant of Powell's underground affiliations and her scathing comments were of a threatening nature. At least he was arrested soon after the quarrel on charges of being a spy. The *Baltimore Sun* for March 15, 1865, carried the following article in the "Local Matters" column:

> *Arrested as a Spy*—Louis [sic] Paine was arrested on Monday last at No. 16 North Eutaw Street, charged with being a rebel spy. Maj. Wiegel made a thorough examination of his case, and there not being sufficient evidence to substantiate the charge, he was released from the charge of being a spy, but held as disloyal. Upon taking the Oath of Allegiance, and engaging to go North of Philadelphia during the war, he was finally released.[9]

Apparently the walls in the Branson house had ears. Why else would Powell have been arrested as a "spy"? He was surely not charged in any way for assault. Nowhere else on record is there known to be any such charge:

March 12, 1865	Lewis Payne
	16 N. Eutaw Street
	Charge Spy
	—Imprisoned—
March 14, 1865	Discharged and ordered north upon taking the Oath of Allegiance[10]

Following the fracas, the maid apparently revealed some pertinent tidbits about Powell to the authorities.

Held under lockup for at last 6 days at the provost marshal's headquarters of the Eighth Army Corps, young Powell was put through a thorough grilling by Maj. H. B. Smith, Chief of Detectives and Assistant Provost Marshal General.

Powell wasn't talking, and when he finally did speak, his story was a fabrication. Again, we can note his cool head and quick thinking under stressful situations:

Baltimore, Md.
March 10, 1865

>Lewis Paine, refugee from Fauquier County, Virginia; my parents reside near Orleans in that county. I am eighteen and a half years old. I have not been out of Virginia since the war commenced, until this time.
>I was never in the rebel army. Mosby used to stay at the house of Joe Blackwell, until his house was burned.
>Willie Tung of Warrenton, Daniel Moffitt of Fauquier County, members of Mosby's command.
>Miss Maggie Branson, with whom I was stopping, is related to me by marriage.
>I bought the coat and vest of grey cloth in this city, since I came here; my pants of grey I bought in Washington.
>I don't remember of hearing any disloyal remarks from any of the boarders at the house No. 16 North Eutaw Street. I whipped a colored woman at that house on Monday last, because she insulted me; her name is Annie.
>(Signed) L. Paine
>Sworn and subscribed to, before me, this 10th day of March, 1865.
>H. B. Smith Lt. and Chief[11]

There *are* some truths in Powell's statement. John S. Mosby *did* use the home of Joe Blackwell as his headquarters in August and September of 1864, and Tung and Moffit did indeed belong to Mosby's command. Also notice that young Powell reiterates that "Miss Maggie Branson ... is related to me by marriage." If indeed Powell was engaged to be married to Maggie's sister Mary, than upon his impending marriage, Maggie would be Powell's sister-in-law—definitely a "relation." (See Appendix K.)

Smith claimed he had a hard time extracting this information from the youth. Powell was no dummy, and a smart spy keeps his mouth shut. The important point is that Smith and the other officers fell for the charade, as would countless others during Powell's trial after the assassination. Obviously, Powell was just as good an actor as Booth.

It was during this agonizingly slow examination of Powell that Mary Branson, accompanied by a boarder, Mr. Shiver, bustled into the office, and to use Smith's words, "pressed right up to my desk."[12]

One can almost see Miss Branson, hoopskirts swaying in agitation, cheeks flushed with indignation, as she strode up to Smith and to Lewis's defense, demanding to know just *why* Mr. Payne was being detained and on what charge. Claiming that the errant youth was her cousin, she insisted Lewis had never been North before. "I at the same time knew he had. I done [sic] this to shield him from harm."[13]

Smith stood up before this spitfire of a young woman and responded in a supercilious manner, as he described later:

>Her word on such matters was not valuable since I had her history for disloyalty in my cabinet. I said to Mr. Shriver, whom I knew to be reckoned as a Loyal man, that he should not have lent his presence.

I was not in a good humor because persons who had promised to testify that Payne had been in Baltimore before had failed to respond. I felt in my bones he was a spy, but could not prove it, and therefore could not hold him, hence my recommendation for his release.[14]

Just who were these "persons who had promised to testify?" The maid, Annie? Who else? Could Smith have been in contact with authorities at Wests Buildings Hospital? The speculation is endless. The fact remains that Smith held Powell for at least two more days—apparently awaiting his witnesses, who never appeared.

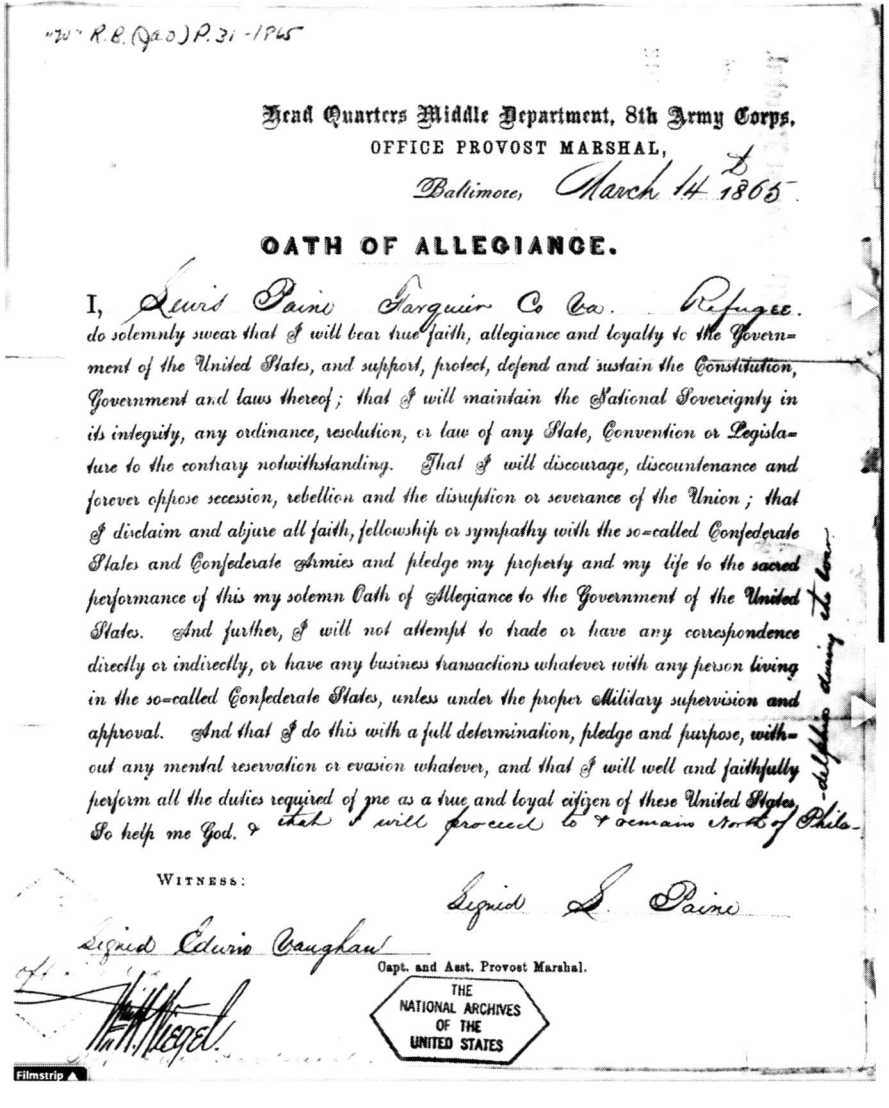

Powell's confirmation copy of the Oath of Allegiance which he took on March 14, 1865. This is the oath he carried when arrested at Mrs. Surratt's house. Erasures can be seen where he obliterated the written orders "to go north of Philadelphia and remain during the war" (National Archives).

On March 14, Powell was issued the Oath of Allegiance, whereby he swore not to bear arms or do anything disloyal against the Union. This, one of two surviving documents which bear his signature, he signed as "L. Paine."

Smith inserted on the confirmation copy of the oath Powell was given a handwritten message requiring him "to go north of Philadelphia and remain during the war." Powell would later erase the inserted order on his copy of the oath—the copy which would be found on him a month later after his arrest at the Surratt boarding house.

Powell, of course, had no idea of obeying this scrap of paper. To him, the oath was meaningless and contemptible. Released with a copy of the oath secure in his pocket, Powell realized that he had to get out of town—and get out quick. With his name on file in the provost marshal's office, he was a marked man who could be arrested for violation of his parole, and Powell had no intention of sitting out the rest of the war in a dank, dingy cell. He had work to do.

Returning to the boarding house, Lewis ate a quick lunch, packed his meager belongings and told Mary and Maggie goodbye. Carpetbag in hand, he made a hurried trip to Mr. Parr's shop. Mary's erroneous "impression" was that he went from there directly to New York. Somehow, Surratt had apparently been informed of Powell's misdeed, because the following telegram was left for Lewis in Mr. Parr's capable hands:

TO: D. Preston Parr
210 W. Baltimore Street Baltimore, Md.
March 14, 1865, 11:40 a.m.
    Immediately telegraph if my friend is disengaged and can see me this evening in Washington.
    (Signed) Harrison Surratt
    541 H Street, bet. 6 & 7 Sts.[15]

Lewis stepped unobtrusively into the fashionable china shop and waited by the door.

The proprietor noticed his uneasy "customer" and approaching him, fished out the telegram. "Do you know anything about that?"

The youth nodded: "Yes. Will you telegraph him for me and say, 'She will be over this afternoon?'"[16]

Parr agreeably did as he was asked and dispatched the following telegram on Lewis Powell's behalf, making *sure* not to include the youth's name, gender or any reference to him:

    TO: Harrison Surratt
    541 H Street, Bet. 6 & 7 Streets
Washington, D.C.
    March 14, 1865
    She will be over in the six P.M. train.
    (Signed) Parr

As far as is known, this is Parr's last recorded transaction with Powell. Lewis would have to lie low for now.

7. "The Nest That Hatched the Egg"

A damp, light breeze blew across the narrow width of H Street. In its dampness was a breath of coming spring, like a lingering spirit with a promise of balmy days to come. The tall young man walking north down H Street peered at the house numbers in the glow of twilight. He remembered the house—541 H Street, a tall, three-story whitewashed brick. That was it, straight ahead.

Lewis Powell climbed up the steep front steps for the second time in three weeks and faced the weathered panel door. There was a faint glow through the transom glass, small and soft in the evening light. Powell shifted his carpetbag from one hand to another, straightened his new slouch hat to a jaunty angle over his eye and adjusted his cravat. He reached out and pulled the doorbell. There was a faint silvery jangle inside. Powell waited. Footsteps sounded soft on the runner in the hallway. The door cracked open slowly to reveal Mrs. Surratt's star boarder, Louis Weichmann.

"Good evening, sir." Powell smiled and touched the brim of his hat politely. "Is Mr. Surratt at home?"

The inquisitive Weichmann eyed the caller suspiciously. He had seen the fellow before, but could not remember his name. To quote Weichmann: "I met the same man whom I had seen some weeks before. His first visit however, had produced so little impression on my mind that I had forgotten his name."[1]

Powell promptly remedied the situation by blandly introducing himself as Mr. Lewis Paine—the *Reverend* Mr. Paine.

Once again, Surratt was not at home, and Reverend Paine expressed a desire to speak to the lady of the house. Ushered into the parlor, Powell put his best manners to advantage. Bowing politely to the ladies and then seating himself, he struck up a lively social conversation, explaining that he was a Baptist minister who had "been in prison in Baltimore for about a week; that he had taken the Oath of Allegiance and was now going to become a good and loyal citizen."[2]

The Catholic household thought it strange that a fundamentalist Baptist minister would seek refuge under their roof but laughed it off as an odd coincidence, and he was accepted into their midst.

Expensively dressed in a new grey suit and black silk necktie, Powell looked more the part of a dashing gallant than that of a pious preacher. Dimples flashing in a boyish grin, he apparently charmed Mrs. Surratt, who remarked that he was a "great looking Baptist preacher."[3] Turning to the landlady, Powell urbanely "made some excuse to Mrs. Surratt, saying he would like to have been there on the 4th of March but could not get there."[4] Weichmann's ears perked up at this bit of information. For what reason had the minister wanted to be there "earlier"? And what was the tie-in with Surratt? Ever watchful, Weichmann looked on as, later in the evening, Powell asked Annie Surratt to play the piano for him. The "Reverend Paine" gallantly pulled out the stool for her and lifted the piano lid, turning the music pages as she played and sang a few musical pieces for the entertainment of the group.

After the little musicale was over, the young people sat down to a game of euchre. This in itself was a most unpreacher-like pastime! Eliza Holohan, one of the lady boarders, noted Powell's joviality and teasing remarks directed at the young ladies. "Queer preacher," she commented self-righteously. "I don't think *he* will convert many souls!"[5]

In the course of the evening, one of the women chanced to call Powell "Mr. Wood," the assumed name by which he went on his previous visit. This didn't escape the inquisitive Mr. Weichmann. Wood! That was it! This very same fellow who had claimed just three weeks previously to be a clerk in a china shop now appeared as a gentleman preacher. What was going on? One can imagine Weichmann just being eaten up with curiosity.

When the household retired for the night, Powell was shown upstairs to the attic room where he had previously stayed. Apparently, Weichmann escorted him to his quarters, even going so far as to watch him unpack his bag. The star boarder claimed his baggage consisted of two linen shirts and a linen coat.

It wasn't until the following afternoon that John Surratt returned home, presumably from Richmond as he was in the habit of traveling back and forth to and from the flagging Confederate capital.[6] Quite understandably, Surratt had wanted to get things straight before meeting with Powell. Weichmann, in his testimony at the conspiracy trial, gave a somewhat piqued description of Powell's meeting with Surratt: "The following day, March 14, Surratt returned home late in the afternoon." (Weichmann here errs in his recollection of the date. Powell was released from the Federal authorities on the afternoon of March 14 and spent the first night of his stay at the Surratt house. Naturally, the "following day" after Powell's arrival would be March 15.) He continued: "While I was in my room seated at my table, writing, Paine walked in. Surratt at the time was lying on the bed. Paine looked at him and said, 'Is this Mr. Surratt?' I answered, 'Yes, sir, it is.' Paine then observed, 'I would like to talk privately with Mr. Surratt.' I then arose and left the room."[7]

Weichmann went on: "I have come to regard this performance as a part of their work. I have not the slightest doubt that Surratt knew who Paine was when he opened the door and stalked into my room, and this was another of their tricks to deceive me." Of course Surratt knew who Powell was. To again quote Mr. Weichmann: "He [Powell] appeared to be kindly treated by Mr. Surratt, as if he was an old acquaintance."[8]

Things were starting to move within Booth's little group. In addition to Surratt and Powell, several others were involved. Samuel Bland Arnold and Michael O'Laughlen were old school chums of Booth. Both had served the Confederate Army and both were out of uniform, paroled and loitering about Baltimore with nothing much to do. Enter John Wilkes Booth. Suddenly Arnold, later to be a commissary clerk at Fortress Monroe, Virginia, was "flush." It had to do with a letter he had received, a letter with a fifty-dollar bank note attached, preceded by a meeting in Baltimore with an old schoolmate, Mr. J. Wilkes Booth, stage star. Mr. Booth met Mr. Arnold at Barnum's Hotel in Baltimore and introduced him to yet another old friend, Michael O'Laughlen. Soon the three were discussing the Confederacy. Wined and dined and no doubt furnished aplenty with information concerning a kidnapping venture backed by the underground, Arnold and O'Laughlen chewed over the idea along with their steak and oysters. The monetary rewards were promising. In Arnold's case, it surpassed pay received for working on his brother's farm. And O'Laughlen, who liked to live fast, decided that a clerkship in a feed store wasn't so exciting after all, and the pay was nothing to write home about.

Here was something important and exciting. Backed by the Confederate underground, a plan to abduct President Lincoln just might work with the help of resourceful operatives.

Arnold and O'Laughlen agreed to cooperate, and the pact was theoretically signed, sealed and dropped right in Booth's lap. These were no doubt Booth's first recruits.[9] There then ensued Booth's quick trip to Montreal, Canada, and New York for conferences no doubt with rebel agents. Upon his return Arnold and O'Laughlen found themselves the custodians of a big trunk containing guns, knives and ammunition for use in the kidnapping venture.

David E. Herold was a young D.C. druggist's clerk out of work. The fact that he was unemployed did not worry Davy in the least. He had seven sisters to keep him in pocket money, and he preferred hanging about the barrooms and stables to having a steady job. His passion was hunting. Clever and cunning with a shotgun, he had hunted extensively throughout southern Maryland and could pick the eye out of a quail at thirty feet. He knew all the backwoods routes in Maryland and was quite good at handling a horse, too. Davy prided himself on knowing just about every family and farm in southern Maryland. Stables and saloons were handy places in which to gather information from the folk who frequented them. Take, for instance, George Andrew Atzerodt. George, a German immigrant who went by the nickname of "Port Tobacco" in reference to his hometown, Port Tobacco, Maryland, had a carriage-painting trade when he worked at it. Most of his time though, was spent ferrying passengers back and forth across the Potomac, mostly agents on missions for the Confederate underground. The rest of his time was spent with stable hands and saloon roustabouts. Davy had known Atzerodt for about five years.[10] Both men knew John Surratt, Confederate courier, and their various underground connections also made them aware that John Wilkes Booth, stage star, was a Confederate agent. Herold had known Booth for two years, Atzerodt for a somewhat lesser period of time. Both men were Southern sympathizers. It would seem doubtful though, that the Confederate hierarchy would place its trust in their inexperienced hands. More than likely, Surratt and Booth were permitted to handpick their associates for the upcoming venture.

In November 1864, John's mother, Mrs. Mary E. Surratt, moved to Washington City to open a boarding house, leaving her tavern rented out in the incapable hands of John M. Lloyd, a former District policeman turned alcoholic, who would manage the tap room and property. Mrs. Surratt at the same time began placing ads in the *Washington Star* for gentlemen boarders.[11] George Atzerodt was one of the first to apply for a room; whether or not he did so at the insistence of John Surratt is unclear. According to Mrs. Surratt, "He remained several days. I do not know how many days. He was not in the house, but a few times. I found in his room bottles of liquor, and when my son came home, I told him that I did not want this man to board; that he kept bottles of liquor and I did not want him there. That is all of my acquaintance with Port Tobacco."[12] Atzerodt did not remain long at 541 H Street after his drinking habits were discovered by the landlady.

John Wilkes Booth's visits to the H Street house were more than welcome. John Surratt had bragged to a young cousin named Belle of the ladies "brushing and fixing" upon the illustrious Mr. Booth's arrival being announced. John's sister, Anna, seemingly had a crush of sorts on the handsome, polished actor.

If there were any protestations against Lewis Powell's visits, they went unvoiced, and so far as is known, Herold did not frequent the boarding house. Much to Weichmann's annoyance, Powell and Surratt remained in the latter's room and talked for quite a while on that particular March evening. After a bit, the pudgy busybody returned upstairs to his room to find it empty. He paused, noticing something odd lying on his table, a medium-sized false mustache of thick black hair. Weichmann picked it up gingerly. It wasn't his or John's, so it must belong to that Paine fellow. That "preacher business" was poppycock. Paine was no more a preacher than Surratt was the pope. To quote Weichmann: "Not thinking much about it, and intending to have a little fun with it, I threw it into a box that stood there."[13]

Perhaps Powell was a bit leery of Weichmann and decided that his room would be a better place to talk. Surratt had some things to show him—things better revealed where there would be less chance of interruption. Fully indoctrinated in Confederate Secret Service directives by this time, Powell and Surratt, no doubt, went over details.

The original plans called for Lincoln to be abducted from Ford's Theater during a theatrical performance. Silly? Perhaps so—and highly impractical. The project called for the group to enter Lincoln's theater box while someone cut the gas lighting. In the ensuing darkness and confusion, Lincoln could be trussed and spirited away in a closed carriage waiting out back in the alley. Powell may have considered the idea an absurd risk—but then service with Mosby had not exactly been fun and games. More than likely, as a hardened soldier who was remembered as being "keyed up for any new sensations," the young Ranger turned agent probably liked the element of risk and rose to meet the challenge.

All was in readiness. Herold traveled the thirteen miles out to Surrattsville with guns, rope and a wrench to be used in the plot. These articles were later stored at the tavern owned by John's mother and were to be available for immediate use. Surratt had certain things to show Powell, and in a short time, Lewis found a small arsenal deposited on his bed—two revolvers, two Bowie knives and eight pairs of new spurs. The two looked over the articles, and no doubt each picked the weapons he would use when the proper time arose.

Now a little melodrama enters the picture. According to Weichmann, he blundered upstairs to the little attic room where Powell boarded. His account leaves it uncertain whether he was on some errand or just snooping around. Although he makes much about Lewis Powell's "stalking" unbidden into *his* room, Weichmann seems to have thought nothing about his own conduct in entering Powell's room with nary a knock at the door. What he saw there aroused his curiosity enough to send him clattering back downstairs to question the landlady. As the door to his room swung open, Powell sprang to his feet, a heavy revolver in his hand. Surratt made a poor attempt to hide the miniature arsenal by sprawling on top of it. Powell just stood there gawking, the gun in his hand at his side. Weichmann stared at them and quickly pulled the door closed. Ferret-like, he hastened downstairs to seek out the landlady. "I at once went downstairs and sought Mrs. Surratt and told her what I had discovered, and that I had seen John and Payne with those weapons, and added, 'Mrs. Surratt, I do not like this.' She told me that I should not think anything of it, that I knew John was in the habit of riding into the country and that he had to have these things as a protection."[14] The memory of those weapons would soon return to haunt Mr. Weichmann.

Surratt and Powell were seemingly not too alarmed by the intrusion and, if they were, they weren't going to let it worry them. That night, Surratt had something else in store for Powell—a theater party to Ford's Theater arranged by none other than Mr. Booth. In a boastful manner, Surratt had already shown Weichmann a ten-dollar theater ticket for the evening performance of *Jane Shore* to be performed at Ford's. Weichmann expressed a desire to go, but Surratt said it was to be a "private" affair.

After supper, the party consisting of Miss Honora Fitzpatrick, a young lady boarder, and a Miss Apolonia Dean, age nine, living at Mrs. Surratt's house while attending school, departed. Powell was Miss Fitzpatrick's escort, and he was arrayed for the occasion in Weichmann's heavy, blue military cape—a loan from the star boarder.

This was to be much more than a mere social outing. Arriving at Ford's in a hired hack, the party was shown to their reserved seats—in the presidential box. Near the end of the play, John Wilkes Booth entered the box and after social amenities, motioned for the men to step outside a moment. At the trial of John Surratt in 1867, Miss Fitzpatrick remembered: "Mr. Booth came there and spoke to Mr. Surratt. They both stepped outside the box and stood there at the door." Asked if anyone else joined the two men: "Mr. Wood [Lewis Paine] ... they remained there a few minutes." Miss Fitzpatrick was more interested in the play than in the conversation of the three men. What were they discussing? Undoubtedly, Powell and Surratt went to Ford's to "case it" in anticipation of the kidnapping. Booth also administered a gentle prod to be sure the men would attend a meeting after the play at Gautier's Saloon.

When the final curtain went down, Surratt and Powell escorted the ladies home. Weichmann remembered that Surratt secured a pack of playing cards and then left the house with his companion, Powell. Gautier's fashionable saloon and restaurant located at the corner of Thirteenth Street and Pennsylvania Avenue was nearly empty. Eleven-thirty at night was not a popular hour. Powell and Surratt went through the dimly lit hallway to the back of the establishment where Booth had engaged a private room with instructions that his party was not to be disturbed. The room was a large one; and a buffet to the side of the door was heaped with cheeses, cold slices of meats and oysters. Numerous liquors and champagnes were on another table alongside. Booth always did things on a grand scale.

So far as can be determined, this was the only time Booth and all of his men were together for a meeting. Arnold and O'Laughlen were there along with Atzerodt and Herold, and finally Surratt and Powell sauntered in. Powell went by the nickname of "Mosby" within the group in deference to his service with Mosby's elite outfit, leaving one once again with the impression that he had been dispatched from Mosby's group to work as an agent in the kidnapping plot.

After a hearty supper, all went well until Booth started with the business at hand. Arnold was in a sullen mood and had had enough of foolish talk about tussling with Lincoln in a darkened theater box. A heated discussion broke out amongst the group. Years later, Arnold wrote:

> Then commenced the plan. Each had his part to perform. First, I was to rush in the box and seize the President whilst Atzerodt, alias "Port Tobacco" and John Wilkes Booth were to handcuff him and lower him on the stage, whilst "Mosby" was to catch him and hold him until we all got down. Surratt and an unknown [were] to be on the other side of the bridge to facilitate [sic] escape, afterward changed to Mosby and Booth to catch him in the box, throw him down to me on the stage. O'Laughlen and an unknown to put the gas out. Surratt, Atzerodt alias Port Tobacco [were] to be on the other side of the bridge. I was opposed to the whole proceeding. Said it could not be done or accomplished.[15]

Strong words were bandied back and forth within the group. The atmosphere was strained, and tension shot through the room like summer lightening. Most of the men present agreed with Arnold, who adamantly asserted that if something wasn't carried out by the end of the week, he was quitting. "Whereupon J. Wilkes Booth remarked in a stern, commanding, and angry voice, 'Do you know you are liable to be shot?—your oath!'"[16]

Arnold coolly eyed Booth. "Two can play *that* game!"

The enraged actor simmered down a bit, apologizing for the outburst and blaming it on the liquor. An alternative plan was then discussed. Booth had heard through theater grapevine and backstage gossip that a matinee performance of *Still Waters Run Deep* was scheduled to be given at Campbell Hospital on Friday, March 17, for the benefit of the convalescent wounded. The guest of honor was to be none other than President Lincoln.[17]

Due to its isolated location on the road leading to the Soldiers' Home, the hospital would be ideally suited for Booth's abduction plan. The conspirators seemed to have settled down and accepted this alternate idea readily. The plans having been revised and agreed upon, the meeting resolved itself into a poker game that did not break up until 5:00 a.m. Meanwhile, the group had one day left in which to make preparation.

8. The Road to Ruin

After months of planning, after all the doubt and hope and nagging fear, everything was in readiness, and all they had to do was wait. The weapons were a few miles south of the Surrattsville tavern, in Davy Herold's capable hands at a place called TB. Atzerodt had a skiff waiting at the Potomac. The mounts were available—Booth had seen to that. Early in November, the actor had made the acquaintance of Dr. Samuel A. Mudd, a country physician residing near Bryantown, Maryland, and a staunch Southern sympathizer. Through various connections, Booth had managed to purchase a saddle horse—a dark bay with a starred forehead and one white foot. The gelding was a pacer, akin to a Standardbred trotter, large and powerful, but blind in one eye. The animal subsequently wound up in Atzerodt's and then Powell's possession. Each man generally furnished his own mount, either by livery or ownership. Powell knew good horseflesh. His stint with Mosby had seen to that, and the young son of Dr. Alban S. Payne had described in colorful terms Powell's fine blood bay mare, the animal he had owned while serving under the Gray Ghost and which he subsequently sold in Alexandria before crossing the lines. Work in his father's smithy as a small boy also undoubtedly gave Lewis an early acquaintanceship with horses. What Powell thought of the one-eyed nag, which was considered uncomfortable to ride, assigned to him by Booth can only be imagined, although he would continue to use the gelding throughout their association.

According to Samuel Arnold, the abduction plans were to "seize him [the president] and his carriage ... and to drive him around by way of Bladensburg to Surrattsville or TB, there to meet Herold and to convey him to the Potomac. It had been decided for the first attempt that ropes were to be stretched across the road for the purpose of tripping up the horses in case of pursuit."[1]

Booth wasn't taking any chances. Arnold revealed that the actor made good use of the meddlesome Louis Weichmann to dig out War Department information pertaining to the number of Confederate prisoners held by U.S. authorities—totaling thirty to thirty-five thousand men.[2] Thirty to thirty-five thousand men could more than build up the flagging Confederate forces, and Booth considered the possible result worth the risk—as no doubt did higher-ups in the Confederate echelon.

This glut of information makes one wonder if Weichmann actually knew what was going on. Certainly he wasn't the innocent he proclaimed to be. For instance, there was the incident concerning the false moustache. Weichmann found it lying on a table in his room the day after Powell came to board, and according to Weichmann "Reverend Payne" claimed the disguise as his. "He felt around for it with his hand and said, 'Where is my moustache?'"[3] With the sparse beard of youth, did the downy-cheeked Powell intend to use the disguise during the abduction? Sharp-eyed Mr. Weichmann must have known the minister bit was a sham. What else did he know? Just how much did the others trust him? One wonders. Seemingly, Lewis Powell did not regard him too highly. Likewise, what about the landlady herself?

In an 1892 newspaper article authored by the son of Powell's spiritual advisor, Lewis was quoted as having confessed to the minister concerning Mrs. Surratt: "Payne spoke with great feeling. Of prior knowledge of their later deeds he declared her innocent, but did not, of course, *deny her interest in their original actions and plans.*"[4] Undoubtedly, Mrs. Surratt knew her son was involved with the Secret Service. She would also not remain in the dark as to the comings and goings of her son's friends. Not much can go on in an eight-room house and remain unnoticed for long. An old undated clipping from the *New York World* gives a contrary impression: "One evening on the occasion of his [Powell's] last visit at Mrs. Surratt's, he made a remark to Surratt in the parlor from which the plan to abduct might be inferred when immediately, Surratt took Payne out of the parlor and told him never to say anything of that kind again in the presence of his mother or sister, as they knew nothing about the affair and should not."[5] Could this be just another instance of chivalry on the part of Powell in his last hours, an attempt to clear Mrs. Surratt of blame and assure himself of a clean conscience? Later developments concerning the abduction scheme make one wonder about the innocence of the widow Surratt.

Friday, March 17, dawned with excitement in the Surratt household on H Street. No doubt Lewis Powell and Surratt were up early to attend to matters. Details of that morning are lacking, but, it is known that the group was scheduled to meet at 2:00 p.m.[6] The plan called for the men to ride out to Seventh Street singly rather than in a group which might attract attention. They were to waylay the presidential coach on a lonely stretch of wooded road leading to Campbell Hospital. One can almost picture Lewis Powell and John Surratt checking their side arms and drawing on their riding gloves as the time grew near. With spurs clinking at their heels as they clumped down the steep wooden front steps, they mounted their waiting horses and rode off down H Street in a transport of excitement.

There seems to be some confusion about what actually occurred then. Most historians believe that Booth and his men actually did waylay an official-looking coach, but Sam Arnold remembered otherwise:

> After dinner, we met Booth and accompanied him to a livery stable near the Patent Office at which place Booth obtained horses for us. O'Laughlin [sic] and myself rode to our room on D Street and made all our necessary arrangements. Each arming himself, O'Laughlin [sic] and myself rode out to where the performance was to take place. We stopped at a restaurant at the foot of the hill to await the arrival of the other parties. They not arriving as soon as expected, we remounted our horses and rode out the road about a mile. We then returned and stopped at the same restaurant. Whilst in there, Atzerodt came in who had just arrived with Payne. A short time after, Booth and Surratt came in and we drank together.[7]

After a dram or so, Booth strode out of the establishment, mounted his horse and rode out to the hospital to check up on matters, leaving his cohorts in the restaurant to await further orders. They didn't have long to wait. Booth was back in a short while, fuming with frustration. The president hadn't shown up.

Actor E. L. Davenport recalled meeting an elegantly attired Booth on horseback at the hospital. Booth expressed great concern over Lincoln's appearance, and upon discovering that the president had not attended, the disgusted thespian had wheeled his horse back down the road. "The Old Man," as Booth sneeringly referred to Lincoln, had other pressing obligations and had sent his regrets for not attending.

"He [Booth] returned immediately, seeming very much excited," Arnold stated, "cautioning care and discretion in our movements, and in a hurried manner advising separation from one another and to return by different routes into the city, as he feared our movements were being overlooked." Powell, disgusted with the outcome, left with O'Laughlen and Arnold, the trio riding leisurely back into town.

Back at the boarding house, Mr. Weichmann had just returned home from work at the War Department. The house was abnormally silent. Where was everyone? The quizzical Weichmann questioned the young black houseboy who worked for the widow. "He replied that Massa Surratt had ridden away from the front of the house in the afternoon about two o'clock with six or seven on horseback."[8] Weichmann pressed for more detail. The party consisted of Mr. Booth, Mr. Paine, Mr. Atzerodt, young Mr. Surratt and three others the youth didn't recognize—Arnold, O'Laughlen and Herold.

Weichmann was in for an additional shock when he went down to supper and encountered the landlady weeping in the hallway. "John is gone away!" Why the tears? Weichmann could put two and two together: "Here was a distinct avowal on the part of this woman that her son had gone away ... on some dangerous errand."[9] This seemed to be proof that Mrs. Surratt knew what her son and his cronies were up to.

The dinner table was made conspicuous by the two vacant chairs. Surratt and the Reverend Paine had not partaken of the evening repast with the rest of the family and boarders. After dinner, Weichmann retired to his room and was engrossed in Dickens' novel *Pickwick Papers*. A door slammed downstairs, and heavy footsteps pounded upstairs. Surratt clumped loudly into his room, flustered and angry.

Alarmed, Weichmann noticed his companion carried a small revolver. Surratt was in a dangerously excited mood. After a few seconds, the door slammed for a second time. Lewis Powell trudged sullenly and dejectedly up the stairs, his trouser legs tucked into his mud-splattered boot tops, his face flushed from drink and rage. He strolled into Surratt's room and glanced at the astonished Weichmann wordlessly.

One of Powell's suspenders had worked loose, and when he raised his vest to adjust the galluses, an innocent enough gesture, Weichmann's eye hovered over the top of the book he was reading and came to rest on Powell's gun-weighted hip.

Booth ambled into the room and Weichmann looked up for a third time. What was going on? Powell and Surratt fidgeted nervously, silent and sullen as Booth strode in small circles, slapping in frustration at his boot tops with a riding crop. He spoke politely to Weichmann and motioned for Powell and Surratt to leave the room, and the trio went up to Powell's quarters in the attic. They stayed closeted in Powell's room for about thirty minutes, after which the three men left the house—Powell with carpetbag in hand. Arrangements were made by Booth for Powell and himself to leave town until things cooled down a bit. Booth would leave for New York the following night, after his last theatrical performance at Ford's Theater on March 18. Powell would make a side trip to Baltimore before proceeding farther north to New York.

Seemingly, there would be one major attraction to draw Powell back to the Monumental City aside from a secret service briefing, and its name was Miss Mary Branson. Logically, it would seem that the incentive would have to be quite strong to entice him back to the city he had left so hurriedly under fear of arrest only four days previously! Or were there others Powell had to alert to the kidnapping failure? Mary's father, for instance, who was supposedly also in on the plot? The romantic-minded Confederate agent could kill two birds with one stone—a briefing with Papa Branson and a dalliance with his sweetheart, Mary! (See Appendix K.)

Whatever the occasion, Powell didn't linger long in Baltimore. Two days later, March 20, he was writing Surratt from the fashionable Revere House Hotel, 604–608 Broadway, corner of Houston Street in New York. At the then exorbitant rate of rooming for $2 a day, the Revere House was considered a pretty posh hotel.[10] With regard to the receipt of this letter, Weichmann remembered the occasion distinctly:

> I happened on my way home to meet Surratt about half past four o'clock in the afternoon at the corner of Seventh and F Streets near the post office. Surratt stepped up to the delivery window of the office and inquired for a letter addressed to him under the name of James Sturdy. The clerk handed him such a letter. It was signed "Wood." Surratt foolishly showed me the signature. I saw enough of the letter to recognize that it was in a very bad handwriting, though I am ignorant of its contents. On being questioned, Surratt admitted that the "Wood" who wrote was the same man [Paine] who had stayed at his mother's house.[11]
>
> An account published in the *New York Herald Tribune* for May 19, 1865, expanded the testimony to include "...the letter was signed 'Wood,' and the writer stated that he was at the Revere House in New York, that he was looking for something to do, but would probably go to some boarding house in Grand Street, I think West Grand Street, that was the whole substance of the letter." One would think that Powell more than had his hands full with possible goings on from the Confederate Cabinet in Canada as well as what was transpiring in New York with the Copperheads as well.

Apparently Lewis was quite a prolific letter writer during this period. Mary had also received one of his missives, although she did not reveal its contents other than to say that Lewis requested she write him care of the Revere House in New York. Mary did, in fact, answer Lewis's letter but never received a reply, or so she testified.[12]

While in New York, Powell presumably added yet another pseudonym to his collection—alias "Jim Moore." Colonel H. H. Wells stated in a letter written on May 11, 1865, to the chief of the New York Detective Police, John Young, that "Lewis Paine" carried such an alias, and from a subsequent grilling of the Branson sisters it became evident that this was more than likely the name that Powell went under while in New York.[13]

Could Powell have traveled to Canada during this time? There are some reasons to speculate what he did. A conference with Confederate operatives there would be almost a must if Booth and his men were actually working under orders issued from an echelon there. Richard Montgomery, a spy or counterspy familiar with the Confederate Canadian setup and its resources, claimed to have seen Powell in Toronto. Although Montgomery gives October 1864 as the date of his first meeting with "Paine" at the "Falls" (a period when Powell was with Mosby in Virginia), there is the thought-provoking possibility that Powell could have been dispatched by Mosby for an initiation briefing into the underground at that time.

Montgomery mentioned another meeting with Lewis Paine at an unspecified date in Toronto:

> I saw him again and had some words with him at the Queen's Hotel in Toronto. I had an interview with Mr. Thompson and on leaving the room, I met this man Payne, in the passageway, talking with Mr. Clement C. Clay ... while Mr. Clay was away, I spoke to this man Payne,

and asked him who he was. I commenced talking about some of the topics usually spoken of in conversation amongst these men. He rather hesitated about telling me who he was. He said, "O, I am a Canadian." By which I understood that I was not to question him further. In about half an hour afterward, I asked Mr. Clay who this man Payne was, and he said, "What did he say?" I told him that he said he was a Canadian. Mr. Clay laughed and said, "That is so; he is a Canadian," and he added, "We trust him."[14]

Montgomery explained further: "The term 'Canadian' was a common expression among the Confederates there and was applied to those who were in the habit of visiting the States; and I understood from Mr. Clay's laugh that their intercourse was of a confidential nature."[15]

At the Surratt trial in 1867, William E. Wheeler, a liveryman in Chicopee, Massachusetts, claimed to have seen John Wilkes Booth and another gentleman in Montreal—a man whose brief description loosely resembles Powell:

Q. Will you describe the person in whose company you saw him at that time?
A. He was a large man, thick-set with a flushed red face.
Q. What was the color of his hair?
A. I cannot remember as to that. It was rather dark I think.[16]

Perhaps Booth and Powell *did* journey to Canada. When he was captured, a handful of Canadian coins were found in Powell's pockets.[17]

Details of what Powell and Booth did in New York are lacking of course. However, it can be stated confidently that when they came back to Washington around March 27, they returned with something much more serious than kidnapping on their minds.

9. Countdown to Tragedy

At the corner of Ninth and F streets, opposite the Patent Office in Washington, D.C., stood the Herndon House, a rooming house with all the trappings of a second-rate hotel. Under the proprietorship of an Irishman, Patrick Murray, and his wife Martha, it catered to a middle-class clientele.

Miss Anna Ward, a young teacher at the Catholic Female School on Tenth Street, knew the Murrays. She also knew the Surratts and attended the same church as the Surratt family.[1] Oddly, she had virtually the very same name as the African American maid whom Powell had previously beaten at the Branson boarding house. (See Appendix K.)

On March 19, following the kidnapping fiasco, Surratt decided to pay a call on Miss Ward. The ever-present Weichmann accompanied him.

> The same evening he [Surratt] asked me to take a walk with him. The first place he visited was a Catholic School at the corner of 10th and G Streets, and there he called for one of the teachers, Miss Annie Ward. He had some conversation with her, of which I am ignorant. After leaving her he went as far as the corner of 9th and F Streets. Here he went into the Herndon House and I followed him. He called for Mrs. Murray, the mistress of the hotel, and when this lady came to him, he expressed a desire to talk with her privately, but she did not seem to comprehend what he said, being somewhat hard of hearing. Then Surratt spoke out a little more boldly. "Perhaps Miss Annie Ward has spoken to you about a room. Did she not speak to you about engaging a room for a delicate gentleman who was to have his meals sent up to him?" He told her furthermore that he wanted the room for the following Monday, which was the 27th of March, 1865. Mrs. Murray then recollected and said such a room had been engaged by Miss Annie Ward and that it would be ready at that time. Accordingly on that day, March 27, Lewis Paine returned from New York to Washington and occupied the room at the Herndon House which had been secured for him by the joint efforts of Miss Annie Ward and John H. Surratt.
>
> Surratt took good care not to mention to me the name of the individual who was to occupy the room. I was, however, not left long in the dark as to that. Happening to meet Atzerodt on the street one day, curiosity prompted me to ask him, "Is it Payne who is staying at the Herndon House?" He responded, "Yes." I communicated that fact to Mrs. Surratt and she became quite angry that I should have found it out.[2]

So Powell was to return to Washington on March 27. More than likely, Powell wished Surratt to make arrangements for him although when placed on the witness stand, Mrs. Murray would claim that she had not talked to Surratt and that Powell had directly applied to her for a room. Nevertheless, Lewis arrived at the Herndon House on the designated day, about eleven o'clock or twelve noon, after just coming in "on the cars"; i.e., horse-drawn street car. With regard to Powell being a gentleman "invalid," one wonders if Mrs. Murray found it believable that the husky, robust youngster was "sickly." Apparently the young black waiter who brought up Lewis' meals didn't seem to think so, noting that Powell had a huge appetite and "would have eaten a young pig—bones and all."[3]

9. Countdown to Tragedy

Signing the register with yet another alias, "Mr. Kincheloe," the name of an officer in one of Mosby's units, Powell was shown upstairs to his quarters, Room 6, the front room right on the corner of Ninth Street, third floor.[4] Here Powell would remain until the fatal night of April 14. Recent findings seem to suggest that Powell may have gone out for a night on the town on his return to the capital—or did he simply have an evening meeting with Booth?

When Powell was captured after the assassination attempt, a search of his pockets revealed, amidst a varied assortment of personal effects, a ticket to Ford's Theater for the Monday, March 27 performance of *La Farza del Destino* (*The Force of Destiny*), Max Maretek's grand Italian opera.[5] The twenty-five-cent pink ticket stub, now in the archives of the Lincoln Memorial University in Harrogate, Tennessee, is the portion that the theater patron retains and has clearly been detached and punched by the ticket attendant at the door. From all appearances, Powell did attend the performance. Lewis was probably not overly fond of Italian opera; however, John Wilkes Booth *was* generous with complimentary theater tickets, and the seat was a good one in the orchestra section.[6] Perhaps a backstage interview with the actor was arranged for after or during the performance. One can be sure the conversation at such a meeting would not consist of mere theater gossip.

Powell did receive some visits during his stay at the Herndon House. Not long after his arrival, Mrs. Surratt paid a call; something that would be considered demeaning in the rigid, repressed Victorian era. Unattended ladies simply did not make social calls on virile young men in their bedrooms—no matter their age. Weichmann, who was accompanying the widow at the time, remembered the incident vividly:

The Herndon House—9th and F streets, Washington, D.C., where Powell boarded at the time of the assassination (courtesy the late James O. Hall and Surratt House Museum).

> In a very few days, Mrs. Surratt called on Payne at the Herndon House. I cannot recall the particular evening on which she did so, but it was after the 27th of March, and sometime during Lent. Mrs. Surratt, Miss Annie Surratt, Miss Olivia Jenkins, a niece of Mrs. Surratt, Miss Fitzpatrick, and myself had been to Saint Patrick's Church at the corner of 10th and F Streets. After leaving church, and on our way home, Mrs. Surratt stopped at the Herndon House and remarked that she was going in to see Payne. She left us all on the outside and in the meantime we took a walk around the square. When we returned to the Herndon House, she was descending the front steps and then we started home together.[7]

Under oath, Honora Fitzpatrick also confirmed the visit, although she claimed Mrs. Surratt had said she was "just going into the Herndon House to see someone," and she did not say whom she was going to visit.

Mrs. Murray, the landlady, did not remember Mrs. Surratt's visit—indeed, she claimed she did not even know her! Weichmann posed a rhetorical question: "Whom then, did she visit if not Payne?" The remaining question could be why did Mrs. Surratt visit the house at all?

The date that the kidnapping scheme turned to murder is unknown. However, if Maj. Thomas T. Eckert, Assistant Secretary of War, is to be believed, something akin to murder was afoot as far back as January 1865, and Lewis Powell was certainly in the picture from the start.

Eckert had been appointed by Stanton to try to get a statement out of the taciturn prisoner, and in testimony given during the Surratt trial in 1867, Eckert gave under oath a smattering of the various revelations which Powell had confessed to during the conspiracy proceedings of 1865. This "confession," if it can be called such, also appears in a bit more detailed account in a book, *Lincoln in the Telegraph Office* by David Homer Bates, a telegraph operator who worked under Eckert.

> Payne told Eckert of three occasions when he was close to Lincoln and could have shot him if so inclined. Once, during the winter of 1865, Booth and Payne had walked through the White House grounds in the daytime. Booth urged Payne to send a card in to Lincoln, using any name he might see fit and when he went into the room, to shoot the President. Payne said he refused and Booth berated him soundly for cowardice.[8]

Another occurrence was at night in January 1865. The hour was late, and the weather was icy and cold. There had been sleet during the day and evening, and a thin rime of ice crusted the ground. Supposedly, Powell crouched behind some bushes on the White House grounds and pistol in hand, waited for Lincoln to appear. When the president finally came into view, walking from the War Department with a companion, Powell suddenly lost his nerve and ran away through the concealing ice-encrusted shrubs.

Eckert even confirmed the occasion by claiming to be the man accompanying President Lincoln that night. Under grilling, Powell turned to Eckert and said, "Major, were you not the man walking with the President through the White House grounds late one frosty night last winter?"[9]

If this confession is true, then kidnapping or murder was the prime goal from the beginning. Eckert's testimony and the subsequent recollections were written after the fact. Pressed for specific information, Eckert admitted under oath that he had not made any written statement, although he had meant to do so at the insistence of Secretary of State Seward. Never finding time, he had just jotted down a few pertinent thoughts in a memorandum. The rest of what he revealed was just recollection of what young Powell had told him in 1865—and these recollections were related anywhere from two years after at the Surratt trial to forty-two years later, in 1907. Add to the fact that Powell was away from the Branson Boarding House only one night in January 1865, when he stayed at the Surratt Boarding House.[10]

And then there are Powell's assertions that he did not know of the plan to murder until 8:00 p.m. on the night of April 14. However, such a drastic endeavor seemingly would necessarily involve more depth of planning. The trip to New York taken by Booth and Powell was no mere diversion—a last-minute decision to kill three or four victims would not have involved the week-long scheming which seems to have taken place.

And then there was the matter of the horses. Booth had apparently left the care of the horses to Powell. Although Surratt supposedly claimed ownership, according to Weichmann, Atzerodt told the War Department clerk that one horse belonged to him and one horse belonged to Booth. These animals, a small sorrel horse and the larger one-eyed gelding assigned for Lewis Powell's use, were apparently shifted around through various owners' hands quite a bit.

As an ex-cavalryman, Powell could be depended on to do whatever was required for the animals' upkeep. Weichmann confirmed Powell's hand in this when, at the request of the widow Surratt, he went to see Atzerodt about hiring one of "John's horses" for the temporary use of Mrs. Surratt's brother, Zadock Jenkins: "I called on Atzerodt at the Pennsylvania House that afternoon with Mr. Jenkins and stated my message. His reply was that before he could loan Mr. Jenkins one of the horses, he would have to see Mr. Payne about it."[11] The astonished Weichmann asked, "What has Payne to do with the horses?" To which Atzerodt coolly replied, "Payne has a heap to do with them." Atzerodt, Weichmann and Jenkins then walked over to Ninth and F Streets to the Herndon House. While Weichmann and Jenkins waited on the sidewalk, Atzerodt went into the hotel to see Powell. Shortly thereafter, he returned with a flat-out refusal on the part of Powell. For some reason, "Mr. Payne" would not consent to the loan of the horses.

Weichmann was disgruntled. He would have good cause later on to remember the incident. The countdown to tragedy was beginning.

10. April 14, 1865

The Confederacy was fast crumbling to dust in that spring of 1865. By April, the death knell had sounded, and for John Wilkes Booth, Lewis Powell and other like-minded rebels, if anything was to be done, it had to be done quickly.

No one knows how Powell received the news of Richmond's fall on April 3—or of Lee's surrender on April 9. Booth is said to have wept over the headlines, but if Powell expressed such grief it remains unrecorded. That Powell was embittered with the thought of his slain brother and the looming defeat of the Confederate cause is certain. There was most probably a streak of revenge in his decision to assist Booth, although he had apparently not yet nerved himself to commit murder, despite the actor's prodding. In the death cell, young Powell would tell Dr. Gillette that he "expected a promotion and the everlasting gratitude of the southern people if he succeeded." In other words, the boy was led to believe that he would be a southern hero; a "freedom fighter" of sorts.[1]

On April 11, President Lincoln gave a speech from the White House portico to a jubilant crowd taking part in the week-long celebrations commemorating the fall of Richmond and the surrender of Lee. Among the revelers drunk with elation were three men who stood sullen, not participating in the cheering and reflected glory. John Wilkes Booth, David Herold and Lewis Powell listened glumly to the president's reconstruction speech in which he recommended giving "elective franchise," i.e., the right to vote, to intelligent blacks and to those blacks who had served in the military. Accordingly, Booth muttered, "That is the last speech he will ever make! Now by God, I'll put him through!" The enraged actor grasped Powell's arm and urged him to draw his revolver and shoot Lincoln on the spot. Powell, alarmed at his companion's outburst, flatly refused to commit such a foolish and unreasonable act. According to what Powell told Eckert after his capture, he (Powell) walked away from Booth and away from the crowd. He would reconsider—and with deadly results—three days later.

Somehow, somewhere, the wheels apparently started turning between April 11 and April 13. The group had dwindled to only Powell, Herold and Atzerodt. Surratt had left on April 2 for Richmond to carry dispatches to Montreal for Confederate Secretary of State Judah Benjamin. Arnold and O'Laughlen had long since called the whole affair quits.

Early on Thursday morning, the day before the assassination, Powell, or a man fitting his description, was seen near the Secretary of State's house, No. 17 Madison Place, on Lafayette Square. Supposedly, previous to the attack as well, Powell was seen talking to and "flattering" a Seward maid, supposedly one Margaret Coleman. According to Atzerodt's Lost Confession, he stated, "I overheard Booth when in conversation with Wood say that he visited a chambermaid at Seward's House & that she was pretty. He said he had a great mind to give her his diamond pin."[2] Secretary Seward had been involved in a carriage accident

10. April 14, 1865

The home of William H. Seward, on Lafayette Square at Fifteen and One-half Street, facing the White House, was known as the "Old Club House" in 1865 (courtesy Dr. John Lattimer Collection).

on April 5 which had left the sixty-four-year-old statesman with a dislocated jaw and a broken arm. In great pain, Seward was confined to bed, attended by Dr. Tullio S. Verdi and an invalid soldier, Pvt. George F. Robinson, who acted as a male nurse.

Interviewed after the attack on Seward, Robinson remembered: "A man came to the window of the dining room of the Seward house on the morning of the 13th and 14th of April, and inquired each day about the health of the Secretary. [He was a] large man, no beard, and had a black hat on and light colored clothes. When I first saw the man at the door of Mr. Seward's room at the time of the attack, I thought I recognized him to be the same person."[3] Was this indeed Powell, or just a strange coincidence? Supposedly, Powell was assigned the task of disposing of the Secretary of State at 8:00 p.m. on April 14, or so Powell told Eckert. He would later tell his spiritual adviser an entirely different story: "Until the *morning* of the fatal day, no crime more serious than the abduction had been contemplated. It was *early in that day* that he was instructed as to what was expected of him."[4]

Booth was for drastic action—it was decided to wipe out the top Federal leaders from the president on down: president, vice president, secretary of state *and* General Grant! Why was the Secretary of State designated for assassination? The reasons were probably many and varied. William H. Seward was a much maligned man. Southerners feared and abhorred Seward, whose opinions on abolition were well known and whose violation of commitments regarding Fort Sumter in 1861 had made them distrust him.[5] Also, it was the duty of the Secretary of State "by law upon the death of said President and Vice President of the United States aforesaid, to cause an election to be held for electors of the President of the United States."[6]

As to the reason for Powell's complicity in the plot:

> Powell insisted that he was a Confederate soldier, and for months previous, while in the Secret Service of the Confederacy, he had journeyed back and forth from Richmond to Washington and Baltimore in conference with prominent men in the latter city, whom of course, he did not name. These gentlemen had kept him in funds, encouraging him in many ways and especially with dreams of glory and the lasting gratitude of the Southern people ... the moment, the consummation of months of anxious contemplation, determination, lost opportunities, chances and changes had come, and he believed that its frenzy would have prevailed over many more obstacles than there opposed him ... the powerful and secret friends of the Confederacy within the Northern lines had played upon his imagination with visions of triumph for the Southern Cause and immortal fame for himself. He had been their honored guest in palatial homes and with means which they had supplied, he had come and gone at their bidding.[7]

Was Booth also a pawn, a puppet in this deadly game?

Whatever their reasons, the little group was in a high state of animation on April 14. Hearing that General Grant was to accompany Lincoln to Ford's Theater that night for Laura Keene's performance of *Our American Cousin,* Booth was in a frenzy. Here was the perfect chance to kill both of them—a devastating blow for the North and an opportunity for a Confederate resurgence.[8]

After spending the morning performing various errands, Booth arranged to get his remaining trio together for a briefing that afternoon. Apparently, Herold had been sent to the Herndon House to notify Powell. M. P. Pope, a livery owner, recalled that particular afternoon:

> I keep a livery stable. I know David Herold. He kept his horse at my stable ... I saw him last on the evening of the murder about two o'clock in the afternoon. There was another man with him mounted on a large blind one-eyed horse. They put their horses in my stable. Herold was on a medium sized roan, "spotted-like." Herold's companion was taller than he, and I think dressed in light clothes. They went down the street. I don't know where they went. They came for their horses again in a couple of hours and rode away. It was 4:30 to 5:00 o'clock when they left.[9]

Another gentleman, however, one Benjamin F. Queen, later gave testimony on April 27, to the effect that he thought that the man accompanying Herold riding a bay horse was George Atzerodt. A kinsman, Andrew Forrest Queen, reiterated in a statement on the very same day that he saw Herold and "another man running after a streetcar into which they got at the junction of 8th and K Street and Virginia Avenue. It was from four to five o'clock in the evening. The other man had on black pants and a light coat nearly gray. The man was taller than Herold." Both of these gentlemen had known Herold "for a long time" and had apparently, as boys, been playmates of Herold as well.[10] Inasmuch as Herold and Atzerodt were pretty much the very same height, it could very well have been Powell accompanying Herold about town on horseback as well as chasing down streetcars on the afternoon of the murder, although there is no definite proof.

Where did they go? There is a good speculation that can be reasonably confirmed on two accounts. Benjamin W. Vanderpoel, a lieutenant of the Fifty-ninth New York Volunteers and an acquaintance of John Wilkes Booth, was in Washington on the evening of April 14, 1865. Sometime about two to four o'clock in the afternoon, while seeking a little diversion, he was drawn by music and rowdy laughter into a music hall on the south side of Pennsylvania Avenue—either the Metropolitan or Canterbury Music Hall, probably the latter. Both were establishments noted for bawdy, raucous entertainment; a dance hall-saloon catering to transients and patrons whose names would never make the social register.

As he was to testify for the defense at the Surratt trial in 1867, Vanderpoel went upstairs in the music hall where he encountered John Wilkes Booth and three or four men seated at a table drinking and talking. Although he did not speak to them, he noted they seemed to be in dead earnest. One of the men he described as "thick-set and foreign-looking." No doubt this was George Atzerodt. Lieutenant Vanderpoel also thought he recognized one of the men as being John Surratt. This is unlikely. The other two were probably Lewis Powell and Davy Herold. The room was crowded, and with the music and noise he could not hear their conversation, although he sat no more than twenty feet or so away from them.

A woman was dancing on the stage at the back of the room.[11] Two women of questionable virtue, the Gardner or Gardiner sisters, were playing the Canterbury at this time as dance-hall girls. According to a Miss Julia Ross, they boarded at the Lichau House.[12] Later on, when Powell's discarded overcoat was picked up after his attack on Seward, a card or scrap of paper was found in the coat pocket with "Mary J. (some sources state "Mary E.") Gardner, 419" written on it. This name and room number possibly referred to one of the dance-hall girls at the Canterbury and could possibly establish Powell's whereabouts on the afternoon of April 14.[13]

Mrs. Martha Murray, however, would remember a slightly different version of events for the elusive Mr. Powell, alias Mr. Kincheloe. She recalled that on

> the day of the assassination, this man was at our house. We always had a four o'clock dinner. He came into the dining room, or the place where persons generally came in to pay their board, and said that he wanted to pay his bill; that he was going away to Baltimore. He paid his bill, and I ordered dinner for him; or rather, called the man and told him to have his dinner sent up to the dining room earlier than usual. It was then three o'clock. It was done and that was the last I saw of him.[14]

Powell later affirmed that Booth, Atzerodt, Herold, and himself met in his room at the Herndon House at 8:00 p.m. where they were assigned their various tasks for the night. This variation in schedules has never yet failed to confuse writers and students alike. If Lewis Powell did indeed sign out at 3:00 or 4:00 p.m. how could he have returned at 8 p.m. followed by three friends, and closet himself in his old room for a meeting? Could this have been achieved without notice? One wonders.

This writer tends to feel that the appointment and plans were gone over earlier, perhaps at the dance hall. What Powell did from five o'clock to ten o'clock in the evening of April 14 will never be known. A dalliance with Mary J. Gardner in her hotel room at the Lichau House may not be out of the question.

It is certain that the prospective roles were for Powell to murder Secretary of State William H. Seward while Booth took on the job of assassinating the president and Atzerodt killed Vice President Johnson. Booth had learned during the day that General Grant had left town early, eliminating himself from the picture.

Powell was probably fully aware of the Secretary of State's physical condition, accounts of which had been published in the newspapers. And then there were the periodic meanderings on the mornings of April 13 and 14 to ascertain how to go about getting into the house.

Far from being the half-wit he was ordinarily considered, Herold had the solution. As an ex-druggist's clerk, he knew all about prescriptions and how they were delivered. What better guise than for Powell to pose as a doctor's delivery boy? It would justify admittance to the house and probably right to the bedroom of the injured official. According to William Bell's statement, Powell presented "a little package which he had in his hand with a label on it."[15] Much speculation has recently been discussed as to whether or not Herold accompanied Powell to Seward's home on Lafayette Square. According to various sources, including a report of Ogle Tayloe's servant, Ben, who saw Powell ride up and approach Seward's house, the boy was alone and was not accompanied by anyone.[16]

Powell had made sure of his weapons. He would be armed with an 1858 Whitney navy revolver, a large, heavy gun which had been popular during the war. Also, as a precautionary measure, he carried a rather large camp or Bowie knife, inscribed with Rio Grande Camp Knife. Both Booth and Atzerodt had similar knives.[17]

The usual hypothesis makes much of the fact that Powell was uncertain of the escape route out of the city and that Herold was designated to accompany him on his flight, waiting outside of the Seward house with the horses until the job was done. The duo would then ride across the Navy Yard Bridge where they would join Booth and travel with him through Maryland and into Virginia. A further study of this theory raises questions when other areas are probed, as will be seen.

So it was that at the appointed hour of approximately 10:00 p.m. Powell turned his mount towards Lafayette Square—and towards a fatal destiny from which there would be no turning back.

William Henry Seward (1801–1872), secretary of state in Lincoln's cabinet, 1861–1869 (Library of Congress).

11. Blood on the Moon

By early evening on that Good Friday, Booth's action team had been fully briefed, the arms were checked and ready and horses for escape had been obtained. Booth was to kill Lincoln at Ford's Theater, Atzerodt was to kill Vice President Johnson at the Kirkwood House and Powell accompanied by Herold was to go to the Seward home and kill Secretary of State Seward. The attacks were all to take place at approximately 10:00 p.m. and avoid the news spreading in time for warnings and protective action.

During the 1850s the Seward home at 17 Madison Place on Lafayette Square had been used as an exclusive club for members of Congress, and it was in front of the "Club House" as it was then known that New York Congressman Daniel Sickles shot and killed District Attorney Philip Barton Key in 1859 for his affair with the lovely Mrs. Sickles, a scandal that had rocked Victorian Washington to its foundations. The house was thus already tinged with disaster, and Lewis Powell was about to introduce one more incident into its shady history.

As has been previously reiterated, did Powell go alone or was Herold with him? Recent findings seem to suggest that Herold was perhaps simply the "point man," called upon to see that each conspirator went through with his job; thereafter seeing that Powell was at Seward's house, Herold left to go check up on George Atzerodt. Powell knew his way about Washington sufficiently to find Mrs. Surratt's house, the Herndon House, Ford's theatre as well as Seward's house. He needed no escort.

According to witnesses who saw Powell ride up and dismount, it is almost verifiable that he was alone. Ogle Tayloe's young servant, according to a newspaper report in the *National Intelligencer*, dated April 26, 1865, claimed that "he saw the assassin ride up to the door of [Seward's house] and fasten his horse to the lamp post." No mention is made of Powell being accompanied by another rider. Period. An article in the *National Republican* for April 18, 1865, also mentions the same scenario; that Powell was alone.

At any rate, Powell skirted the darkened square. The hour was late. Many citizens were preparing for bed, and lights in windows were few. The equestrian statue of Andrew Jackson in the center of the park stood like a ghost rider above the newly budding trees in Lafayette Square. Halting in front of the house, Powell dismounted and tied the reins to the lamp post. Powell checked the bogus bottle of medicine in his pocket as he walked to the front door. The thick tree trunks half hid the waiting horse. It was approximately 10:15 p.m.

The darkened doorway faced Powell, black and forbidding, its recesses opening up to swallow him in a dim-lit yawn. Frosty light, faint and cold, shone about him from the narrow glass panes which framed the door. Powell knocked and rang at the door then waited. Footsteps reverberated in the hallway, and the latch on the door clicked and inched opened to reveal a young black man in a white coat. This was William Bell, a house servant who had worked for the Seward family for approximately nine months previous to the assassination attempt. At the trial of the conspirators, Bell recalled precisely what happened:

> About a quarter past ten, I presume it was, the bell rung. I went to the door. A tall and heavy built man approached. He seemed to be a young man, so far as I could judge. He said he wanted to see Mr. Seward. I told him that he could not see him from the very fact that Mr. Seward was sick in bed, and the orders were strict not to allow anyone to come in. He said, "I am sent here by Dr. Verdi, Mr. Seward's family physician." He held in his left hand a little package which I supposed to be a prescription. It had a prescription paper on it. He said he wanted to see Mr. Seward. I stated he could not see him. He says, "I must see him; I am sent here by Dr. Verdi to let him know how to take this medicine, and I must see him." I says, "You cannot see him by any means at all. He is asleep just about this time." He insisted that he must see him. *I spoke rather rough to him.* He started to go up; and having spoken rather rough to him, I said to him that I hoped he would excuse me. I had no idea that he was an assassin. *He spoke rather politely to me,* and said, "Oh, that's alright!" I told him that I was just doing my duty. Of course, I had no right to insult him, not knowing who he was.[1]

For half a century, various writers have had a field day with the dialogue between Powell and Bell.

"Get out of my way, Nigger! I'm goin' up," snarls Powell in Philip Van Doren Stern's 1939 novel *The Man Who Killed Lincoln*. Jim Bishop also quoted the same offensive language in his 1954 study *The Day Lincoln Was Shot*. No one knows for sure just *what* Powell said to Bell as he came in. The conversation related in Van Doren Stern was pure fiction. Unfortunately, historians have picked up on this imaginative dialogue over the years. Granted the trial testimony as recorded does get a bit confusing when Bell asserts in one breath "He talked very rough to me in the first place when he came in"[2] and then asserts when questioned by the judge advocate that "he did not talk rough."[3]

Whatever passed between Powell and Bell, Seward's house servant had an eye for detail: "His face was very red at the time he came in, and he had very black, coarse hair."[4]

"He seemed to be excited and talked very fast and very loud ... he was a tall man, I think full six foot ... dark complected and [had] no whiskers or moustache."[5]

"He had on very heavy boots at the time, black pants, light overcoat and a brown hat."[6]

Much of Bell's description was used on the government's "wanted" poster, including the intruder's tone of voice; "small and thin, inclined to tenor." Another important characteristic Bell noticed was Powell's dimpled cheeks—a feature which would later lead to positive identification. One wonders about Powell's "red face" and excited, loud talk. Possibly he was keyed up to do the job by a drink or two of liquor.

Powell started upstairs, and Bell went along in front of him, noticing Powell's new heavy riding boots. They made considerable noise on the stairway and Bell kept admonishing him to walk quietly. Powell apologized with a smile. He was dead set in his determination. Nothing was going to stop him. Frederick Seward, the secretary's son and the assistant secretary of state, heard the commotion on the staircase and went to investigate. Powell trudged resolutely to the third floor with William Bell still at his heels admonishing him. Frederick Seward demanded to know the cause of the ruckus, and Powell persuasively declared his intentions, producing the medical vial and explaining his supposed errand. An argument ensued. Powell was resolute in insisting on his being admitted to see the secretary. He had proceeded too far on his assignment to be deterred by anyone or anything.

Fanny Seward, the twenty-one-year-old daughter of the secretary, was attending her father that night, along with Pvt. George F. Robinson. She heard the voices raised in argument and went to see what was causing the disturbance.

> I hastened to the door, opened it a very little, and found Fred standing close by it, facing me. On his right hand, also close by the door stood a tall young man, in a light hat and long overcoat. I said, "Fred, father is awake now." Something in Fred's manner led me at once to think that he did not wish me to say so, and that I had better not have opened the door. This confused me, and looking around, I was glad to see father going to sleep again. Holding the door as I did, I know the man could not see my father at all, nor could Fred, I think. I do not remember what Fred said to me. The man seemed impatient, and addressing me in a tone that struck me at once as harsh and full of determination more than such a simple question justified asked, "Is the Secretary asleep?" I paused to look at my father and replied, "Almost." Then Fred drew the door shut very quickly. I sat down again. I had no means of telling the errand of the man. I fancied someone had sent him—that he was, perhaps, a messenger from the telegraph office.[7]

Powell now knew the location of the secretary's room and cunningly played out another ruse. Seward's son steadfastly refused him admittance to the sickroom. "I am in charge here. Go back and tell the doctor that I refused to let you see him if you think you cannot entrust me with the medicine."

Powell eyed Seward coolly. "Very well, sir," he shrugged in pretended resignation. "I will go."[8] William Bell started downstairs leading the apparently sullen Powell and still admonishing him to walk quietly. Powell descended one step. Two steps. He was conscious of Bell's looming black shadow on the wall and also his own shadow stalking beside it. Three steps ... Fred Seward still stood at the head of the stairs, his eyes on Powell's retreating back. Suddenly, Powell gripped the heavy revolver in his pocket and, drawing the weapon, spun around with a muttered oath. He leveled the weapon at the astonished assistant secretary's head and pulled the trigger. Instead of an explosion, there was only a dull metallic click. The gun had misfired. In an interview given by an elderly Fred Seward to the *New York Times* for July 8, 1912, Fred stated, "He snapped the pistol close to my temple, and when it missed fire exclaimed, 'That Navy revolver!'"

Aghast, Seward spun around and grabbed at Powell, whose panicked response was to pistol whip his victim about the head. Had Powell thought to cock the gun and continue pulling the trigger, he could have killed five people. During the struggle with Fred Seward, the gun struck the bannister, breaking the ramrod hinge, but this would not have prevented the pistol from working. Bell fled terror-stricken down the stairs and out the front door to summon help from General Augur's headquarters

Frederick Seward, assistant secretary of state, wounded by Powell (Seward Museum, Auburn, New York).

Contemporary woodcut engraving of Powell's attack on Frederick Seward, assistant secretary of state and son of William H. Seward, April 14, 1865 (author's collection).

at the corner of Madison Place. Meanwhile, Powell grappled with Fred Seward, who was bleeding profusely from a severe cranial fracture inflicted by the blows of the gun.[9] Not yet unconscious, the secretary's son clung to Lewis Powell with the persistency of a bulldog, scarlet ribbons of blood disfiguring his face.

Crashing into a wall, Powell sought to disengage the man's iron hold. Together they maneuvered toward the secretary's room, and Powell crashed against the heavy door with his shoulder. His own weight, combined with that of his clinging adversary, burst the door wide open, and together they stumbled across the threshold. Pvt. Robinson, having heard the commotion in the hallway, had started for the door when Powell burst in. The enraged intruder now drew his knife, and, stumbling into Robinson, sent the man reeling across the floor with a quick slash on his forehead. From out of the dimness, Fanny Seward shrieked. Miss Seward relived the horror of that night for the rest of her young life:

> I do not remember how his [Powell's] face looked, his arms were both stretched out, he seemed rushing towards the bed. In the hand nearest me was a pistol, in the right hand a

Lewis Powell's violent bedroom assault on Secretary of State Seward and household, April 14, 1865 (author's collection).

knife. I ran beside him to the bed imploring him to stop. I must have said, "Don't kill him," for father wakened, he says, upon hearing me speak the word "kill," and seeing first me, speaking to someone whom he did not see and then raised himself and had one glimpse of the assassin's face bending over, next felt the blows and by their force (he being on the edge of the bed where fear of hurting his broken arm had caused him to lie for sometime) was thrown to the floor. I cannot remember seeing him—nor seeing Payne—go around the bed—but Anna [her sister-in-law] was in the room and saw it.[10]

According to one later report: "Payne afterward said that if he could have made up his mind to strike her [Fanny Seward] out of his way, he could have accomplished his purpose upon the Secretary, but that her face between his weapon and her father disarmed him; he had not the heart to take her life also."[11] Apparently weakened by the shock of the violent attack upon her father and brother, Fanny succumbed to what was probably consumption in October 1866.

Powell frantically thrust Fanny Seward aside and bounded upon the old gentleman's bed. Placing his left hand on Seward's chest, he struck repeatedly with the knife. As the secretary was supported by a framework backrest, the weapon glanced off the metal in a shower of sparks.[12]

Robinson had by now regained his feet and, attacking Powell from behind, dragged him off the prostrate secretary:

I saw him strike Mr. Seward with the same knife with which he cut my forehead ... I saw him cut Mr. Seward twice that I am sure of, the first time he struck him on the right cheek, and then he seemed to be cutting around his neck. I did not hear the man say anything during this time ... I afterwards examined the wounds, and found one cutting his face from the right cheek down to the neck, and a cut on his neck, which might have been made by the same blow, as Mr. Seward was partially sitting in bed at the time, and another on the left side of the neck. Those were all I noticed, but there may have been more, as it was all bloody when I saw it. Mr. Seward received all of his stabs in bed; but after the man was gone, and I went back to the bed, I found that he had rolled out, and was lying on the floor.

I did not see Mr. Frederick Seward down on the floor; the first I saw of him was after the man was gone when I came back into the room he was inside the door, standing up.[13]

In his counterattack on Robinson, Powell managed to get his arm up just enough to strike the soldier twice in the shoulder, driving the knife to the bone.

We came off on the floor. He got his arm around my neck, and struck me two or three times under the ear with the butt of the revolver, but he was in such a position that he could not hurt me. He then dropped that, and took hold of me, and then took his knife to strike into my breast or bowels. While he was doing this, we became clenched together, face to face. I then tried to throw him over my hip on his back, but my leg being wounded, it was not strong enough to stand the heft of both of us. I succeeded, however, in getting the knife where he couldn't use it. He then tried to get me by the throat, and I tried the same by him, and succeeded so far as to get my hand under his jaw. My object was to get such a hold on him that I could in some way get him into the hall and pitch him over the banisters. I thought that would be the best way to get rid of him.[14]

Major Augustus Seward, the eldest son, having been awakened, stumbled into the room and seized Robinson. Half asleep, and seeing the confusion in the dimly lit room, he thought that the soldier-nurse had gone berserk and was attacking his father. Seward attempted to shove the enclasped pair toward the door, Powell all the while striking the younger Seward over the head with his knife and proclaiming in a low voice, "I'm mad! I'm mad!"

Was this admission of madness a pre-planned ruse, or had the full, horrible realization of what he had done finally dawned upon him? "For God's sake, Major!" Robinson yelled hoarsely, "Let go of me and take the knife out of his hand and cut his throat!"

Powell managed to twist free, knocked Robinson to the floor and tore away from Seward. Bounding down the staircase, he noticed a man's form in the semi-darkness. He slashed at the fleeing man, knocking him to one side. This was a State Department messenger named Emerick Hansell. Slashed in the back, Hansell shrieked at the pain before collapsing on the stairs.

Powell pounded down to the front door gaping ajar in the night breeze. Of the five people he had attacked, two of whom were seriously injured, none would die. Behind him in Seward's room, he had left his broken revolver and his brown slouch hat.

Unlike Booth and Herold, Powell may not have had Virginia in mind as an escape route. In the September 1880 issue of *North*

George F. Robinson, Seward's soldier-nurse (Seward Museum, Auburn, New York).

11. Blood on the Moon

Left: Front of Congressional Medal awarded in 1871 to Sergeant George F. Robinson, USA, for his efforts to save William H. Seward on the night of April 14, 1865 (author's collection). *Right:* Reverse of Congressional Medal shows Powell grappling with Robinson in Seward's sickroom (author's collection).

American Review, J. W. Clampitt, one of Mrs. Surratt's attorneys, related that Powell told him that "he endeavored to make his escape to Baltimore and proceeded in the darkness of night in that direction." (Subsequently, Powell's horse would be found in the outer reaches of Washington, east of the Capitol.) Why Baltimore? Did he plan to meet anyone there? Mary Branson perhaps? Was he then to make his way to Canada—perhaps with Mary in tow? It would have seemed more logical for him to have joined Booth to travel on through the south to Florida and home. The speculation here is endless. Powell could have decided on his own escape route. With the country on a massive manhunt, a group of hard-riding men would certainly appear suspicious.

Bursting from the scene of carnage he had perpetrated, Powell paused just long enough to catch his breath. Then came the heavy sound of boots crunching the cobbles, coming at a run. Shrieks and screams tore from an upper window of the house. With deliberation,

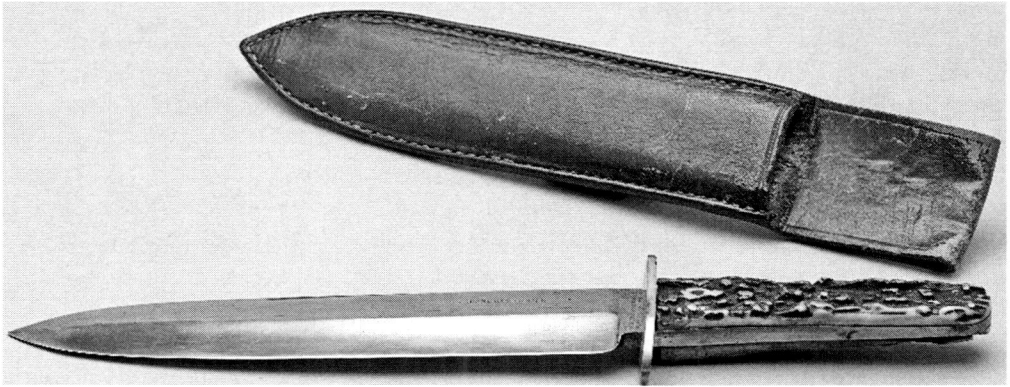

Lewis Powell's Bowie knife inscribed with the words, "Rio Grande Camp Knife" (Huntington Library, San Marino, California).

Powell untied his horse and mounted, and the blood-smeared knife slipped from his grasp and clattered into the gutter where it would be found early the next morning by Robert Nelson.[15]

"That's him! Gettin' on a horse!" William Bell shrieked and pounded around the corner as Powell started off. The youth was dogged and persistent, racing twenty feet behind the assailant's slow-moving horse and piercing the night with his harsh cries of murder. Three soldiers ran out into the poorly lighted street, but Powell was by then almost out of sight.

Alfred Cloughley, a clerk in the second auditor's office, gave testimony before Justice David Cartter on the night of the assassination, and in a statement taken down in shorthand by Corp. James Tanner, related what had happened in Lafayette Square:

> About 10:00 o'clock this evening, I was walking with a lady in Lafayette Square. I heard someone cry out that the gates should be shut and immediately after, the cry of "Murder!" and "Stop, Thief!" There were several voices. We rushed to the gate. Before reaching it, I saw a man on horseback bending forward and putting spurs to his horse and start off. I think the horse was a pacer. The crowd called out, "Stop, thief!"
> The horse was going up 15½ Street, north.[16]

Why Powell made so slow a retreat is puzzling. Suddenly, as if awakening, he clapped spurs to his horse and went at a trot up Fifteen and One-half Street to I Street, where Bell lost sight of him. Here history also lost sight of him until he was later apprehended at Mrs. Surratt's H Street house. Powell was heading out of the city, that much seems certain. Innumerable writers have contended that he was lost in a strange city, but much more acceptable is the contention that he knew his way and was proceeding toward Baltimore, as stated by Clampitt.

History leaves us with the impression that Powell was a cold, calculating cutthroat—a human being without remorse. Certainly, there was an incongruous makeup in the boy's character: one moment a soft-spoken preacher's son, the next a ruthless assassin. Could war have so demoralized him? This assumption in itself would seem unlikely. Hundreds of men had gone through the war and were not affected by its horrors. Having viewed himself as a loyal and patriotically obsessed Confederate, Powell had "higher" motives and was therefore not afraid to be a part of the most outrageous atrocity imaginable against the Unionist government. Powell asserted that he expected promotions and approval from *his* Confederate government and aspired to be a hero to the Southern people. When he was a small boy, his mother had probably told him stories about her father, who had died as a result of the War of 1812. Even his brothers were named for heroic statesmen: George Washington and Benjamin Franklin. And then there was his cousin, the illustrious Brigadier General, John Brown Gordon, C.S.A.

Could Powell have been trying to emulate or surpass this martial glory? The Rev. Dr. Gillette gives a different, perhaps more truthful, view of Powell as he left the Seward home: "He had no sooner mounted his horse and begun his flight than the revulsion came. He saw the crime in its real light and as a crime merely."[17]

"The moment he fled from the house of Secretary Seward and leaped into the saddle of his horse, his mind was quickened into a realizing sense of the horror of the damnable deed which he had perpetrated and he became miserable, wretched—life itself became loathsome."[18] Dr. Gillette also recalled that "without the least arrogance, brag or mock heroism, he still maintained that his deed had made for him a duty when under the spell of its motive.

He did not know that he had ever shed human blood before.... He admitted that he believed it would give peace to the South."[19]

Misguided patriot or no, Powell was bent on escape. Near Fort Bunker Hill, in back of Congressional Cemetery, Powell discarded his blood-splattered overcoat. In the pockets were his riding gloves, a false moustache and, as previously stated, a slip of paper with the name and hotel room number of "Mary E. Gardner." The overcoat was found on the afternoon of April 16 by a private of the Third Massachusetts Infantry, Thomas Price, at a place about three miles northeast of the city on a grassy pathway between two forts.

Powell also abandoned his horse. "He was pursued by the cavalry while attempting to leave the city ... his horse stumbled and partly fell upon him and he then abandoned him and took to the fields ... he lay under a tree less than a mile from the city limits and slept till morning. On Saturday, he went out two or three miles and laid in the woods."[20]

According to various press reports (testimony given to Dr. Gillette on the night before he died, etc.), Lewis was violently thrown from his horse on the escape from Seward's house. Several reports claim that Powell stated that his horse fell or partially fell with him and he was thrown into the road.[21]

Colonel John A. Foster, in a statement given for evidence, claimed that on the night of April 14, 1865, near Fort Bunker Hill, a horseman was heard galloping by, apparently jumping from the high ditch down onto the road below. Shortly thereafter, there was heard the sounds of a man moaning or groaning loudly as if in distress. Several pickets at the Fort were going to check on the source of the sounds when they ceased; therefore they decided to give up the quest. When the groaning sounds had faded, the horse was heard running off in another direction.[22]

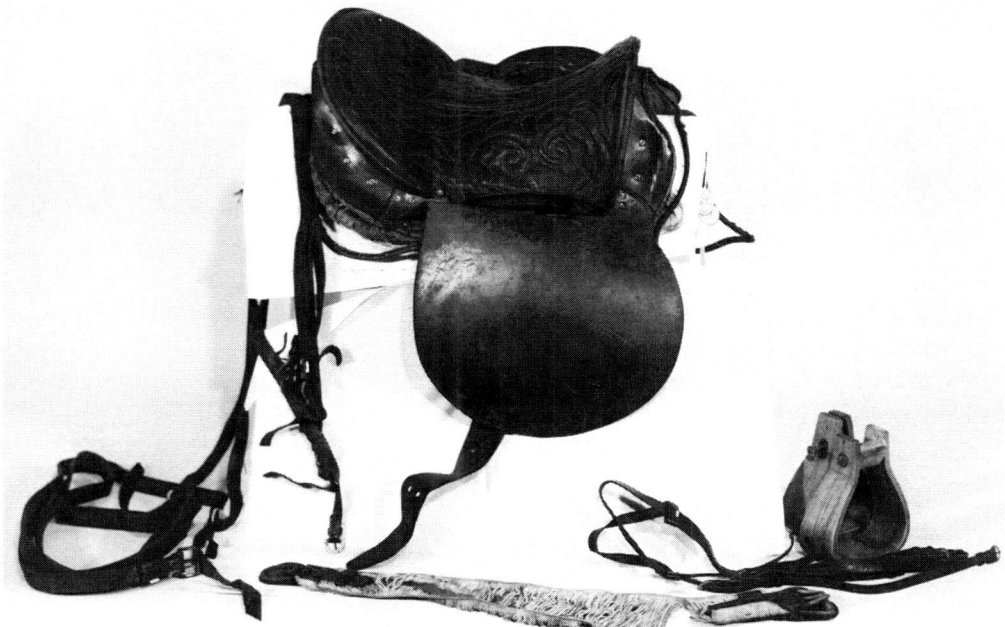

This decorative saddle was used by Powell on the night of the assassination when he fled from the Seward home (National Park Service).

When found, Powell's horse had a cut on its shoulder, its knees were muddy and it was somewhat lame, giving indications of having fallen.[23] Powell was knocked unconscious and it's apparent that he may have had or most probably did have a concussion. That he struck his head is indicated by the facial injuries which appear in his photographs taken after his capture. This could also account for his "hazy recollections" of what happened during the attack on Seward earlier that night. Photographs of Powell taken on board the monitor on April 18 show him with a somewhat swollen and blackened left eye as well as a bruised lower lip and nose. There are also what appear to be abrasions under his chin.[24]

In the meantime,

> for three days and nights, he wandered the woods, without any substance, every moment expecting to be arrested. He felt that he had committed a grievous sin and that he would be pursued and overtaken. On one occasion, a party scouting for him drew very near to where he was secreted. He climbed a tree and found a secure shelter in the topmost branches.[25]
>
> The gray light of the morning soon warned him, however, that it was not safe for him to proceed longer ... a farmhouse was situated not far off, he knew, as the farmer's dogs were baying in the distance. The tree, thick with early spring foliage, was near the roadside and just after daybreak, he heard the rush of cavalry and peering forth, saw them distinctly as they passed by on their search for the murderers. This rush of cavalry continued all day long, and motives of safety compelled him to remain in the tree. The gnawing of hunger were intense and a burning thirst seized upon him.[26]

Powell knew that things were closing in on him and that he couldn't hold out much longer in his desperate situation. In order to avoid being apprehended, he had to have a clean change of clothing and a good substantial meal. Not too well acquainted with the city of Washington and knowing he was a wanted man, he realized there was only one place that he might expect to be treated with hospitality—Mrs. Surratt's boarding house.

Desperate, Powell devised a plan to pose as a day laborer. He needed a hat. In a strict era when propriety demanded that a man cover his head in public, Powell would appear strange without a hat of some sort. He decided to improvise, and by removing his frock coat, vest and dress shirt, he cut a sleeve from his knit undershirt which he placed over his thick dark hair as if it were a stocking cap.

He waited.

"As night again fell upon farmland and city, his hunger and thirst becoming unbearable, he descended and approached the farm house. He did not alarm the inmates, as to do so would be to surrender himself to justice, as by this time the whole country was aroused, and placards descriptive of the murderers and offering large sums for their apprehension were posted in every direction."[27]

Powell spied a pickaxe in a farm yard, and securing it to use as a prop for his disguise as a laborer, he began his long walk toward Mrs. Surratt's boarding house.

12. "How the Game Was Bagged"

Washington was a city draped in black. As the reins of leadership fell from a dying president's hands, they were seized by his successor who intended to exact a punishing vengeance against the murderers. The new president, Andrew Johnson, was but a shadow in the reflected power of Edwin M. Stanton, Secretary of War.

Dictatorial in his authority, Stanton made it clear that punishment for the nation's traitors would be cruel and swift. On the morning of Monday, April 17, Col. Lafayette C. Baker, chief of the National Detective Police and unscrupulous head of the Federal Secret Service, issued a wanted poster. The handbill gave a scant, almost ridiculous description of John Wilkes Booth, but carried a wealth of accurate information in describing the as-yet-unknown assailant of Secretary Seward, even going so far as to describe Powell's tone of voice.

> $30,000 REWARD
> DESCRIPTION
> of
> JOHN WILKES BOOTH!
> Who Assassinated the PRESIDENT on the Evening
> of April 14th, 1865
>
> Height 5 feet, 8 inches; weight 160 pounds; compact built; hair jet black, inclined to curl, medium length, parted behind; eyes black and heavy dark eye-brows, wears a large seal ring on little finger; when talking inclines his head forward; looks down.
>
> Description of the Person who Attempted to Assassinate Hon. W. H. Seward, Secretary of State
> Height 6 feet 1 inch, hair black, thick, full and straight; no beard nor appearance of beard; cheeks red on the jaws; face moderately full; 22 or 23 years of age; eyes, color not known—large eyes, not prominent; brows not heavy, but dark; face not large, but rather round; complexion healthy; nose straight and well formed, medium size; mouth small; lips thin; upper lip protruded when he talked; chin pointed and prominent; head medium size; neck short and of medium length; hands soft and small; fingers tapering; shows no signs of hard labor; broad shoulders; taper waist; straight figure; strong looking man; manner not gentlemanly, but vulgar; Overcoat double-breasted, color mixed of pink and grey spots, small—was a sack overcoat, pockets in side and one on the breast, with lappells or flaps; pants black, common stuff; new heavy boots; voice small and thin, inclined to tenor.
>
> The Common Council of Washington D.C. have offered a reward of $20,000 for the arrest and conviction of these Assassins, in addition to which I will pay $10,000.
> L. C. BAKER,
> Colonel and Agent War Department

The handbill's specifics also appeared in the April 17 *Washington Daily Morning Chronicle*. The government knew what it wanted if not *whom* it wanted. The information on Seward's assailant was supplied through the revelations of William Bell.

The hour was late on this Monday night, close to 10:00 p.m. as Lewis Powell trudged disconsolately through the miles of city streets to Mrs. Surratt's H Street boarding house.

Although writers have gone to great pains to describe young Powell's lack of familiarity with Washington's streets, he seemingly had no trouble whatsoever in finding his way back to the H Street establishment.

Mourning crepe decorated every doorway that he passed en route to his H Street destination. It hung all around, fluttering and gleaming in the mist. Even the lamp posts were swathed in it.

The Surratt house had been under suspicion ever since the morning of the president's death. A month earlier, Louis Weichmann, Mrs. Surratt's star boarder, had hinted to Capt. D. H. E. Gleason of the War Department that strange goings-on were taking place at the Surratt house which principally involved Booth and John Surratt. Immediately after the assassination, the authorities decided to take a closer look at young Surratt and his home which was reportedly a frequent haunt of J. Wilkes Booth, Lincoln's killer.

Early on the morning of April 15, the house was searched under orders of Maj. A. C. Richards of the Metropolitan Police Force. Their objective? Find John H. Surratt! This first search having proved unsuccessful, the house was subjected to another raid on the night of April 17 when all of its residents were rounded up to be taken to military headquarters for questioning.

This second, more successful raid was staged by Federal authorities. Gen. Christopher C. Augur ordered Col. H. S. Olcott, special commissioner of the War Department, to initiate the arrests and seizures, assisted by Capt. W. M. Wermerskirch, Maj. H. W. Smith, and officers Thomas Sampson, C. H. Rosch, Ely DeVoe and R. C. Morgan. The landlady, her daughter Anna, niece Olivia Jenkins and one young lady boarder, Honora Fitzpatrick, were the sole occupants of the house. Louis Weichmann and boarder John T. Holohan had previously left under Richards' orders with officials seeking to track down John Surratt in Canada. Indeed the *Albany Evening Journal* of April 15, 1865, proclaimed that John H. Surratt, a Marylander, was the assassin who had attempted to kill Seward.

Inside the Surratt house, the ladies were getting ready to depart with the Federal detectives. Major Smith had accompanied Mrs. Surratt upstairs to get bonnets and wraps, while Detective DeVoe was keeping an eye on the occupants in the parlor. The doorbell rang, and officers Sampson and Morgan arrived as Captain Wermerskirch was searching the house for incriminating material. Suddenly the steep front steps creaked under the weight of heavy footsteps. Thinking it was the officer arriving with the carriage, Colonel Morgan reached for the door:

> Captain Wermerskirch and myself were standing at the parlor door while Mrs. Surratt and the ladies were putting on their things. They were about ready to start when there was a knock and a ring at the same time. I thought it was the man who had been sent for the carriage. Captain Wermerskirch and myself stepped up to the door and I opened it ... Major Smith came forward. He got there just as I opened it.[1]

Detective Officer C. H. Rosch had been stationed outside, "for the purpose of preventing anyone to come out of the house after the officers had entered, but to *allow anyone to enter*."[2] Apparently Powell didn't see the detective outside in the foggy mist.

Weary and bedraggled, Powell eyed the confusion inside the hallway in mild shock. He had walked right into the open arms of a vengeful justice.

12. "How the Game Was Bagged"

"I ... I guess I'm mistaken," Powell faltered and began to inch away. "Whom do you want to see?" The question was leveled at him with the force of a pistol shot.

"Mrs. Surratt," Powell replied in an uncertain murmur. According to Major Smith, he seemed to hesitate. Instantly there was a sharp click, and Major Smith drew a huge Colt revolver which he shoved into Powell's grimy face.

"You're right. Step in."

Powell trod over the threshold into the dimly lit foyer, and the front door and all chance of escape closed solidly behind him. Smith ordered the youth to put his pickaxe down. "He laid it down or put it into the corner. I took him to the back part of the hall and set two men to stand guard over him. We *then* commenced questioning him and examining him."[3]

Strangely enough, each of the arresting officers gave differing accounts of the arrival of Powell. The varied reports were influenced, no doubt, by the prospect of obtaining the five-thousand-dollar reward on Powell's head. William Wermerskirch's version was less dramatic and more matter-of-fact: "When he came to the house, he was asked to come in, because he refused to come in after he saw strangers present."[4]

R. C. Morgan was the man who actually opened the door: "I replied, 'It is alright; come in.' I passed him in and put him behind the door, standing myself with my hand on the door, open."[5]

The 1867 Surratt trial transcript offers a more detailed account of the occurrences than do the Pitman, Perley Poore or Peterson versions. However, in the two years which passed between the two judicial proceedings many details could have become confused because of faulty memories.

One thing the officers did agree on was Powell's strange get-up which aroused the utmost suspicion, notwithstanding the fact that they believed the late caller with the pickaxe to be a disguised John Surratt returning to his home: "Payne was dressed in a gray coat with a gray vest and black pantaloons. His boots were rather fine and if I remember right, had red tops to the legs ... he had on his head a woolen sleeve, appearing like a night-cap. It turned out to be a woolen sleeve, which he had pulled down over his head, letting the end hang down like a tassel."[6]

The weary youth unconvincingly claimed to be a laborer and in a muffled voice explained that Mrs. Surratt had hired him, a poor man, to dig a gutter in her back yard. Mrs. Surratt, Powell asserted, had stopped him in the street that very morning to ask if he would work for her. He was just stopping by now to determine what time he would start work in the morning. The officers took especial note of the young man's exhausted condition. His statements made little sense, and his clothing, though greatly soiled, appeared to be rather expensive.

"Mrs. Surratt, will you step here a moment?" Smith peered into the parlor where Mrs. Surratt and the young ladies had knelt to pray before leaving the house. Mrs. Surratt arose from her knees and stepped tentatively from the parlor door to confront the dejected, oddly costumed visitor and Major Smith.

"Do you know this man? Did you hire him to dig a ditch for you?" Smith looked inquiringly at the bonneted and shawled widow.

Raising her hands, Mrs. Surratt avowed: "Before God, I do not know this man; I have never seen him. I did not hire him to dig a ditch!" This positive and basically inaccurate assertion would cause Mrs. Surratt's life to be forfeited on the gallows. Although the gas jets were dim, Major Smith asserted that Powell was seated directly under the lamp. As Mrs.

Surratt entered the room, Powell arose from his seat and the light shone down upon his face.[7] According to Smith, Mrs. Surratt was standing about five feet from Powell when she swore he was not known to her.

The carriage arrived, and in the company of two detectives, the four ladies were escorted to the door. Morgan recalled that Mrs. Surratt "leaned her head over toward me and said, 'I am so glad you officers came here tonight, for this man came here with a pickaxe to kill us!' I made no reply, but passed them out the door, and then reclosed it and commenced to question Payne." The dejected youth made no reply. With the women taken care of, the officers turned their full attention to him. They pelted him with questions, but Powell was too exhausted, both mentally and physically, to evade their sharp inquiries convincingly: "I asked him where he was from. He said he was from Fauquier County, Virginia. Previous to this, he had pulled out an Oath of Allegiance on which was written 'Lewis Paine,' Fauquier County, Virginia. I asked him how old he was, whether he had any money."[8]

Detective Officer Thomas Sampson, under special service with Colonel Olcott and the War Department, saw a "big catch" in the detention of Powell. As soon as he laid eyes on the man, Sampson was convinced that he fit the description of the Seward assassin. Although he does not mention Mrs. Surratt at all, Sampson relates the lengthy questioning of Lewis "Paine" Powell which took place:

> Sampson: "I said, 'Where have you been working?'"
> Powell: "Different places."
> Sampson: "What wages do you usually get?"
> Powell: "From a dollar to a dollar and a quarter a day."
> Sampson: "Do you have steady work?"
> Powell: "No. I only get jobs now and again."
> Sampson: "Can you give the names of any person you have worked for?"
> Powell: "No. I cannot give you any names."
> Sampson: "Can you take me to the places?"
> Powell: "No."
> Sampson: "Do you know the names of the streets?"
> Powell: "No."
> Sampson: Would you know the street if you were in it?"
> Powell: "No. I know nothing about it."
> Sampson: "Where is your boarding house?"
> Powell: "I've not got any."
> Sampson: "Where is the balance of your clothes?"
> Powell: "I've got all my clothes on."
> Sampson: Where did you sleep last night?"
> Powell: "At the railroad depot."

When questioned about his wages, Powell muttered, "I've not got any money. How can I get money when I work for a dollar to a dollar and quarter a day and pay any lodgings and housing out of that?"

After asking about his place of residence, Sampson switched back to Powell's "sleeping habits" of the past few nights.

> Sampson: "Where did you sleep last Wednesday night?"
> Powell: "I don't know."
> Sampson: "Thursday night?"

Powell claimed not to know where he slept, and Sampson persisted.

> Sampson: "Friday night?"

12. "How the Game Was Bagged" 77

Again, Powell insisted he had slept at the depot.

> Sampson: "Saturday night?"
> Powell: "I don't know where I slept."
> Sampson: "Well, where did you sleep last night?"
> Powell: "I have been walking about so much that I don't know where I slept last night."[9]

Sampson questioned Powell a bit further about farm work, etc. "Unimportant questions," according to Sampson's deposition. He was particularly aware, as were the other officers, of the prisoner's uncalloused, well-manicured hands. They were certainly not the hands of a man used to rough manual labor.

Soon after, the carriage clattered up to the boarding house door, fresh from the delivery of Mrs. Surratt and ladies to the provost marshal's office. Upon orders, detective officers Sampson, Devoe and Rosch took Powell under armed guard to headquarters for further questioning and examination. At General Augur's headquarters, the exhausted "laborer" was put through a thorough grilling which began with a body search. Powell dug into his pockets and produced a varied and incongruous assortment of personal effects:

> 1 packet of pistol cartridges, unbroken
> 1 pocket compass in a mahogany case
> 1 needle case with threads
> 1 small hair brush and bottle of hair pomade
> 1 folding comb
> 2 tooth brushes 1 small penknife
> 1 Webster's pocket dictionary
> 2 fine white handkerchiefs
> a pocketbook with pennies; Canadian coins, scraps of paper, postage stamps, etc.
> a confirmation copy of an Oath of Allegiance dated March 14, 1865, and signed, "L. Paine."[10]

Powell's gutta-percha folding comb found in his pocket the night of his arrest, April 17, 1865 (National Park Service).

This motley assortment of items was strictly at variance with Powell's assumed employment. To further confuse matters, Rosch included in his list: "one small new revolver; loaded." If Powell was armed with *two* pistols, it seems odd that he resorted to his knife during the attack on Seward. As the other two detectives did not mention a gun, the weapon may have just been a figment of Rosch's imagination. All three officers verified the fact that Powell possessed a pack of pistol cartridges.

One source went so far as to claim that, of the two handkerchiefs found in Powell's pockets, one of them was apparently a woman's, an article for which Powell could give no plausible explanation.[11] If so, was it a souvenir of his sweetheart, Mary Branson, or was it the product of a tryst with an unknown lady? Ever the gentleman, Powell was not about to divulge his romantic interests and implicate a lady.

One also wonders about the pocket dictionary. Author Theodore Roscoe found a good explanation for this item in his immense work *Web of Conspiracy*. A dictionary could be used for Secret Service encoding and deciphering.

There was one personal item which meant much to the prisoner; a small, embroidered pincushion which was also found in his possession.

The arrest of Powell at Mrs. Surratt's H Street boarding house, April 17, 1865 (National Park Service).

This pincushion seemed to hold a great deal of sentiment for the youth; so much so that he begged for its return when taken away from him. It was probably a gift from his mother upon joining the army and part of his soldier's "housewife"; a small sewing or mending kit which both Northern and Southern soldiers carried with them. The pincushion was taken away with the rest of his personal effects and upon his incarceration onboard the monitor, he pleaded desperately to have it returned to him. This was granted by Colonel H. H. Wells, but once he transferred to the Arsenal, the pincushion was again surrendered to be utilized as Evidence No. 13. It was apparently returned to him right before the execution. (See Appendix L.)

The detectives knew they had Powell in deep water. One can almost see Lewis sweating and stumbling over the sharp questions that were shot at him. Not having eaten or slept in over three days, he was practically dead on his feet, and his weary confusion shows. Sampson continues:

> In conversation with him after the search, I asked him whether he had heard the "news."
>
> He asked, "What news?"
>
> I said, "The news of the assassination of Mr. Lincoln and of the attempted assassination of Mr. Seward."
>
> He said he had not heard of it.
>
> Said I, "Why, it is all over the town here—and even in New York!" Said he, "I believe I heard something about it the next day."

Lewis Powell, just after he was arrested at Mrs. Surratt's house, April 17, 1865. This photograph, taken directly after his capture, shows Powell dressed in the suit he was wearing when arrested. He had left his hat behind in Seward's bed chamber (Dr. John Lattimer Collection).

The officers then questioned Lewis about his Oath of Allegiance—whether or not he could read and write. Powell shook his head wearily. "No," he lied. Being a poor man's son, he had been kept hard at work on the farm—he could only manage to write his name. Therefore, he did not understand the written oath.

Sampson's list of Powell's possessions claimed that his wallet contained twenty-five dollars. The detective questioned the captive about his financial status: "Where did you get all the money?" Powell claimed that he had worked for it and when pushed changed his story to the effect that he had *found it.*[12]

Trapped, Powell must have known that it was no use. He was too exhausted to try to evade them. Although he had successfully fended off the questioning when he had been arrested in Baltimore a month before, he was now either too tired or too defeated to care. An account of the capture in the *New York Herald* stated that he "Often contradicted himself and broke down completely in his narrative."[13]

Officer Sampson stated, "While searching, I made him take off his boots. They came off with great difficulty and his stockings were wringing wet. His boots had the appearance as if he had been walking through water." Rosch would remember: "His feet were incased in a very clean pair of socks, with bands tied up on the sides like the highland fashion."[14]

There is one surprising incident regarding Powell's personal appearance which Smith, Wermerskirch, and Sampson all noted: the fact that Powell's trousers were "mud to his knees," "pants rolled up over his boot tops; or at least one boot top," "his boots and lower person were soaking wet and his stockings were wet," etc. In the photographs taken of Powell just after his capture, his boots seem immaculate, as do his black trousers. No traces of mud appear anywhere on his person, indicating that the boots and trousers could have been cleaned for the pictures.

The officers were satisfied that they had the man who tried to murder the secretary of state, but they had to be doubly sure. A check of the man's description in Baker's handbill confirmed it. Not only did they have Seward's assassin, they had also found his horse. On the night of April 14, Lt. John J. Toffey had come upon a large bay horse, blind in one eye, near Camp Barry, about three-quarters of a mile east of the Capitol. The gelding appeared to be slightly lame from a fall, and there was blood on the saddle blanket—blood which had not come from any injury visible on the animal.

The Selena Kansas *Saline County Journal* for July 14, 1881, later detailed how "one of the horses had been captured, nearly exhausted, at the outskirts of the city and that its bridle was covered with blood. The animal was identified as the horse ridden by the assassin from Seward's residence. This gave a good deal of hope that the author of the horrible crime might be captured."

The officers then summoned William Bell, and "The prisoner was taken into a lobby adjoining the front office for some minutes until Secretary Seward's houseboy was brought into the room for the purpose of seeing whether he could identify the prisoner."[15]

Bell remembered:

> It was in the night, about two or three o'clock ... [Mr. Webster] told me he wanted me to go down to General Augur's headquarters; I went down there. There was a light, very bright, in the hall at the time. They asked me how light it was at Mr. Seward's that night; told them it was not light in our hall, that the burner did not give but very little light; they asked me what kind of man the one was who came to see Mr. Seward. I told him he had black hair, thin lips, a fine voice, very tall and broad across the shoulders. There were about twenty or thirty gentlemen in there. They brought in one man and asked me if he was the one, and then brought in another. Neither looked like him, and I told them "No." They then opened the middle door and this man came walking in; at the door the light was turned up very bright. As soon as I saw him, I put my finger right on his face and said, "I know him; that was the man."[16]

Sampson remembered that Bell also exclaimed, "I know his mouth!" Young Bell, who possessed a sharp eye for detail, had remembered Powell's dimpled cheeks. The clothing of

Contemporary woodcut engraving of William Bell's identification of Powell at General Christopher Augur's headquarters (National Park Service).

the suspect also tallied with that worn by the assailant. As Sampson smugly phrased it, "I had never seen a more positive identification in my life."

It didn't take long for the authorities to act. As of 4:30 a.m., April 18, a sullen and silent Lewis "Paine" Powell was confined in chains aboard the ironclad *Saugas*, guarded by a contingent of the Marine Corps. The vessel was at anchor in the eastern branch of the Potomac River, near the Washington Navy Yard. By the next day, April 19, the newspapers headlined the details of the capture of a fugitive whose name was still unknown.

13. In the Belly of the Whale

One by one, the ironclad monitors were fed a daily diet of chained prisoners—shackled men thrown into the darkened bowels of ships. The *Saugus* and her sister ship, *Montauk,* rode their anchors separated by a few yards. Long, low, flat, covered with heavy steel sheet metal, with a round turret and one tall smokestack, they had an eerie appearance in the grey dawn light, looking like partially-submerged sea monsters.

Powell was not alone in his misery. Samuel Arnold, Michael O'Laughlen, George Atzerodt and Ford's Theater scene shifter Edman Spangler had tumbled down into the blackened holds. Hartman Ritcher, cousin of George Atzerodt, at whose home George had been captured, was also consigned to the floating prisons.

Early on the morning following Powell's capture, Maj. Augustus Seward, elder son of the wounded secretary, made his appearance on the *Saugus* for the express purpose of identifying Lewis Powell.

> I saw him on board the monitor the day after he was taken. He was brought up on deck of the monitor and I took hold of him the same way I had hold of him when I shoved him out of the room, and I looked at his face, and he had the same appearance, in every way, that he had the few moments that I saw him by the light in the hall; his size, his proportions, smooth face, no beard, and when he was made to repeat the words, 'I'm mad! I'm mad!' I recognized the same voice, varying only in the intensity.[1]

One rather questionable account in the *New York Times* for April 20, 1865, described the identification of the unnamed captive aboard the monitor not only by Major Seward, but by Miss Fanny Seward, Private George F. Robinson and again by William Bell. This account cannot be substantiated by other sources. However, Dr. Tullio Verdi stated,

> Next morning, I accompanied Miss Fanny and Augustus Seward to the Monitor, where Payne was held a prisoner. What a feeling must have pervaded the bosom of this girl while she was going to meet this assassin, who, before her own eyes, had so brutally assaulted and all but killed her father. She had seen him in a dimly-lighted room, under great excitement. Would she recognize him now? The idea of meeting this man face to face, although where he was harmless, would have excited vain fears in many a girl's heart; but she was composed and her demeanor expressed only the dignity of her own strange position. She met the naval officer on the Monitor with the same calm and gentle manners so natural to her. The officers, on the other hand, felt almost a reverence for this girl who, instead of making a demonstration of her harrowing grief, was commanding self, and in her own unaffected manner received the expressions of their respect and sympathy with unfeigned gratefulness.
>
> Payne gradually rose from the hatchway and with neck exposed, head uncovered, showing a serious if not stolid face and colossal frame, he stood unmoved before this frail girl, who would not even utter a curse upon him. God alone knew what passed in those two hearts at that moment. Strangely quiet, they stood before each other. Were they overwhelmed by the magnitude of a crime that was beyond man's redress? The scene was a solemn one—too solemn for man to utter a sound; a silence, broken only by the hissing wind and surging waves

pervaded the whole ship.... Miss Fanny was hanging on my arm. Did I feel a quiver? Probably I did for I gently drew her from the painful scene. Conscientious even at this trying moment, she could not identify the man for her identification, she thought, might be his death. She had only seen him by a dim light as if a frightful vision. That was all she said.

To the questions of the detectives Payne answered hesitatingly and somewhat evasively. Had he ever seen the lady before? No. Could he pronounce Dr. Verdi's name? He pronounced it so well that it made me shudder. Yet my name was a foreign one, and he a stranger to me. Had he ever seen Dr. Verdi before? No. Such was the assassin Payne ... his answer bespoke only a light degree of fear ... his physique was Herculean.[2]

The photographs of Powell that were taken at about this time depict a sullen, glowering young man with a grim coldness in his eyes—a look reflecting deep, hopeless resignation. Another photograph shows him clad in his frock coat, vest and hat, his hands immobilized by elongated steel shackles known as "lily irons."

Maj. Thomas T. Eckert and Charles Dana, assistant secretaries to Stanton, were assigned the task of interrogating Powell in the hope that he might talk and drop some wanted names, including his own.

Eckert remembered another photography session on board the monitor a few days later on April 27. Powell, sullen and silent, decided to foil photographer Alexander Gardner. Whenever the photographer would remove the lens cap from the camera, Powell would respond with a vigorous head shaking—the results of which would produce a blurred unrecognizable image. Enraged, Col. H. H. Wells, provost marshal of defenses south of the Potomac, struck Powell's arm with his sword or cane. The burly Eckert stepped up at once and reprimanded the officer for his unwarranted action.[3] Watery-eyed, Powell thanked Eckert and said that was the first sympathetic word he had heard since his arrest. The picture taking session came to an abrupt halt.

Colonel Wells had something else in mind—a thorough search of the prisoner.

> I took off his coat, shirt, pants, vest and all his clothing ... he had on a white linen shirt at the time and an undershirt minus one sleeve. I described to him what I supposed his position was when he committed the assault, and said to him that I should find the blood on the coat sleeve inside of the coat he was wearing [the frock coat]. I found it also on the white shirt sleeve. I

Powell in irons aboard the monitor *Saugus* (Library of Congress).

called his attention to it at the time and said, "What do you think now?" He leaned back against the side of the boat and said nothing.

Wells also subjected Powell's fine red-topped boots to a close inspection: "There was then upon them a broad ink stain that is now to be seen on one of them, on the inside. I asked him where he got those boots. He said he bought them in Baltimore and had worn them three months. I called his attention to the falsehood that was apparent from the fact that the boots had only been slightly worn. He made no reply to that."[4]

Wells did not abuse Powell physically on this occasion, although he accused the prisoner of being a liar. The provost marshal noticed blood on the overcoat: "I called the prisoner's attention to the fact, and I said, 'How did that blood come there?' Said he, 'It is not blood!' I said, 'Look and see and say if you can tell me, it is not blood!' He looked at it again and said, 'I do not know how it came there.'"[5]

After removal of his own clothing, Powell was given a dark blue sailor suit consisting of a navy regulation undershirt and "fall-front" bell bottom trousers. This he would wear for the next three months and to his grave. He was also given additional shirts to wear as well; although he retained the trousers. His civilian clothing was confiscated by the United States Government, and what happened to them is not now known, although as late as 1885, "in the office of the Judge-Advocate General of the Army ... mementoes of the tragedy" were kept. "There [is] also a light-colored slouch hat, worn by Payne when he entered Secretary Seward's room, which he lost in the struggle...."[6]

Apparently the prisoners were moved about quite a bit from one ironclad to another in order to keep to a minimum any communication between them. Under Capt. Frank Monroe, a contingent of forty marines was assigned to guard the prisoners confined aboard both the *Saugus* and *Montauk*. Two sergeants, John Peddicord, and Joseph H. Hartley, had special assigned duties while guarding the conspirators.

April 22, Lewis Powell's twenty-first birthday, found him in abject misery. Sergeant Peddicord recalled: "On the deck of the vessel there was a pile of irons for hands and feet, together with an anvil and hammer. As these prisoners were secured, I selected irons to fit and riveted them on the hands; also to one leg with an iron ball and six feet of chain."[7]

Powell was confined in the chain locker, and although he showed a wonderful fortitude, far beyond what might be expected of a twenty-one year old, even one who had braved four years on the battlefield, the effects of his solitary entombment within the monitor began to

The handcuffs worn by Powell throughout much of his incarceration. These heavy, restrictive shackles, commonly called "lily irons," prevented any joint movement of the hands (Dr. John Lattimer Collection).

strain his nerves to the breaking point. But there was yet another nightmare he was to be subjected to—a blackness far more terrifying than the monitor's darkened hold:

April 22, 1865
Commander J. B. Montgomery
Commandant, Navy Yard
Washington, DC
    The Secretary of War requests that the prisoners on board the iron clads belonging to his department shall have for better security against conversation, a canvas bag put over the head of each and tied around the neck with a hole for proper breathing and eating, but not for seeing—and that Payne be secured to prevent self destruction.
    G. V. Fox[8]

Marine Sergeant Peddicord was responsible for placing the hoods on the prisoners, and although all of those thus subjected to this inhumane cruelty were "affected," Peddicord remembered that Powell actually wept. "Even stalwart Payne, who never said a word before, asked me, 'What is *that* for?' I replied that I was there to obey orders, not to answer questions; and as I forced the hood down ... I noticed a tear start and roll down his cheek. These hoods had small openings at the nose for breathing and were raised a bit during their meals."[9]

One is left with the impression that the hooding punishment, not much different from being buried alive, had turned Powell into a frightened, dejected youth—a person tottering on the edge of insanity. Although he would exhibit a devil-may-care attitude while on trial, his imperturbability in the prisoner's dock may have been pure bravado.

Peddicord remembered something else:

One evening, I noticed that the officers were looking for something to come up the river and when I awoke Sergeant Hartley at midnight, I told him of this and turned in to sleep until 6 o'clock in the morning when he called me, saying, "Come out here! I have something for you." I turned out on deck and went to where he was, alongside a carpenter's bench on which lay the body of a man wrapped about with a soldier's blanket. My order from Hartley was, "Take charge of this body and allow no one to touch it without orders from Colonel Baker." ... it was the body of the assassin, John Wilkes Booth, which had been brought up the river during the night by the detachment of troops who had captured him.[10]

On April 26, a Federal cavalry group had finally caught up with Booth and Herold at a small farm near Port Royal, Virginia, owned by the Richard Garrett family. David Herold had given himself up, but Booth had refused to surrender and was fatally shot by an eccentric sergeant named Boston Corbett. The postmortem examination of the fugitive actor was held on deck of the *Montauk,* with Herold being confined in chains below deck. The round-up of the alleged conspirators was just about complete to the satisfaction of the government—only John H. Surratt remained at large.[11]

On April 26, the day of Booth's death and Herold's capture, the newspapers had some sensational headlines:

Attempted Suicide of Paine

Washington, April 25
Special to the Philadelphia Press
    Paine, the alleged assailant of Mr. Seward, who was arrested a few days ago, while entering the house of Surratt, in this city, attempted to commit suicide last night by butting out his brains against the walls of his prison. The bumping attracted the attention of his jailor, who found on examination, that the prisoner had seriously injured himself. To prevent further

injury, his hands were confined and a cap, stuffed full and large so as to act as a pad, was fastened upon his head.[12]

Serious questions arise over Powell's reported suicide attempt. Did an actual attempt occur, or was there a cover-up to conceal an injury intentionally inflicted during interrogation? The suicide charge seems somewhat incongruous in view of the fact that Powell was heavily ironed from the time he was imprisoned. Orders for the hooding were issued on April 22, and more than likely, they were immediately put into effect.

It is possible that Powell, under deep pangs of remorse for what he had done, would want to take his own life. Two months later, the young prisoner would be observed in his prison cell handling the ball attached to his leg and placing it against his head. This could have constituted his best effort toward a second suicide attempt, but the facts will never be known.

The coffle of dejected prisoners was finally conveyed to the old Arsenal Prison at Greenleaf's Point on the night of April 29, after almost two weeks in the bellies of the monitors. It may be noted here that neither Mrs. Surratt nor Dr. Samuel A. Mudd was ever confined on the monitors, nor were they hooded as the rest of the prisoners.

Thomas T. Eckert had spent time with Powell on board the monitor trying to induce him to talk. Once he brought Lewis a chew of tobacco; the only thing the prisoner still craved. Slipping it through the mouth opening in Powell's hood, Eckert received the youth's gratitude with the expression that he had never had anything to taste so good as that piece of tobacco.[13]

Powell told Eckert many conflicting stories, one of which concerned the Confederate plot to burn New York City in November of 1864. Supposedly Powell was a part of this venture—but at that time he was serving with Mosby in the Shenandoah Valley. Some of Powell's tales do seem a bit farfetched. In another instance, Lewis claimed to have attended a meeting at a gambling place in Baltimore where the secretary of the meeting was a physician on Fayette Street. The inquisitive Eckert went to the aforementioned gambling saloon, and scratching around in a fireplace grate, found a scrap of paper describing an abduction plot and bearing the name of Dr. Samuel A. Mudd.[14] Of such is the stuff that "penny dreadfuls" were made of!

Granted, some of the accounts do have a ring of truth to them, such as Booth's trying to induce Powell to shoot Lincoln on the White House grounds, an incident which was also mentioned by Herold in a disclosure to his attorney, Frederick Stone.

When time came to leave the ironclads, Eckert accompanied Powell, whose swollen feet were clad in a pair of carpet slippers for the short trip ashore, the shackles having irritated his feet unmercifully. Inasmuch as his boots had been confiscated as evidence, he probably would have been provided with slippers, regardless of the condition of his feet. Samuel Arnold dwelt on the terror of the night as the prisoners left the monitors: "As the silent hour of midnight drew near, the dragging and clanking of chains were heard overhead as victim after victim passed to and fro to the place provided for his reception and then all became silent as death again."[15]

Eckert remembered, "As they neared the gang-plank of the vessel, it was necessary for each one to lower his head to prevent being struck by the crosspiece; the tide being very low ... Payne could not see the obstruction and I placed my hand on Payne's head and pressed it down so as to prevent his striking the crosspiece."[16]

13. In the Belly of the Whale

The arrival of Powell at the Arsenal Prison (National Defense University Library, Visual Learning and Special Collections Branch, Fort McNair, D.C.).

Rebuilt in 1817, after being burned during the War of 1812, the Arsenal had been used since 1831 as a Federal prison. It was turned over to the War Department under orders from President Lincoln in 1862, to be used as a place of storage for ordnance supplies. Now, in 1865, because of its isolated location and tight security, it was to be used as a prison again. The tiers of cells were quickly made ready to receive the prisoners implicated in the murder of the president.[17]

After the autopsy, the body of the ringleader, John Wilkes Booth, was promptly buried under the floor of a warehouse in the prison building between the warden's quarters and the main cellblock. The second-and third-floor tiers of cellblocks were to hold Booth's cohorts.

Ferried from the monitors by steamer, the wretched prisoners were compelled to march through a double row of armed soldiers, "a long distance through mud and water," with iron shackles biting into the flesh of their ankles and every step a misery. Samuel Arnold remembered being "conducted up and down long flights of stairs and finally being thrust into a damp and narrow cell in which was a mattress and blanket."

Mrs. Surratt was conveyed by carriage at 5:00 p.m. on the evening of April 29 from the Old Capitol Prison and taken directly to the Arsenal. Dr. Mudd was similarly transported.

As a precaution, each of the accused was placed in a cell separated by empty compartments on either side and attended by two armed guards. There would be no chance of communication and even less chance of escape. For Lewis Powell, and for the other seven defendants, the nightmare had begun.

14. Blind Justice

There was a busting excitement throughout the old Arsenal as it prepared for the trial of the accused assassins.

> A large room in the northeast corner of the third story of the penitentiary, near the cells in which the prisoners were confined, was fitted up for the trial. It was about thirty by forty-five feet square, with a ceiling about eleven feet high, supported by three wooden pillars. Four windows, with heavy iron gratings, afforded tolerable ventilation, and there were two anterooms for the accommodation of the court and witnesses. The room was whitewashed and painted for the occasion, a prisoner's dock was constructed along the western side, the floor was covered with cocoa matting, and the tables and chairs were new. Gas was introduced, in case the court should protract its sittings until after dark.[1]

A youthful Bvt.-Maj. Gen. John F. Hartranft, who had been in command of a division at Alexandria, received his orders from the War Department by direction of President Andrew Johnson to act as "Special Provost Marshal General" in preparation for the trial. He was to report to Maj. Gen. W. S. Hancock, then commanding the Middle Military Division, United States Volunteers, Washington, D.C.

Hartranft brought with him his aide-de-camp, Capt. R. A. Watts. Also from Hartranft's division were "Lt. Colonel W. H. McCall of the 200th Pennsylvania, Lt. Colonel G. W. Frederick of the 209th, Colonel Dodd of the 211th and Lieutenant G. W. Geishinger of the 208th."[2]

The Arsenal grounds were guarded by a brigade of infantry, an artillery battery and even a battalion of cavalry, all ready and willing to enforce the proper security. No one could enter or leave without a written pass from the secretary of war.[3]

In his logbook, Hartranft provides a clear picture of what went on at the prison day by day:

> I took charge of eight prisoners in the cells of this prison about 2 O'clock on the 29th of April. I immediately swept out the cells and removed all nails from the walls and searched the persons of the prisoners and took the articles mentioned and marked "A" from their persons which I enclose.
>
> At 8 O'clock A.M., breakfast was given to the prisoners in my presence and under my personal supervision, which consisted of coffee, soft bread and salt meat. After they had finished breakfast, the bowl containing the coffee was removed. No other article was taken into the cell. The same system has been observed at each subsequent meal. At this same hour [8:00 a.m. I also made a personal inspection of all the cells and prisoners, and found them as comfortable as could be expected under the circumstances. At 2:30 P.M., Dr. G. L. Porter reported by authority of the Secretary of War, for his daily inspection of prison and prisoners; he inspected the prisoners in my presence. I also made a personal examination of the cells and prisoners at this time.[4]

The same "menu" was served without variation four times a day—salted pork, beef or beef soup with bread, coffee or water. This unbalanced diet would have noticeably dire effects on young Powell's digestive system.

The "old Arsenal" on Greenleaf's Point where the conspirators were incarcerated, showing the prison yard. The gallows was erected close to the brick wall facing the entrance of the buildings (Library of Congress).

To guard against sudden illnesses or suicide attempts, Dr. Porter would make nightly periodic checkups on the condition of the prisoners.

On May 2, 1865, Major Thomas T. Eckert visited the Arsenal for a considerable period of time, trying to induce Powell to talk about his actions: "The conversation was at his own instance. I kept him [Powell] off for four or five days after he expressed a desire for an interview with me. Finally, he became so much distressed that I listened to him; but it was simply a statement of his own action the night of the assassination, of his feelings while in the room and after he left the room, and where he went up until the time of his arrest." It is unfortunate that Major Eckert didn't write down the statements in full as he had promised Secretary Seward.

Powell was no name dropper. He was very close-mouthed about the various goings-on previous to the assassination, although he did tell Eckert that he had first met Booth in Richmond, and Eckert afterwards thought that the year involved was 1863. As the major put it: "He was very particular when I put a question, not to allow any information affecting others to be drawn out of him he did once speak of Herold and his remark was that he was a 'little blab.' Said he, 'I never was satisfied with him myself and so expressed myself to Booth.'"

When questioned by the chairman of the Impeachment Committee whether or not Powell had implicated others in the plot, Eckert asserted:

> The reply he made to me in answer to that question ... besides implicating John Surratt was, "All I can say about that is that you have not got the one-half-of them!" ... I asked him if he left Gettysburg with a view to go to Baltimore to meet Booth. He said he did not. I questioned him very strongly on that and he laughingly replied that I must believe him; that his meeting with Booth in Baltimore was accidental ... he called him "Captain." I asked him if Booth held a commission. He replied that he did not know ... he did recognize him as his superior officer.[5]

The prison cellblock in the old Arsenal as depicted in *Harper's Weekly*, July 8, 1865 (author's collection).

It is doubtful that Eckert received all the information just mentioned during this one particular interview, inasmuch as Hartranft says Eckert was in Powell's cell, number 195, for only about an hour:

> At 8:50 p.m. I opened cell 195, removed the hood from the prisoner and Major Eckert entered the cell. I closed the door (not locking it), and removed the sentinel and allowed no one in hearing distance of the conversation in the cell.
> At 9:43 p.m. Major Eckert came out of the cell and Charles Couner (accompanying Eckert) passed to the cell and looked upon the prisoner through the open door, after which he passed away. The hood of the prisoner was then replaced and the door closed and locked at 9:50 p.m.[6]

Eckert would visit Powell frequently and regularly throughout the trial—up until the day before the executions.

Now comes a matter of the utmost importance—the trial of the eight alleged conspirators. As this was a touchy matter of sorts, President Andrew Johnson went through the formality of asking Attorney General James Speed whether the persons charged with the offense of having assassinated the president should be tried before a military tribunal or a civil court (civil courts being fully operational in Washington at that time). The attorney general then rendered the following decision:

> That if the persons who are charged with the assassination of the President committed the deed as public enemies, as I believe they did, and whether they did or not is a question to be decided by the tribunal before which they are tried, they not only can, but ought to be, tried

by a military tribunal. If the persons charged have offended against the laws of war, it would be palpably wrong for the military to hand them over to the civil courts as it would be wrong in a civil court to convict a man of murder who had in time of war, killed another in battle.

In Speed's opinion, the conspirators were enemy agents—not specifically civilians who came under the jurisdiction of the military. In other words, they were not civilians under constitutional law, since their crimes had been violations of the laws of war.

Johnson breathed easier after receiving approval for a military proceeding and felt authorized to issue the following presidential order:

Whereas the Attorney-General of the United States hath given his opinion:
That the persons implicated in the murder of the late President Abraham Lincoln, and the attempted assassination of the Honorable William H. Seward, Secretary of State, and in an alleged conspiracy to assassinate other officers of the Federal government at Washington city, and their aides and abettors are subject to the jurisdiction of and lawfully triable before a military commission.

The assistant adjutant general lost no time in appointing the "nine competent military officers" to serve as a commission.

Hartranft decided to initiate preparations for the trial permitting the prisoners to take much needed baths. One can imagine how the wretched prisoners felt. This was May 4, and a long, hot summer was setting in. Trussed up in a steaming hood and manacled with stiff shackles, the accused men were in torment. The opportunity to bathe must have seemed a godsend.

From 4:50 to 7 p.m. the prisoners in cells 184, 195, 205, 170, 181 and 209 were taken into an adjoining cell with a blanket placed over the door, the hood and irons were removed, and they washed their persons with water provided for that purpose. They were afterwards furnished

The alleged conspirators were tried by a commission of nine military generals under the direction of Secretary of War Edwin M. Stanton. The Military Commission was presided over by Gen. David Hunter and assisted by Judge Advocate John Bingham and Assist. Judge Advocate Joseph Holt. Standing, left to right: Brig. Gen. Thomas M. Harris, Maj. Gen. Lew Wallace, Maj. Gen. August V. Kautz, and Henry L. Burnett. Seated, left to right: Lt. Col. David R. Clendenin, Col. C.H. Tompkins, Brig. Gen. Albion P. Howe, Brig. Gen. James Ekin, Maj. Gen. David Hunter, Brig. Gen. Robert S. Foster, John A. Bingham, and Brig. Gen. Joseph Holt (Library of Congress).

with clean underclothing and clean bedding. Only two cells were opened at one time, and the prisoners did their washing in the presence of myself or one of my field officers.[7]

Samuel Arnold would remember that, as welcome as his bath was, the water was cold as ice.[8]

Lewis Powell apparently had a crying need to talk to someone, but the cynical Hartranft did not wish to talk, or perhaps was prohibited from conversing with the prisoner: "The prisoner in 195 [Powell], after he had finished washing himself, as I was about leaving the cell, and about to lock the door, said, 'General, I would like to talk to you if you would consent to do so—I do not mean now, but when you have time.' I answered, 'I have no time.'"

One gets the uncomfortable impression of Powell, hooded and chained, locked in his tomb-like cell, begging for an ungranted interview, just wanting someone—anyone—to talk with. The mind-boggling psychological effect of the treatment accorded the prisoners must have been profoundly adverse.

On the morning of May 9, the prisoners had the charges and specifications read to them, and the morning of May 10 saw the start of the first day of their trial. For Powell and three others, it was the beginning of the end.

Brought into the courtroom at 11 a.m. on the morning of May 10, the prisoners were arraigned before a court of nine immaculately attired generals in full dress uniform. Judge Advocate General Joseph Holt, with assistance from Assistant Judge Advocates John A. Bingham and Col. H. L. Burnett were in charge of the prosecution.

The prisoners had to secure their own counsel, and, according to various press reports, Powell initially "selected" Mason Campbell, "a lawyer of the Baltimore bar," who had had "considerable practice and is a son-in-law of Judge Tanney [sic]." The article also states: "It is a considerable comment that Payne, the contract murderer from Canada, should have singled him out. He has taken the Oath and is presumed to be loyal. He has some reputation here, being frequently engaged in the Supreme Court. He has not yet appeared, and it is hardly probable he will."[9]

One wonders who proposed the name of Campbell. The Branson ladies? Would they have had connections of some sort? Again, we recall the card found in Powell's coat pocket, "Mary J. Gardner." There was a cousin of General Gardner, C.S.A., a young lady by the name of Mary Gardner. What was the connection here, if any? We will probably never know.[10]

One wonders how a somewhat penniless youth would have selected such a prominent (and obviously expensive) lawyer to represent him when asked whom he selected for council.

How did Powell know Campbell or even hear of him? The choice is obvious when one considers young Powell's Baltimore connections.

Powell attended St. Barnabas Episcopal Church while living in Baltimore. This was the family church of the Branson family in whose house he boarded. He also attended Dr. Fuller's Seventh Baptist Church from time to time as well. He heard Dr. Abram Dunn Gillette preach there on a snowy Sunday in February of 1865. However, young Powell apparently became a frequent visitor at St. Barnabas Church, attending, according to one reference, both morning and evening.[11] The rector, Reverend Augustus P. Stryker, was an ardent Southerner who had previously been reprimanded by the Bishop for refusing to pray for Union troops. In this, Stryker and the young Confederate soldier, Powell, had much in common. Powell thus became intimate with Stryker and visited him frequently, the older pastor finding the young man "gentlemanly, intelligent and earnest."[12]

As a frequent visitor to both Stryker's church as more than likely his home as well, the

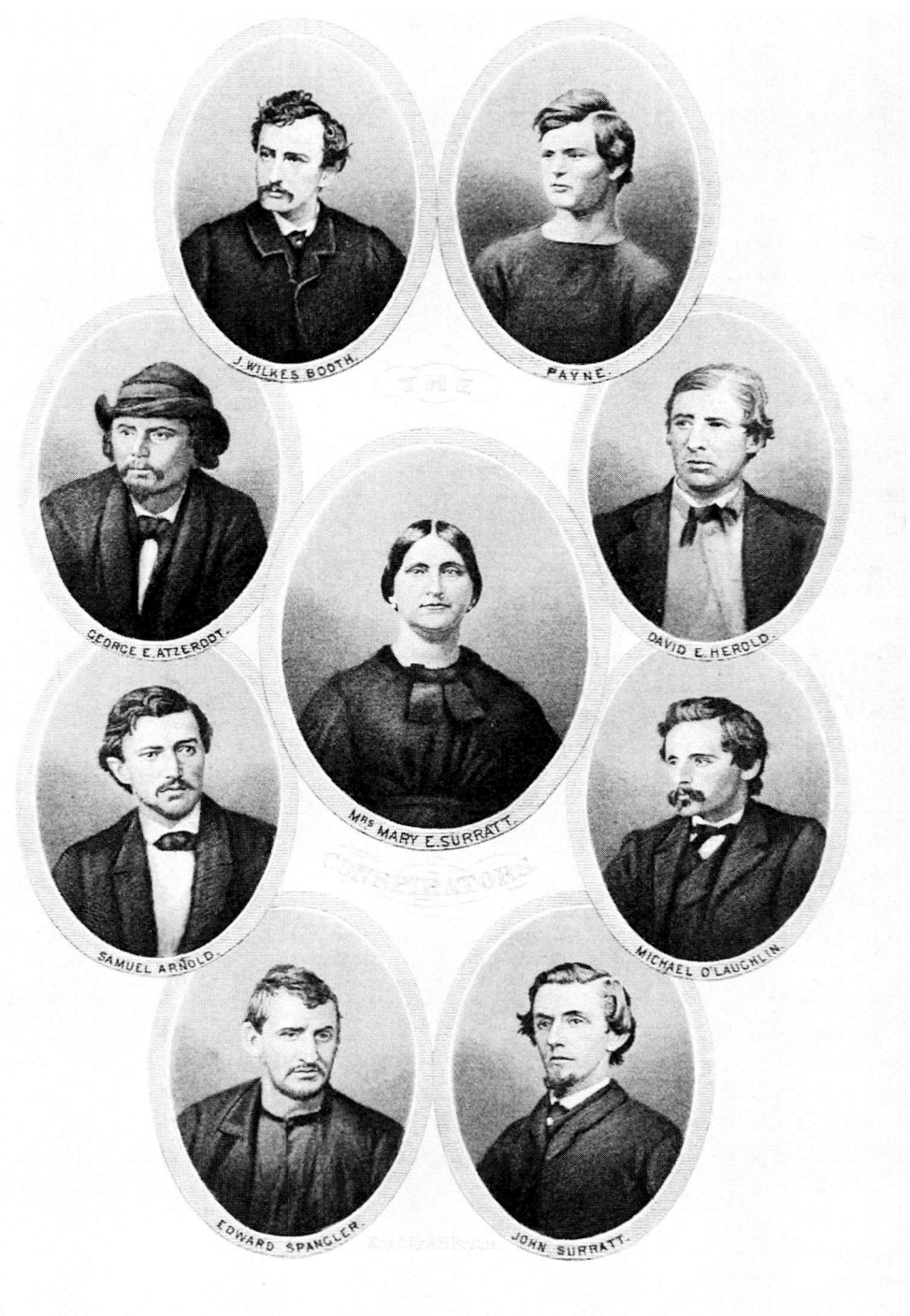

Popular engraving of the accused conspirators which first appeared in the official bound volume of the conspiracy trial transcript by Benn Pitman, 1865 (Library of Congress).

youth became familiar with Stryker's family. Stryker was the son-in-law of Mr. Mason Campbell, prominent attorney and kinsman of Statesman, Roger Tanney. Campbell also attended St. Barnabas Church.

This of course, made him Powell's apparent choice for representation. Needless to say, Campbell refused to have anything to do with the suspected young "Seward Assassin."

The Branson family was also in great difficulty with the military at this particular time. Major H. B. Smith reported: "Immediately upon the identification of Paine, I arrested the Bransons and all the occupants of their fashionable boarding house, No. 16 N. Eutaw Street. Following is a list of the persons arrested:

> Mrs. M. A. Branson
> Miss M. A. Branson (Mary)
> Miss Maggie Branson
> Mrs. Early
> Mrs. Croyean
> Mrs. Thomas Hall
> Miss Josephine Hall
> Mr. Joseph Branson, Jr.
> Mr. C. H. Morgan
> Mr. C. S. Shriver
> Mr. Charles Ewart
> Mr. C. E. Barnet[13] [sic]
> Mr. J. C. Hall
> Mr. W. H. Ward
> Mr. E. A. Willer
> Mr. Augustus Thomas
> Mr. Winchester
> Mr. Thomas Hall
> Mr. S. T. Morgan
> Mr. H. D. Shriver

I began my examination of the individuals in the house, seeking to find who, if any, were intimate with Paine, and might, therefore have had some knowledge of the crime before the fact.

Not all of these people were known to be disloyal. Messrs. C. H. Morgan, J. C. Shriver, and H. D. Shriver are marked on my list as "loyal" and there may have been others. [Strangely, head of household, Joseph Branson, Sr., is missing from the list.]

I have [in 1911] a led [sic] pencil memorandum of the examination in the house [No. 16 N. Eutaw Street], but it is so disjointed as to be unintelligible.... Finding that the most valuable source of information was the Bransons, I released all others, resuming the examination of Miss Maggie Branson in my office where I could be more deliberate ... when she had finished, she was anxious to learn what I thought the government would do to her ... Miss Branson was detained a long time.[14]

Included in the list of those subpoenaed for questioning was the maid with whom Powell had the altercation in Baltimore in March of 1865—Annie Ward. Although subpoenaed, she was never called to testify. One wonders why. (See Appendix K.)

Two days after the opening of the trial, Powell was without counsel. Major William E. Doster, a graduate of Harvard, and a former provost marshal of the City of Washington, had been engaged by John Atzerodt as counsel for his errant brother, George, who like Powell was on trial before the Military Commission. Aware that Powell "Paine" was without legal counsel, the dapper Major Doster was requested by Assistant Judge Advocate General Burnett to defend Powell as well.

Colonel William E. Doster, former Washington, D.C., provost marshal and Powell's court-appointed attorney, as he appeared while a student at Yale and Harvard universities in the late 1850s (courtesy the late James O. Hall and Surratt House Museum).

Maggie Branson would eventually testify at the trial in Powell's defense, and it is a minor mystery why Mary did not do likewise, she being the more intimate with Powell. Perhaps with both sisters to choose from, Doster decided that Maggie would be the more effective witness. However, it has now been determined that Mary Branson was ill with "female trouble" from which she would later die at age 40 in 1871. There is also some speculation that she could have possibly been pregnant with Powell's child. (See Appendix K.)

Doster was reluctant to take Powell on as a client.

> This I at first refused to do on the ground that I had my hands more than full with one considering the excited state of public feeling, and that, in fact, this was a contest in which *a few lawyers were on one side and the whole United States on the other—a case in which, of course, the verdict was known beforehand* [author's italics]. I finally allowed my name to go down for Payne temporarily, but with the understanding that as soon as he could secure counsel for himself, I might and would, withdraw.
>
> He never secured other counsel, and I had to do the best I could for both clients.[15]

Major Doster would become increasingly intrigued by Powell. A resourceful attorney, he took considerable time and effort to try to make as strong a case as possible in defense of his youthful and mysterious client.

The trial of the century had begun.

15. "Hero Villainy": A Field Day for the Media

The third day of the trial was noticeably different from the first two. After sitting behind closed doors for two days, the court decided to admit the press and the general public. The nation would now get a firsthand look at the motley crew of "assassins." Indeed, the papers were full of the proceedings, and in no time at all, all manner of improbable stories began to appear.

The ringleader, John Wilkes Booth, was dead, and the press needed a substitute target upon which to vent its rage. It found the perfect quarry in the mysterious Seward attacker. Taciturn and aloof, darkly handsome, young Powell made the perfect "villain." As early as May 11, a story appeared in the *Louisville Union Press* bearing the title, "Career of an Assassin. Payne Described by One Who Knows Him," in which the youthful assailant was portrayed as a member of the notorious Payne family of Kentucky and one of a group of murderous brothers and swindlers by that name. These Payne brothers allegedly participated in the St. Alban's raid in Vermont in October 1864.[1] Speculation would continue to swirl around Powell all during his trial, and he became a prime target for the pens of journalists:

> It is 10 o'clock and the court is soon to sit. The members ride down in superb ambulances and bring their friends along to show them the majesty of justice. A perfect park of carriages stand by the door to the left, and from these dismount Major Generals' wives in rustling silks, daughters of congressmen, attired like the lilies of the milliner; little girls who hope to be young ladies and have come with "Pa" to look at the assassins; even brides are here ... these tender creatures have a weakness for the ring of manacles, the sight of folk to be suspended in the air; the face of a woman confederate in blood....
>
> They chat with their polite guides, many of whom are gallant Captains, and go one after another up the little flight of steps which leads to the room of the officer of the day. He passes them, if he pleases, up the crooked stairways, and when they have climbed three of these, they enter a sort of garret room, oblong, and plastered white, and about as large as an ordinary townhouse parlor. Four doors open into it—that by which we have entered, two from the left, where the witnesses wait, and one at the end, near the left far corner, which is the outlet from the cells. A railing close up to the stairway door gives a little space in the foreground for witnesses; two tables, transverse to this rail, are for the commission and the press, the first named being to the right. Between these are a raised platform and pivot armchair for the witness; below are the sworn phonographers and the counsel for the accused, and then another rail like that separating the crowd from the court, holds behind it the accused and their guards.[2]

Thus was the opening of court described by one of the most colorful Victorian journalists, George Alfred Townsend (GATH), special correspondent to the *New York World*. Townsend was intrigued by Powell, as was the entire court. Day after day, Powell would sit erect in the prisoner's dock, leaning his head back against the wall, sweeping his large blue eyes across the courtroom or gazing dreamily out of the grated window.

Rare carte de visite lithograph of the accused seated in the prisoners' dock before the Military Commission. Powell sits between Atzerodt on his right and Herold seated on his left (author's collection).

Seven men sat sandwiched between guards in the prisoners' dock. A lone woman sat outside the dock railing near the prison door leading to the cells. Of them all, the two who attracted the most attention were Lewis "Paine" Powell and Mrs. Mary E. Surratt. Powell sat stiffly and glared at the faces that glared back. The court watched Powell, his movements, the stubborn, proud lift of his chin. There was something about the man that engaged the imagination—an obstinate dignity, a proud and military bearing that was not discernible in any of the others. Call it what you would—dignity, good breeding, brazenness—it immediately focused one's attention on him. This, combined with the fact that he was obviously the youngest prisoner in the dock, made him the most dramatically interesting person of the eight.

Townsend gave the bloodthirsty public what it craved with his tidbits of gossipy yellow journalism:

> Taller by a whole head than either his companions or the sentries, Payne the Assassin, sits erect and flings his barbarian eye to and fro, radiating the tremendous energy of his colossal physique. He is the only man worthy to have murdered Mr. Seward ... the mystery attending Payne's home and parentage still exists to make him more incomprehensible ... with this man's face before me as I write, I am reminded of some Maori Chief waging war from the lust of blood or the pride of local dominion. His complexion is bloodless yet so healthy that a passing observer would afterward speak of it as ruddy. His face is broad, with a character nose, sensual lips, and very high cheekbones ... while the head runs back to an abnormal apex at the tip of his cerebellum. His straight, lusterless black hair, duly parted, is at the summit so disturbed that tufts of it rise up like Red Jacket's or Tecumseh's; but the head is kept well up, and rests upon a wonderfully broad throat, muscular as one's thigh, and without any trace, as he sits, of the protuberance called Adam's Apple. Withal, the eye is the man Payne's power. It is dark and speechless and rolls here and there like that of a beast in a cage which strives in vain to understand the language of its captors. Payne looks at none of his fellow prisoners; assas-

sins caught seldom care to recognize each other—for while there is faithfulness among thieves, there is none among murderers. His great white eyeball never roves to anybody's in the dock, nor theirs to his. He has confessed his crime and they know it; so they have no mutual hope; they listen to the evidence because it concerns them; he looks at it only because it cannot save him. He is entirely beardless, yet in his boyish chin, more of a man physically than all the rest combined ... his dress which we scarcely notice in the grander contrast of his pose and stature, is an old shirt of woolen blue, with a white nap at the buttonholes, and upon his knees of black cloth he twirls, as if for relaxation between his powerful manacles, a soiled white handkerchief ... his heavy handcuffs make his broad shoulders more narrow. Yet we can see by the outline of the sleeves what girth the muscle has, and the hand at the end of the long and bony arm is wide and huge, as if it could wield a claymore as well as a dirk. He also wears carpet slippers, but his ankles are clogged with so heavy irons that two men must carry them when he enters or leaves the dock. The flesh on his face is hard, as if cast rather than generated, and while we see how he towers above the entire court, we watch him in wonder, as if he were some maniac denizen of a zone where men without minds grow to the stature and power of fiends.³

After reading Townsend's blood and thunder verbiage, one wonders if he wasn't describing Shelley's Frankenstein monster.

The reading public loved Gath's bombast, however, and clamoring for more, got what they wanted by the pageful. Strangely enough, although he would claim that for Powell "there can be no sentiment," Townsend portrayed the fellow with sympathy and sensitivity after his execution.

On the morning of May 13, Powell and his companions encountered a courtroom packed with upturned faces; eager, searching and leering, with fingers pointing at the prisoners while whispering their comments.

Testimony concerning Powell got under way with Louis J. Weichmann taking the stand for the prosecution. The War Department clerk had a field day before the court as he related in minute detail the unusual occurrences at the Surratt boarding house, before and after Powell's stay there, as well as when he occupied a room at the Herndon House. Weichmann was proving himself to be a very effective witness—in fact, too good a witness. He spoke too readily, too eagerly, obviously wanting to please the Commission—to make a good impression at all costs.

During Weichmann's testimony, according to one account, "Payne seemed amused when Weichmann related as to Payne's disguise as a Baptist preacher and with apparent difficulty, suppressed a laugh."⁴ One thing was certain, Powell was making a highly favorable impression upon the

Contemporary artist's conception of Powell on trial before the Military Commission (National Park Service).

spectators. Every eye in the courtroom rested upon his erect figure. He was proud, sleek and handsome. In spite of his soiled clothing, his appearance was very much in contrast with that of his fellow male prisoners—a thoroughbred amongst plow horses. His unconcerned courtroom demeanor provided a vast field for the reporters' imaginations, and they composed fanciful sensation stories about him. Indeed, one finds more press coverage allotted to Powell than to Booth.

> Atzerodt and Payne seemed the most unconcerned of the prisoners. Atzerodt advanced to the bar in front of the raised seats and leaning his elbow on the rail, conversed at length with his counsel, Mr. William E. Doster. Payne directed a cool, impudent stare by turns upon every person in the room. His bold eye, prominent under jaw and athletic figure gave all the marks of a bold, desperate villain, but not one capable of planning a deed of cunning. When he advanced to the bar to converse with his counsel, he rested his manacled wrists on the rail, and stooping over in a boyish style, his coal-black hair fell over his eyes in masses, adding to the savage desperation of his look. He scowled as he talked, and once or twice a grim smile appeared about his mouth, but seemed to find no lodgment about the fierce eye. He seems to affect as rowdyish a dress as possible, and today, appeared in nothing but a close-fitting collarless blue woolen undershirt, pants of the same color and material, stockings and shoes. On Saturday, he wore a steel-mixed outer shirt, or gray, with collar, but as today—with no coat or vest. As he sat with his head defiantly thrown back against the wall, his tall form towered preponderously above those of his fellow prisoners on the bench.[5]

The preceding excerpt seems to condemn Powell as if he were responsible for his attire. It would be hard to surmise, in the rigidly formal Victorian era of the 1860s where a gentleman would not appear in public in shirtsleeves, just how much his dress during the trial was used as prejudice against him.[6]

Gentlemen in the Victorian era did not expose their bare neck or throat in mixed society. It was something that just was not done—certainly not considered "genteel" in the strictest sense. Although Powell did get a change of clothing from time to time, for the most part he sat in his shirt sleeves in either a woolen or flannel shirt with exposed neck. It has always been supposed that he wore this same suit consistently throughout his incarceration to his death three months later. Not so.

Lewis Powell's dress in the courtroom from May 10, 1865, until his death on July 7, 1865, varied. He did not wear the same clothing day after day, but was able to change his shirt and occasionally his pants as well. One day he might wear the regulation navy undershirt, and on another day, he might appear in a shirt complete with collar and collar button, while then again on a different day he would wear a gray shirt or a blue shirt with a button placket front and black pants instead of the navy drop front bell bottomed ones. Never, however, did he appear in a suit coat, vest or white dress shirt as did the majority of his fellow prisoners. In early summer within the stuffy courtroom though, he did appear once with his handkerchief tied around his neck. Apparently, on the lunch hour before court reconvened, the youth sought to cool off by soaking his handkerchief in cold water and placing it around his neck as a sort of early ice pack. This was something that was also done frequently by soldiers on the march in the army.[7]

The young man consistently wore his stockings and slippers into the courtroom inasmuch as his feet had swelled much under the constant chafing and pressure of his leg irons that he could no longer get his boots on. He was therefore given carpet slippers to wear. According to the prison commandant, John F. Hartranft's letter book, the prisoners were given clean clothing and underwear, and their clothing was also laundered from time to time. Their relatives also brought them apparel. Young Powell, who had no family near, even received the gift of a personal item, a pocket handkerchief, from a concerned woman who had observed the youth sweating profusely in the prisoner's dock.

His standard clothing however, was the blue sailor suit, consisting of pull-over undershirt and drop fly front bell bottomed pants of the same material and color, flannel drawers, brown stockings with white tips to the toes and a white handkerchief. This was also the same attire which he wore to his death.

"Monstrum Horridum" headlined the *Chicago Tribune,* with the *New York Times* indicating hearty agreement:

> An increased crowd was in attendance at the assassination trial today, and the room was uncomfortably crowded. The first question asked by the newcomers, "Which is Payne?" he being by common consent the king villain of them all. He absorbs the greater part of the attention of the audience and you hear continually such expressions as, "Did you ever see such a perfect type of cut-throat? What a monster he is to be sure. Had Booth hunted the world over, he could not have found a more fitting tool for his work. He is constitutionally an assassin," etc.[8]

Practitioners of phrenology, the art of analyzing character by studying the shape of the head, were out in full force—indeed, most of the so-called studies of the conspirators made by reporters and journalists literally smack of this quackery.

Mrs. Jane Swisshelm, a lady chronicler, wrote that Powell resembled a bovine in appearance and was "without that swell behind the ear which is said to indicate the social affection in the human head."[9] One wonders if Mrs. Swisshelm actually checked behind Powell's ears! A particular mannerism of Powell which Mrs. Swisshelm observed was "his peculiar motion in tossing aside his hair," a characteristic which was also commented on by others.

Perhaps the strangest story to come out of the whole journalistic hodgepodge was the assertion that "Paine" was the illegitimate son of Jefferson Davis! This ridiculous canard widely published in romantic detail by the press was a base and baseless fiction. (See Appendix G.)

By this time, the nation was beginning to understand that the name "Paine" or "Payne" was an assumed misnomer.

"Who and what this man Payne is, is the great mystery of the day. There have been various reports concerning him and his antecedents, but it is believed that all are lost concerning him; and it is doubtful if his real name is Payne."[10] Even his attorney, William E. Doster, was puzzled as to who his mysterious client really was. Powell would say nothing and would just lean his head back against the wall in the prisoner's dock, staring at the crowds. Doster could get nothing whatsoever out of him.

The *Albany Evening Journal* had it half right on June 6, 1865, when it stated:

> The conspiracy trial still drags its slow length along, with much of repetition and very little of interest in the testimony. The counsel for Payne, whose case presents so many romantic features, are doing their best to establish a theory of insanity in his behalf; but thus far, with very little success. It has transpired that his real name is Powell, and that he has highly aristocratic relations at the South. It is scarcely possible that the trial will continue longer than during the present week. Its close will be a relief to the press and the public.

Young Powell was, of course, second cousin to General John Brown Gordon.

A week would pass before the court heard testimony directly affecting Powell and concerning his attack on Seward.

William Bell was put on the witness stand and emphatically asserted that "Paine" was the man who attacked Secretary Seward. "The identity of the accused was completed by the testimony of Major Seward, Robinson, and the mulatto boy." Major Seward unhesitatingly testified that Powell was his father's attacker beyond a shadow of a doubt.

Powell sat unconcerned in the dock during the testimony until George Robinson took the stand. The wounded male nurse gave an emotionally charged account that seemingly engaged Powell's rapt attention. He sat bolt upright, his face flushed a deep red, and his teeth clinched tightly together. His chest heaved under his light knit shirt as Robinson picked up Powell's huge Bowie knife and demonstrated the manner in which Powell had wielded the weapon. Ordered to stand up in the prisoner's dock while Robinson gave his testimony, Powell was red-faced but unflinching.

William Bell was once again called to the witness stand: "The manacles were taken off from Payne's wrists under the direction of Major General Hartranft and the coats and hat which he wore in his assault on the Sewards put on him that he might be recognized ... the prisoner seemed to enjoy the freedom of his arms keenly. His fingers taper and his hands are finely shaped, soft and white as a woman's. When identified, he would wrinkle his brow and bite his nails nervously."[11]

All eyes were again upon the star prisoner as he tried on the gray frock coat and overcoat. The brown felt slouch hat was handed to him, and he placed it on his thick glossy hair, turning it at a jaunty angle over his eye. Now he faced the court, cheeks tinged in a slight blush, his lips curled in a bashful dimpled smile. The court was awed in its fascination with the enigmatic prisoner. The ladies in the courtroom were thrilled with his handsomeness. Slowly Lewis turned and faced the witness. Young Bell shook his head. "Oh, he knows me right well! If he has confessed to everything, you can ask him if I am not the one that let him in!"

This homely assertion caused the court to rock with laughter—and Powell gave in to the humor, joining his laughter with that of the court. The spectators were stunned to see him laugh.[12]

Further testimony by Mrs. Murray told of Powell's stay at the Herndon House. Thomas Price described Powell's coat and Detective Rosch and Colonel Wells paraded themselves before the court to describe Powell's arrest and subsequent search.

Powell's red-topped boots were placed on exhibition and examined. A large ink stain was reportedly discovered in the inner top of one of the boots, and removal of the ink revealed the imprinted name of John Wilkes Booth. Was Powell wearing a pair of Wilkes Booth's cast-off boots? Booth was reputed to have had large feet, while Powell's were supposedly small for a man of his size, thus explaining how Powell could wear the boots of a man of medium stature. It is conceivable that this evidence was fabricated to prove Powell's tie-in with the assassin. Powell told Colonel Wells that he had bought the red-topped boots in Baltimore and had worn them for three months previous to the assassination, so *someone* was obviously lying.

Through it all, Powell sat silently, "entirely unmoved either by anything said or done in the room, and never speaking to the counsel; not bold and defiant, but composed; indifferent and self-possessed."[13]

The special correspondent of the *New York World* summed up the questions plaguing the entire country: "Who is this man? Has he any friends? Where did he come from? What is his real name?"

Perhaps no one was more puzzled than Powell's attorney, William E. Doster. Doster didn't know just how to present his case and began to wonder if his client wasn't insane. The prisoner wouldn't talk and refused to volunteer any information about himself. Insanity seemed to be Doster's only hope; unless the prisoner decided to break his silence.

16. In the Shadow of Death

May was drawing to a stifling, sultry close—hot and sticky. Lewis Powell sat with his fellow prisoners day after day, listening to the unending testimony. The members of the Commission, attired in their heavy woolen and gilt uniforms, were torpid with the heat and the droning narratives of the witnesses. Some of the members, like Maj. Gen. Lew Wallace, were plainly bored. Wallace, later to gain world renown as the author of *Ben Hur,* doodled and drew likenesses of the prisoners throughout the trial. Sketching away through the evidence, he left behind what are perhaps the most notable pencil portraits of the conspirators drawn from life. A somewhat competent artist, he made two sketches of Lewis Powell, one a portrait and the other a grotesque caricature which bears a hardly recognizable resemblance. Incorrectly labeled as "Mrs. Surratt," the pencil portrait shows a long-haired boyish youth with a detached, dreamy facial expression—quite different from the way he was otherwise described.[1]

As soon as Powell's courtroom demeanor and his appearance appeared in the papers, ladies were clamoring at the doors to see him. Each day, more and more women filled the courtroom eager to get a look at the boyish would-be assassin. Their comments and chattering embarrassed Powell, and the more determined of them would sometimes press close against the dock railing before court convened: "As the prisoners were brought in, the spectators pushed forward as usual, and the ladies especially crowded with such eagerness about the bar of the dock—uttering lively ejaculations at the time as Payne entered that he visibly lost countenance for the moment, blushing like a girl."[2]

Powell had quite a following by the ladies. This was emphasized by the *Washington Evening Star* for May 29, 1865: "Payne is amusing himself by returning stare for stare of all given him so abundantly by the lady visitors." A few days later, on June 13, 1865, that same paper stated: "A fresh impetus to the interest felt by the lady spectators in the prisoner Payne is given this morning by the appearance in a New York paper of a sensation article, broaching the theory that Payne is the illegitimate son of Jeff Davis." (See Appendix G.)

Marian "Clover" Hooper Adams went with friends to see the trial at least twice and like the rest of the ladies, was impressed with the youngest conspirator.

> Annette and I drag Mr. Rogers to the court again. It's crowded; but we squeeze in and get some reporters' chairs. Mr. Rogers waits outside and reads the paper. Being a woman has its advantages on this occasion. The evidence is not very interesting, but it is to see the prisoners. Mrs. Surratt only shows her eyes, keeping her fan to her face. All the men except Paine have weak, low faces. Paine is handsome but utterly brutal, and sits there a head higher than all the others, his great gray eyes rolling about restlessly, not fixing on anything, looking like a wild animal at bay. It is a sad impressive sight.... The trial was interesting—not imposing enough. A moderate sized room—at one end the row of prisoners with a low paling in front—then the tables with reporters, judges in such a few seats—a side door eight feet from Mrs. Surratt

where one entered—with an uncomfortable trying to take out your eye-glass—and scrutinize your fellow creatures—as if they were something apart from the rest of humanity. Mrs. Surratt looked as if she might be a comely rather buxom woman of eighty [sic]—a thin veil over her face and fan partly screening it. A guard between each of the prisoners—the only interesting one Payne. He looked like a fierce animal at bay—defiant—brutal—as if he'd do it again without scruple. I heard that severity had no effect upon him, but that kindness touched him. He is said to have some education. He has a splendid physique—but a low brow and fierce restless gray eyes that turn from side to side.[3]

Day by day, the journalists noticed the dispirited, hangdog countenances of the six other men, creatures beaten into hopelessness beneath this cruel farce of a trial—for it was a farce. The entire Confederate government, without any substantial evidence, was accused of being involved in the conspiracy, while Jefferson Davis and members of his cabinet were tried in absentia. Untruthful witnesses and irrelevant evidence were accepted without objection by the Commissioners.

One by one the witnesses appeared at the prosecution's bequest to point their accusing fingers in Powell's face. Seward's son, Seward's doctors, the detectives who arrested him, people who had found his knife and Lt. John Toffey who had found Powell's runaway horse. One and all, they came day after day to confront and rail against him—and Powell sat through it all with an easy indifference, his only reaction being an occasional long drawn-out sigh and a slightly reddened face.

At times, the prisoner did seem to be interested in some of the courtroom proceedings, according to the *New York Times* of May 16, 1865: "Payne was extremely vigilant, bending forward eagerly to catch a glimpse at the newspapers which the counsel read in front of the dock, as if anxious to see what the world thinks of him."

One can almost sense William Doster's frustration in trying to defend his bewildering, imperturbable client. To let Doster tell it:

During the first two weeks of the trial, I could get nothing out of Payne, either as to his previous history, or as to anything he might have to say in his own defense, or as to whether he wished to be defended at all. During all this time, I knew very little more of him than the public generally, and not near as much as the prosecution, and was in great doubt whether to explain his conduct by lunacy, unparalleled stupidity or fear of prejudicing his cause by communications with his counsel.[4]

The turning point proving Powell's guilt came when he was positively identified by Seward's houseboy. This damning testimony rattled him a bit, and, to use Doster's expression, "thawed him out."

"One Saturday afternoon, he asked me what the next day was. I answered, 'Sunday.' He then said if I could get down to the Arsenal and could procure a private interview with him, he would like to tell me something." Doster agreed and on the following day, presented a pass to see both of his clients, Powell and Atzerodt. At 1:00 p.m. "Payne was unhooded and taken into the courtroom where Mr. Doster had an interview with him until 2:20 p.m. under the usual restrictions for counsel."[5]

With sentinels posted outside the empty courtroom, the prisoner began by giving Doster a "disconnected" account of his life, indicating great hesitancy in speaking out about what had transpired between the conspirators as to "his share in the transaction," as Doster phrased it. Powell anxiously inquired about the condition of Fred Seward, whom he had pistol-whipped, and, when told that his victim was progressing from his wounds, expressed remorse over having hurt the young man and stated that he owed him an apology. Powell reportedly suffered anguish over this pistol whipping. Doster was somewhat puzzled. The youth seemed dull, "his mind seemed of the lowest order ... and his moral faculties equally low." Powell was not a moronic half-wit as he has been portrayed. If his intelligence seemed "low," it was probably confusion resulting from the traumatic hooding. Powell had demonstrated considerable guile and intelligence before his imprisonment, and encasing his head in such an inconceivable torture device for hours and weeks on end could easily have dire effects on his mental and emotional processes. Powell apparently had been terrified of the hooding from the first. Add to this the unending anguish of a one-sided trial—a trial with sure death as the only verdict. The result of such a combination of situations would be mind-numbing.

Doster would also recall Powell's inability to remember either his age or the name of the state in which he was born. These mental blocks *could* have been an intentional effort to feign loss of memory not dissimilar to the "dummy" act which he staged during Major Smith's questioning a month earlier following his arrest in Baltimore. Powell could have been unwilling to bring his parents' names into the limelight. By this time, the prisoner must have known what the outcome of the trial would be. The trial itself was a mere formality.

One thing is sure: Powell did reveal his true name to Doster at this time—and more than likely told the attorney that his father was the Rev. George C. Powell of Live Oak, Florida.

That Doster may not have believed everything his client told him seems apparent by the fact that four weeks would pass before the attorney would write the Rev. Mr. Powell in regard to his son, Lewis.[6] Many years later, Doster would commit to writing his recollection that

> on hearing the narrative, I immediately concluded that the only thing possible to be done on his behalf was to let the court know all that I knew about his mental and moral nature and his previous education. This, by rules of evidence, which were strictly enforced against the prisoners, but relaxed in favor of the prosecution, could only be done under the plea of insanity, which was accordingly adopted. Under the plea of not guilty, I had no recourse except to show that he was not the man Seward's Negro took him to be, and I could not show that. Even under the plea of insanity, I could not let the court talk to the prisoner and find out for itself what a phenomenon he was. That was to be done by experts.[7]

Powell's defense lawyer decided to plead insanity on behalf of his client. Actually, there was nothing else he could do in his effort to stave off capital punishment. As early as May 31, 1865, a headline-seeking journalist for the *Boston Daily Advertiser* predicted:

> Desperate as his case seems, a defense will be attempted by his counsel—a defense the precise line of which I am not at liberty to indicate, but the audacity of which will be apt to create quite a sensation in the community ... I may remark here that it is now seriously proposed to put Payne on the witness stand for the defense of the other prisoners. The design may either be carried out or abandoned before this reaches you. Such a proceeding would certainly create a sensation in the courtroom.

That Powell had asked that his father appear during his trial is revealed in an article taken from the June 1 *New York World:*

> The prisoner Payne today, for the first time almost, appeared to belong to our common humanity ... today he actually asked that three witnesses might be called in his favor. A lady and a doctor living in Warrenton, Virginia, and a minister of the Gospel living in Florida....

During the proceedings, Payne leaned forward in his seat, with his face alternately white and flushed and drew a long breath of relief when it was announced that the witnesses would be summoned.

The witnesses from Warrenton were no doubt Dr. Albin S. Payne, and Mrs. John Grant who testified as to Powell's altercation with the Union soldiers in whose behalf he interceded. (See Appendix F.)

The proceedings of June 2 brought forth a witness who probably caught Powell's interest. Maggie Branson took the stand in his defense. Detailing the prisoner's work at the Gettysburg hospital, Maggie declared that Powell was "very kind to the sick and wounded." When questioned as to how Powell spent his time at her parents' boarding house, Maggie told the court that the taciturn boarder passed much of his time reading medical books and while there seemed to be "depressed" in spirits. The young woman also described Lewis's run-in with the "exceedingly impudent" servant girl, Annie Ward.

One wonders why no effort was ever made to elicit information from Joseph Branson, Sr., the Branson patriarch, who was, according to Powell, more or less involved in the abduction plot.[8] What did Mr. Branson know, and why were there no statements extracted from him? Maggie, Mary and their mother, Mrs. M. A. Branson, were all incarcerated in the Old Capitol Prison in D.C. after being placed under house arrest and examined by the Federal authorities. Why not Mr. Branson? A review of Major Smith's list of those arrested does not even include Mr. Joseph Branson, Sr., although the name of Joseph, Jr., does appear. Where was this "head of the household"? Did Smith simply forget to list the name? Or were there implications of a more sordid sort? An esteemed member of the Baltimore City Council, was Branson above arrest and questioning? Yet he allows his entire family and household to be held? A check of the LAS files show that one Joseph Branson was selling goods to both the Confederacy as well as the Union. Apparently he was double dealing as late as 1864 with both sides of the conflict.[9] Could someone have been protecting him? Or did he possibly escape to Canada, leaving family behind to suffer the consequences?

That Branson Sr. was still alive is certain: a check of the 1870 Baltimore census confirms this by listing Joseph Branson as a seventy-three-year-old boarding house keeper. Branson would die in 1872 at his daughter Maggie and son-in-law's home in Brooklyn, New York. He is buried in Brooklyn's Green-Wood Cemetery—alone, in a plot intended for Maggie and her husband, Charles Barnett. In the 1880s, the Barnetts moved back to the Baltimore, Maryland, area where Charles Barnett opened and operated a prosperous business college. The family is buried in Baltimore. (See Appendix K.)

In the middle of Maggie Branson's testimony, Doster disclosed his decision to set up an insanity plea for Powell. Assistant Judge Advocate Bingham claimed no foundation for such a plea had yet been laid. Doster retorted, "I claim that the whole conduct of the alleged murderer, from beginning to end, is the work of an insane man, and that any further declarations I may prove, are merely in support of that theory and of that foundation as laid by the prosecution."[10] A reporter observed that Powell "appears to be as much astonished and amused as anybody, at the idea of making it appear that he is mad. When the matter was referred to in the first instance, Payne smiled and then blushed up into the hair of his head. He hung his head with a faint indication of shame when testimony was given which showed that he knocked a servant girl down and stamped upon her, for refusing to clean up his room in the house where he was boarding in February last."[11]

Dr. Charles H. Nichols, superintendent of the Government Hospital for the Insane, was then called to the stand by Doster, but Dr. Nichols's answers to questions regarding "moral insanity" seemed to be utterly irrelevant. Powell had been severely constipated for the previous four weeks, and Doster's hint that this in itself indicated insanity was upheld by Dr. Nichols. The strict unvarying bread and broth diet, combined with mental and emotional anguish, would seem to be a much more realistic cause for this condition.

That same afternoon, after Powell was returned to his cell, "the sentinel over the cell of Payne discovered the prisoner handling the balls attached to his limbs, placing them against his head."[12] Taking no chances on the prisoner injuring himself, Hartranft quickly unfastened the balls from the shackles and removed them from the cell. A suicide attempt? Or a repeat of an earlier one? Could Powell have become distressed over the day's courtroom occurrences?

Two sentinels who stood guard over Powell's cell were called to the witness stand on June 3, apparently to "prove" the prisoner's insanity.

JOHN B. HUBBARD
Q. State whether at times you are in charge of the prisoner, Payne?
A. I am.
Q. Have you at any time during his confinement had any conversation with him?
A. I have.
Q. State what was the substance of that conversation?
A. I was taking him out of the courtroom the other day when he said he wished they would make haste and hang him; that he was tired of life and that he would rather be hanged than come back here.

John F. Roberts, the other guard, testified along the same lines: "On the day that Major Seward was examined here, and the prisoner was dressed in a coat and hat, as I was putting the irons on him again, he told me that they were tracking him pretty close and that he wanted to die."[13]

Rather than substantiating Powell's "insanity," Roberts's testimony gives a clear indication of Powell's state of mental anguish, an anguish which he was able to conceal most of the time.

Capt. Christian Rath remembered quite a different Powell from that which the press presented. Having served under General Wilcox of the Ninth Army Corps as provost marshal, Rath was initially ordered to report to the prison for duty as a provost. Later he would serve as executioner. To quote Rath: "Had I known what I would have to do there, I would never have taken the office."[14] When the trial began, Rath's job was to "see that no one entered the courtroom without the necessary credentials." Rath's duties brought him in contact with Lewis Powell. "Payne never complained—no matter what you did to him, he never said a word, and I grew fond of the fellow and was sorry for his predicament. There was a mystery about Payne. He was a great big fellow, and as brave as a lion."[15]

Rath seems to have gotten along well with young Powell, and the two soon acquired a liking for each other.

> Payne had a grim sense of humor. One day, we were discussing our nerve and afterwards I threw myself on the bed for a little sleep. Suddenly I awakened, feeling as if an icy hand had gripped my heart. There was Payne, looking down at me with an ugly expression on his face. I wondered how he had gotten out of his cell, and just then saw Lt. Colonel McCall in a cor-

ner, laughing. Payne laughed and I knew they were only trying my nerve. I was not afraid, though I was startled for a time.

Towards the end of the trial when the conspirators were given outdoor exercise in the prison yard, Powell competed against Rath in quoit games and according to Rath, "I participated in some close contests."[16] Rath further described Powell in the prisoners' dock of the stuffy courtroom: "Payne never murmured. The perspiration ran down his forehead, into his eyes and over his nose ... he was satisfied apparently ... he never complained."

A humid summer was beginning to fasten itself on the Washington area. Hartranft noted that "the prisoners are suffering very much from the padded hoods and I would respectfully request that they be removed from all the prisoners except 195 [Powell]. This prisoner does not suffer as much as the others, and there may be some necessity for his wearing it."[17]

Powell did suffer from the heat, as much as or more than everyone else: "Either from languor from the great heat or from some other cause, the heretofore erect figure of Payne is somewhat drooping ... it is said that he expresses the greatest aversion to sitting on exhibition in the prisoner's dock."[18]

Noticing Powell's discomfort in the hot, stuffy prisoner's dock day after day, at least one of the women spectators took remedial action when a "Christian lady" made him the gift of a pocket handkerchief, sending it to him along with an accompanying note, saying that she "should pray for him and that others prayed for him." Powell was deeply touched by the gesture and "received the present with the air and bearing of a gentleman, returning his thanks, and as to the prayers, he said no one praying for him should labor alone; that he prayed for himself. This last remark was made with much emotion; his eyes filling with tears."[19]

Another report reiterated just how stuffy the courtroom was: "As the morning grows on, the heat in the room becomes oppressive. Water is passed the thirsty prisoners in a large dish of tin."[20] Although Mrs. Surratt, in preference to her gender, had a glass tumbler from which to drink, the male prisoners drank like animals from a communal tin bowl. Likewise, the Commission, attorneys and reporters also received glass tumblers freshened with cool water from a charcoal filtered tin water cooler.

Occasionally, there was some diversion, as when Dr. Mary Walker visited the court. Dr. Walker, the only woman doctor in the Federal Army, and later a recipient of the Congressional Medal of Honor, was an avid advocate of women's rights and insisted upon wearing trousers under short, tunic-like skirts, an almost unheard of female attire in the mid-nineteenth century. Powell and the rest of the male prisoners snickered and smirked to see a woman in pants.[21]

Powell seemingly found another diversion in the appearance of a young soldier of fortune, Henry Kyd Douglas, an officer on the staff of Stonewall Jackson. Arrested shortly after the surrender for having his photograph taken in Confederate uniform, young Douglas soon found himself conveyed to Washington and incarcerated where he was to be a witness of sorts with regard to the absurd accusation that Wilkes Booth had been in touch with Stonewall Jackson! Day in and day out, Douglas would sit in the courtroom listening to the testimony along with the spectators.

> One day, I observed that [Payne] seemed to recognize me. I asked General Hartranft to find out in his next visit to his cell who he was. He reported that Payne's name was Powell, that he was the son of a Baptist clergyman, that he had been a private in the Second Florida Regi-

ment, wounded at Gettysburg as I was; a prisoner in Wests Buildings Hospital at Baltimore when I was, and that he had seen me there; that he subsequently had escaped and never returned to the army. I saw that Hartranft had taken great interest in him as a character study. He said Payne seemed to him a man of iron will, cool and fearless, a typical desperado and singularly truthful.[22]

Douglas expressed the opinion that, with the exception of Powell, the men were a "sorry looking lot."

If Hartranft found Powell "truthful," Doster had his doubts. Doster's insanity plea was about to unravel. Various medical men came and went to examine Powell in his cell, and in a room outside of the courtroom. Doctor James C. Hall examined Powell and found his memory "slow." Whether this resulted from the hooding or whether it was a pose is impossible to tell. Dr. Hall also found Powell to have a "very feeble, inert mind." An absurd allegation, considering the circumstances! "He [Powell] could not remember the maiden name of his mother. He said her first name was Caroline, but he could not remember her maiden name." Surgeon General J. K. Barnes found "no evidence of insanity—none whatsoever." Doctors Basil Norris, Hall and Assistant Surgeon Porter agreed that there was "no sufficient evidence of insanity."[23]

Doster's insanity plea thus fell apart. Such a plea was doomed from the start.

17. The Last Mile

Washington
June 23, 1865
Rev. George C. Powell
Live Oak, Florida
Dear Sir:
    The duty I have to perform is so repugnant to my feelings that only absolute necessity and the request of your son has driven me to it. The person who is now on trial here for assault upon Secretary Seward on the evening of the 14th of April says his name is Lewis Thornton Powell, and that the name of his father is George C. Powell of Live Oak Station, Florida; that he enlisted in the 2nd Florida Infantry and deserted from the Southern Army. He begs you to come on at once. Your safety is guaranteed.
                    Very Truly, W. E. Doster
                      Counsel for Powell[1]

Doster was at the end of his rope. What to do with Paine? His last resort and final decision was to accept his client at face value and write the prisoner's father—if father he indeed was. Strange that the attorney would wait until the end of the proceedings to comply with his client's vitally important request.

The trial was approaching its conclusion, and by late June the satiated public was beginning to lose interest. Even the press reports were starting to "dry out." Coverage of the Grand Review staged in Washington on May 23 overshadowed the court proceedings.

Major Eckert and General Hitchcock were continuing to haunt Powell's cell, obviously seeking more information, as if Doster was totally incapable of such work. Granted, the attorney had his hands more than full defending both Atzerodt and Powell, conscientiously leaving no stone unturned in two almost hopeless cases. Seemingly, Doster was trying harder with Powell's case.

On June 16, an old Negro woman was permitted entrance into Powell's cell, and upon seeing the youth, she embraced him, smothering him with endearments. Powell was embarrassed and perturbed, trying to extricate himself from an awkward situation: "Go away, woman! I don't know you!"

The woman was sent by someone to buttress the contention that Powell was the son of Dan Murray Lee, who's Mammy she had been. Such an alleged relationship was, of course, ridiculous—another obvious canard.

On June 21, Doster had presented his arguments in defense of Powell and Atzerodt. He painted a panoramic picture of Powell's life, full of melodramatic renderings in the best Victorian tradition: "Mr. Doster proceeded to describe and narrate in animated language the manner in which Booth, step by step, worked on the mind of the victim. Mr. Doster argued that Payne at the time had no will of his own, but has surrendered his will completely to Booth." He concluded with the following:

He has killed no man and if he be put to death, we shall have the anomaly of the victim surviving the murderer and under law, he can be punished only for assault and battery with intent to kill, and therefore imprisoned. Mr. Doster proceeded with other considerations why the prisoner's life should be saved, and before concluding, spoke of the many good qualities he had found in the prisoner by his intercourse with him; his frank, manly bearing, his disinclination for notoriety and his indisposition to screen himself from punishment. His only prominent anxiety was lest people should think him a hired assassin or a brute....[2] [See Appendix H.]

Upon commencement of Mr. Doster's argument, the prisoner Payne (or Powell) moved uneasily once or twice in his seat, and after casting his eyes slowly about the room, fixed them with a steady look on his counsel but with an air of unconcern strikingly in comparison with the interest manifested by the other prisoners. Arnold ceased to look through the grated window by which he was sitting, and leaned forward as if to catch every word of Payne's history; while Herold, seated immediately on Payne's right, turned half around and watched the face of the latter with a sort of half amazed stare. The allusions to Payne's early life, the teachings of his mother and the social influences of his sisters seemed to move the prisoner. His eyes grew misty and assumed a vacant look, and his fingers toyed with each other nervously. Finally, Payne dropped his head and maintained that posture until the conclusion of the argument, with the exception of an occasional sidelong glance. Once, he raised his eyes and his face flushed during the narration of his experience in the Rebel army and his destitution in Baltimore. At the conclusion of the argument in his defense, he crossed his legs and rested his manacled hands on his knees, slowly sweeping the room with his eyes and finally settling down into an easy posture, as if relieved by the termination of his case.[3]

The court recessed for lunch after Powell's defense, and one of the members of the Commission remarked matter-of-factly, "Well Payne seems to want to be hung, so I guess we might as well hang him."[4]

The *New Orleans Tribune* for June 29, 1865, erroneously stated, "The conspirator Payne, who attempted to kill Seward, was ordered to be shot by the Military Commission. The sentence was commuted to five years in the Ohio Penitentiary."

Despite the obvious biographical inaccuracies, Doster made an uncommonly valiant effort to save his young client, and his failure to do so was most certainly not for the lack of trying. On June 27, Special Judge Advocate John A. Bingham delivered a caustic response to the various defense arguments in which he emphatically upheld the evidence produced by the prosecution.

The trial was over.

The Commission met behind closed doors to deliberate on the testimony and reach a verdict. Mrs. Surratt was a thorn in the side of the Commission. A few of the judges were against the death sentence, but pressure prevailed, and after both Stanton and President Johnson had reviewed the findings, the sentences were approved. Four were to die—Mrs. Surratt, Herold, Atzerodt and Powell.

July 6 had all the makings of a sweltering summer's day. On this particular morning, the prisoners were not given their usual exercise session in the prison yard. For the previous few days, the accused were given an hour each morning and evening to stroll about the enclosure or play a game of quoits. This hour went fast for the athletic Powell, who liked to engage in quoit-pitching contests with Rath and Spangler.[5] There would be no quoit games on July 6—or ever again for three of the male prisoners. Major General Hancock, in company with Major General Hartranft, made his rounds of the prison cells between 11:00 a.m. and noon.

Of the four to die, Powell was the first to be informed of the sentence:

Lewis Payne—Finding of the specifications, guilty, except combining, confederating and conspiring with Edward [sic] Spangler; of this, not guilty.

SENTENCE—And the said Commission does therefore, sentence him, the said Lewis Payne, to be hung by the neck until he be dead, at such time and place as the President of the U.S. shall direct, two-thirds of the Commission concurring therein.

President Johnson had already given directions that the sentences be carried out "under the direction of the Secretary of War, on the 7th day of July, 1865, between the hours of 10 o'clock a.m., and 2 o'clock p.m. of that day."

When the prison authorities entered his cell, Powell rose from his mattress and "conversed with intelligent politeness." He listened stoically to the execution order, chin up, shoulders squared. Although he only had about twenty-four hours to live, he showed no emotion. The sentence was what he had expected all along, and it held no shock or surprise for him.

Hartranft asked Powell if he had any friends or relatives he wished summoned. Powell shook his head and replied that his friends and family were too far away and could not "get there in season."[6] However, he did express a desire to see the Rev. Augustus P. Stryker, an Episcopal minister and rector of St. Barnabas Church in Baltimore. Attending services at St. Barnabas with the Bransons, Powell had made the acquaintance of Stryker, finding in the minister a Southern sympathizer whose sentiments matched his own.[7] Lewis also asked to see Major Eckert who, he said, had promised to supply the services of a Baptist minister.

From the moment that he was informed of his death sentence, Powell was in a frenzy concerning Mrs. Surratt. Powell blamed himself for her fate. He had been captured at her house, on her very doorstep, and his fabrication of having come there disguised as a laborer to dig in her garden involved her deeply, perhaps fatally in the conspiracy.

Throughout the trial, Mrs. Surratt's defense witnesses maintained that the widow had bad eyesight: "she had not been able to thread a needle for years." Daughter Anna took the stand to state that her mother had defective eyesight and was too proud to wear spectacles.

One wonders what to make of all of the testimony concerning Mrs. Surratt's eyesight. Powell *had* boarded at her house for three days and had visited once previous to his tenure at the boarding house. The widow had also visited Powell at the Herndon House, if we are to believe the testimony of Louis Weichmann and Honora Fitzpatrick. Certainly she should have recognized his voice if not his person. The probability, while not conclusive, is that she recognized Powell the night of her arrest. His face was undisguised. We must also consider Powell's assertions that she may have known of the abduction plot. Fathers Wiget and Walter, spiritual advisors to Mrs. Surratt, visited Powell during his final hours. Father Wiget "embraced the favorable moment to ask him a question unheard of by the others, 'Laying my hand on his [Powell's] shoulder, so, I said in a quick low tone, 'Tell me my friend, is Mrs. Surratt guilty?' Just as quick, he answered, 'No, she is not!' Then suddenly leaning forward and putting his lips to my ear he whispered, 'She might have known that something was going on, but she did not know what.'" The *New York Times* for July 7, 1865, asserted that Powell "stated that he would *do* anything, *say* anything, if Mrs. Surratt and her daughter would be able to remain together."

By midday, after the sentences had been pronounced, Mrs. Surratt's daughter, Annie, had been summoned to her mother's side and her shrieks and sobs rang throughout the prison walls, undoubtedly penetrating into Lewis Powell's cell to make his anguish even keener.

According to one reporter, Powell "says John Surratt is acting cowardly and most villainously in failing to appear and die with his mother ... he expressed deepest regret that Mrs. Surratt is to be a sufferer for any reason of his, and evidences a solicitude for her not unlike that of a tender child for its parent, seemingly thinking only of her fate and of her suffering."[8]

The Reverend Doctor Abram Dunn Gillette was greatly puzzled. On the afternoon of July 6, Assistant Secretary of War Thomas T. Eckert arrived at Dr. Gillette's front door in a carriage and asked the pastor of Washington's First Baptist Church to attend to the doomed conspirators at the Arsenal. Seward's assailant, Lewis Paine, had personally asked for Dr. Gillette by name and desired his spiritual attendance and consolation.[9]

Upon reaching the Arsenal, the perplexed but willing and kindly minister was conducted at once to Powell's cell. The good clergyman knew nothing of the condemned man and was "much concerned to learn why he had chosen him, a loyalist, in preference to other clergymen of his own faith who were in admitted sympathy with the Southern Cause."[10]

Powell explained that he had heard him preach not long before:

> Do you remember a bitter, sleety Sunday last February, when you preached in the Reverend Doctor Fuller's church in Baltimore? It was then I heard you. I sat with two ladies in one of the end pews to the right of the pulpit. There were scarcely more than a score of people in the church as the walking was so icy and dangerous. My companions and myself were the only occupants of the end pews on either side of the chancel. I had hoped that perhaps you might remember the circumstances, as you frequently turned towards us as though addressing us.[11]
>
> According to the "Local Matters" section in the *Baltimore Sun* for February 13, 1865, this would be Sunday, February 12. A huge snowstorm enveloped Baltimore early that morning, and by 10:00 a.m., with several inches already on the ground, "several churches were closed entirely and those where services were held, were but slightly attended."[12]

Powell related that he was the son of a Baptist minister and in conversation pertaining to his mother and family, broke down in tears, weeping bitterly for the first time since his sentence had been pronounced. Regaining his composure somewhat, Powell revealed his background and initiation into the kidnap-assassination plot.

In conversation with Powell, Dr. Gillette claimed that the prisoner told him that

> he thought he was doing right in attempting to kill Secretary Seward, *as he still claimed to be a Confederate soldier* [author's italics]; aside from that, he admitted that he believed it would give peace to the South. He thinks now that it was all wrong, and blames Rebel leaders for his death, though he did not fear to die. Several times he expressed his thanks for the kind treatment which he received from officers while in prison. He stated that he was led into the conspiracy by Booth and John Surratt.[13]

Powell continued to agonize over Mrs. Surratt, telling Reverend Gillette: "She at least, does not deserve to die with us. If I had no other reason, Doctor—she is a woman, and men do not make war on women." (See Appendix I.)

In a last desperate effort, Powell sent for his friend, Captain Rath:

> That night, Payne sent for me and said, "Captain, if I had two lives to give, I'd give one gladly to save Mrs. Surratt. I know that she is innocent and would never die in this way if I hadn't been found in her house. She knew nothing about the conspiracy at all, and is an innocent woman."

> I hastily conferred with Major Eckert, telling him what Payne had told me. We hurriedly sent word to the War Department, and in an hour had orders to take Payne's statement."

Dr. Gillette remembered the following:

> As for his own doom—if he did not welcome it in the form it came to him—he never uttered a word of protest or expressed a pang, except as it left the cruel iron in the hearts at home...
>
> "My course is run," Powell regretted. "I know now how foolish, vain and wholly useless it is and must have been, and were I set at liberty this morning, I should hope to be dead by sunset, as all men must hereafter point at me as a murderer."[14] [See Appendix I.]

Powell's personal effects, at least some of them, were returned to him by this time. "He had a few small articles, a knife and a Bible, which he desired the clergyman to send to his people ... in the Bible were some flowers he had pressed, white convolvulus and blue larkspur, which had grown in his prison yard. He was entirely resigned to his fate and said he could never again enjoy life, even if he were pardoned."

Dr. Gillette was impressed with Powell's intelligence in direct contrast with the newspaper accounts which portrayed him as a coldblooded killer with a moronic mentality. Lewis requested the clergyman to write to his parents and tell them he had repented and had his hope of heavenly—if not earthly—pardon. Throughout the long night, the prisoner took special advantage of Dr. Gillette's ministrations, alternately praying and weeping.[15] "His last prayer was, as suggested by his friend, Doctor Gillette, 'Lord Jesus, receive my spirit.'" Finally towards dawn, emotionally drained, Powell was able to get about three hours of sleep.

General Hartranft had ordered extra tight security measures for Friday, July 7—a hangman's holiday. If the Arsenal was well guarded during the trial, it was impenetrable and impregnable now. Four members of the Veteran Reserve Corps—William Coxhall, D. F. Shoupe, G. F. Taylor and F. B. Haslett—were assigned the task of knocking the props out from under the gallows.

The noise of hammers and saws made ominous music to greet the dawn—a sultry, sullen morning with temperatures in the eighties and a promise of higher temperatures later on.

Inside the Arsenal, the hustle was greater than ever, the prayers, sobs, weeping and ministrations continuing in the four cells. Breakfast was provided as usual, but none of the doomed four partook of it. Various accounts describe Powell as consuming a hearty breakfast, the only one of the four able to do so. However, Dr. Gillette emphatically asserted that Powell partook of nothing, neither food nor drink, on the fatal day. Stimulants such as Wine of Valerian and Brandy were administered to Herold, Atzerodt and Mrs. Surratt, but Powell steadily refused, saying "that he wished to die with an unclouded mind."[16]

Powell was still making his appeals for mercy to be shown Mrs. Surratt and early in the morning he summoned General Hartranft, who persuaded by the pleas of the condemned youth, wrote a memorandum to President Johnson, a missive which was blatantly ignored:

> Washington Arsenal
> Military Prison
> Washington, DC
> July 7, 1865
>
> Mr. Payne stated to me this morning that he was convinced Mrs. Surratt was innocent of the murder of the President or any knowledge thereof and as to the abduction of the Presi-

dent, he did not know that she was connected with it, although he had frequent conversations with her, during his stay at her house.
    I think Payne would state the truth in this matter.
J. F. Hartranft
Bvt. Major General
Comdt. Prison

George Atzerodt also found a champion in Powell: "Atzerodt, he stated, was innocent of any attempt to murder, and at the Herndon House, where Booth, Atzerodt, Herold and himself met on the evening of the 14th, he heard Atzerodt declare, when ordered by Booth to kill the Vice President, that he would not do it."[17]

At 9:00 a.m. William E. Doster visited his clients for a last interview. The four condemned prisoners had been moved from their cramped cells to a large room on the first floor. The corridor outside the room was full of wailing relatives and friends—Herold's seven sisters, Atzerodt's brother and common-law wife, and Mrs. Surratt's Annie. There was no one to see Powell. It was impossible for his parents to journey from Florida, and Doster had sent his summons to Powell's father only two weeks before. There was no way in which the Rev. Mr. Powell could reach Washington quickly enough through the war-torn South to see his son alive.

Powell asked permission to bid good-bye to his counsel and officers of the penitentiary, and "desires that two or three persons from Baltimore shall be admitted, if they call, though he does not send for them."[18]

Two or three persons from Baltimore? Who were they? Maggie and Mary Branson, no doubt. But the third? This could be the Rev. Mr. Stryker. That good gentleman had endeavored to secure a pass to see Powell, upon hearing of his desire for his services, but it would be noon before he was finally admitted.[19] Powell's Baltimore lady friends never materialized. Mary Branson was, according to reports, desperately ill. Sister Maggie apparently remained home with her and their mother in Baltimore. Whether or not Reverend Stryker conveyed this to Powell remains unknown. Stryker never wrote anything which can be found regarding his visit to the death cell.

Unknown to Powell, someone *may* have journeyed from afar to see him—his forgotten sweetheart Bettie Meredith. According to Lewis Edmonds Payne, his young cousin Bettie "went to Washington during the trial, but did not succeed in seeing Powell. She wrote to him, but does not believe her letters were delivered as she received no response to her letters. She applied to Secretary Stanton, but he refused her permission to visit the jail ... and all efforts to see her lover were in vain."[20]

When Doster entered Powell's cell for the final visit, he found the condemned youth visibly upset and saw that "even his fortitude was shaken by the hurried way in which he was to be executed." He had heard clearly the noise of the hammers on the scaffolding outside, and was sitting crouched in the far corner of his cell, staring into space with reddened eyes. Powell sincerely thanked the attorney for services rendered.

Doster then asked Powell if he had any messages he wished to leave. Powell stated, "None except I want you to give my love to my parents and tell them that I die in peace with God and man. I do not want to live, even if the President will spare my life, I do not want it. My only regret is that in leaving the world now, I will not be able to reward or show my gratitude to you for your services in my behalf."[21]

Lewis Powell on the morning of his execution—July 7, 1865. His appearance in the death cell was sketched by a *National Police Gazette* artist (National Park Service).

Powell offered his penknife to Doster "as the only earthly thing he had to give." Doster declined the gift.

By mid-morning, the gallows structure was completed. Next on the agenda was the digging of the graves. As the prison personnel were too superstitious to perform this duty, soldiers were recruited to complete the task under a sluggish, blistering sun.

Inside the prison, a last minute attempt was being made to save Mrs. Surratt, her attorneys having applied for a writ of habeas corpus. From inside also came the shrieks of daughter Annie and the wailing chorus of David Herold's seven sisters.

The sun reached its zenith and baked the newly turned earth of the four raw graves. Reprieves could and would not wait—nothing could be done to save the woman, neither Powell's agonized pleas nor writs of any type. "At the very last [Powell] asked if no respite had come to her, and the pitiless fate of the woman seemed his chiefest regret."

The life spans of the four now dwindled down into hours—then minutes. Officers came to each cell to bind the arms of the doomed in preparation of the march to the scaffold, and handcuffs were loosened for the last time. Powell gave his minister the copy of the death warrant which Hartranft had furnished him. Dr. Gillette had procured a straw hat for Powell as a protection against the sun's rays and placed it upon the youth's head just before the death march began.[22]

The prison yard was fast filling with reporters and military personnel, hungry to see the hanging. As this was not a public execution, one had to have an official pass and a legitimate reason to attend. Mere curiosity seekers were turned away. One person present was Doctor Mary Walker, the only female surgeon in the U.S. Army. (She was strongly censured by the press for riding her horse astride to witness the executions.)

Beneath the scaffold, weary with the heat and somewhat nauseated by the tension, the four Reserve Corps veterans stood in readiness to knock out the props when the time came. Shoupe and Coxshall were under the drop which would contain Powell and Mrs. Surratt, while Taylor and Haslett were under the other. About 1 p.m. the attending "audience" pressed closer to the hollow square of soldiers surrounding the gallows and at about 1:10 p.m. a muffled ten-drum cadence struck its slow, melancholy beat. Thus, the last "music" that ever reached the ears of the hapless foursome on July 7, 1865, was a military cadence (not a full band), but a drumbeat, deadly and steady. There are no records that Hartranft ever had a band stationed on site at the Arsenal.[23]

> Suddenly the wicket opens, the troops spring to their feet and stand to order arms; the flags go up First came a woman, pinioned—a middle aged woman dressed in black, bonneted and veiled, walking between two bareheaded priests.... Four soldiers with muskets at shoulder followed, and a captain led the way to the gallows. The second party escorted a small shambling German ... preceded by two officers, flanked by a Lutheran clergyman, and followed, as by his predecessor, by an armed squad.... The third, preacher and party, clustered about a shabby boy whose limbs tottered as he progressed.[24]

The Reverend Dr. Abram Dunn Gillette, pastor of Washington's First Baptist Church and comforter to Powell in the death cell and on the gallows (Library of Congress).

The last prisoner to enter the yard was the one all eyes turned to: Lewis Powell. Accompanied by one of Colonel Baker's detectives and Sergeant Grover, Company D, Eighteenth Veteran Reserve Corp, in addition to Dr. Gillette and the Rev. A. D. Stryker, who had finally arrived about noon, Powell walked erect, proud, chin up and without any tremor in his firm step.[25] "Payne's face and eyes presented an unusual color and appearance."[26] Although his eyes were swollen and red from weeping, Powell's face, also reddened, seemed to betray no fear, and he seemed the most collected of the four, conducting himself with quiet dignity.

Slowly the entourage, about twenty in number, ascended the creaking steps. Seated in an arm chair on the gallows platform between Mrs. Surratt and Herold, Powell "now and then ... looked half-pityingly at the woman, and only once moved his lips as if in supplication. Few who looked at him, forgetful of his crime, did not respect him. He seemed to feel that no man was more than his peer and one of his last commands was a word of regret to Mr. Seward."[27]

The *National Republican's* reporter, R. F. Boiseau, had been intrigued all during the trial with the "dark faced" Payne, as he referred to the young conspirator. Boiseau, present in front of the gallows, stated in a report for the *National Republican,* "The Executions," dated July 8, 1865, that the doomed youth was not as courageous on the gallows as stated:

> Payne, the bloody minded assassin, who broke into Mr. Seward's sick chamber and tried to murder him in his bed, walked to the scaffold with as firm a tread as any criminal we ever saw, but even he broke down before the curtain fell, sitting with his strong neck slanted upward, in the position he has maintained throughout the assassination trials, with his eyes directed towards some part of the sky, where he may have imagined the heaven of traitors to be located. He maintained for a time the imperturbable expression he has so constantly worn since his arrest, but before the ceremony was over, his face was suffused with crimson and tears streamed down his cheeks. The wretched being must have reflected in those moments upon the fiendish cruelty of his assault with dagger and pistol upon an old man who had for weeks been disabled by severe injuries. There was more than this underneath that dark face, perhaps. He might have been thinking how vast was the failure of the great plot which he had participated in, and which promised such great results to the rebel cause. Whatever he was thinking of, he betrayed more emotion in that last hour than he had done during all his imprisonment and trial, and the spectators wondered more than ever before who he was and what was in his mind.

A puff of wind struggled through the oppressive heat and dislodged Lewis's straw hat, which Dr. Gillette retrieved and placed back on his head. "Thank you, Doctor," Powell whispered. "I shall not need it much longer."

Shielded by umbrellas, General Hartranft read the findings of the court, and with, that official duty over, the closing religious exercises took place. Dr. Gillette advanced to the front of the platform to publicly thank, at the request of Lewis Powell, the officers of the prison and all who had had charge of him for their uniform kindness.

The minister then delivered a fervent prayer in behalf of Powell:

> Almighty God, our Heavenly Father, we pray thee help this dear friend to commit his soul into thy hands as unto the hands of a faithful Creator—dependent upon all the mercy and merits of our Lord Jesus Christ in hope of eternal life, through faith in Him. Grant him forgiveness for all his sins, an easy passage out of this world, and if consistent with thy purposes of mercy, a share of those delights thou has in store for thy people. Receive him into thy presence, we humbly ask, through Jesus Christ, our Lord and Redeemer. Amen.[28]

Powell was visibly affected during the prayer, his eyes filling with tears as he listened to the minister's words. One reporter stated that "Payne [sic] throughout wore an air of contrition as well as courage and thereby excited the pity of the spectators."[29]

Statements of gratitude and prayers for the other condemned followed, after which the four prisoners were asked to rise and step forward. Mrs. Surratt had to be assisted to rise from her chair. The limbs of the condemned were bound and chairs pushed back on the platform.

Powell was the first to receive the noose, and "held back his head and was particular about having the noose adjusted and secured by tightening above his 'Adam's Apple,' as if it had been the adjustment of a cravat for a festive occasion."[30]

"I want you to die quick, Paine," Captain Rath said, adjusting the noose under the youth's left ear.

Contemporary sketch of the doomed conspirators on the scaffold and preparations for the hanging. Note the sadistic inaccuracy of the "meat hooks" over the heads of the condemned (Library of Congress).

Rare photograph of the condemned seated on the scaffold—Powell sits in the center with bowed head, while a gentleman, possibly the Reverend A. Stryker, kneels at Powell's feet. The Reverend Dr. Gillette stands behind Powell holding the umbrella (author's collection).

17. The Last Mile   121

The trap spring, July 7, 1865. Lewis Powell is next to Mrs. Mary Surratt on the far left (Library of Congress).

"You know best, Captain." Powell's voice was calm and matter of fact.

The white hanging hoods were pulled down over their faces for the last time, and still Powell stood straight, head high. Herold and Atzerodt whimpered and trembled, while Mrs. Surratt plaintively implored the officials not to let her fall.

Powell murmured to Rath through his hood, "I thank you; goodbye."[31]

"At twenty-five minutes past one, the signal was given by General Hartranft through Captain Rath, the drops were knocked suddenly away ... and fell."[32]

Down shot the four bodies, and they jerked to and fro in dreadful twisting circles. Powell would not die instantly or easily. Slowly he strangled to death, writhing horribly at the end of the rope for approximately five to eight minutes, chest heaving; his exposed wrists purpling dark with restricted blood flow. Similarly, Herold also died hard. Mrs. Surratt and Atzerodt did not suffer much—their necks were broken. They hung and twirled for about twenty minutes before examination by medical personnel pronounced all four dead. Dr. Gillette, sickened by the proceedings, was seemingly heart sore over young Powell's death. The trying experience left him troubled and sleepless for weeks afterward. The bodies were cut down and without ceremony placed in plain pine gun boxes and hastily buried.

"It was a dishonored death for a most unsoldierly deed. At least Payne gave to it something of dignity by calmness, modesty and silence."[33]

18. Afterword

The Civil War left deep wounds in many people—in body and soul. To the Rev. George C. Powell and his family in Live Oak, Florida, the war was a crushing blow that maimed them permanently.

Doster's letter, asking that Mr. Powell come to Washington, arrived July 6, on the very eve of the executions, thus making it impossible for any member of the family to get to Washington in time. The Reverend George Powell, nevertheless, attempted to do so. Arising from a sick bed where he had been recently confined, the clergyman journeyed one hundred miles by train to Jacksonville, where he learned of his youngest son's execution. The grief-stricken father returned home to break the tragic news to his wife and remaining children.

One can sense how much of a devastating blow this was to the family. With one son killed in the war, and the elder boy, George, a crippled veteran, the old clergyman had prayed that his youngest son, declared as a prisoner of war since the battle of Gettysburg, would return home. Now Lewis, "his only hope in his old age," had been executed for a heinous crime.

Dr. Gillette kept his promise to young Lewis Powell and wrote to his father as to the spiritual role he had played at his doomed son's request. The Reverend Powell was hungry for news, begging for detailed information concerning his son's final hours and of his spiritual status when he died. (See Appendix I.) "Please write as early as possible ... as everything in reference to my son is very interesting to us."

The last of the series of letters from Live Oak, written in March 1866, requested that Lewis's personal effects; Bible, autograph and some money be sent to Mr. Powell: "Please inform me if it is possible if I would be permitted to get and remove the remains of my son from Washington, D.C., to my home in Florida." The minister added that he would not press for the return of the body unless Federal authorities were agreeable to the request. So far as is known, Lewis's parents did receive their son's personal effects. According to family legend, these articles were destroyed in a house fire in the 1920s.[1] However, the Powell family made no further attempts to move Lewis's remains to Live Oak, so far as is known although the father did conduct a memorial service for Lewis and "urged that his son had been hanged in a good cause."[2]

Lewis's mother, deeply affected by her youngest son's violent death and the death of at least one other child in the war, "was almost frantic with grief." Family history claims Patience Caroline took to her bed after receiving the news of Lewis's death and did not recover from the shock for over two years.[3]

The War Department was not about to forget Lewis Powell's ghost. It would seem that someone (Stanton perhaps?) still had doubts concerning young Powell—enough to initiate an investigation of sorts. In August of 1865, a month after Powell's death, General Ethan

18. Afterword

Allen Hitchcock instructed Capt. Adam C. Nutt, military commander of Lake City, Florida, to travel to Live Oak, Florida, to ascertain whether Powell had told the truth about his home and family. It didn't take long for him to locate the family, and his report to Capt. M. Henry, forwarded to the War Department, follows:

> Lake City, Florida
> August 26, 1865
>
> Captain:
>
> I have the honor to submit the following report. In obedience to orders contained in endorsements on the accompanying papers, I proceeded on the 24th inst. to Live Oak (not White Oak) Station, twenty-six miles west from Lake City on the Pensacola and Florida Railroad; found one George C. Powell, who at the commencement of the Rebellion lived half a mile from Live Oak Station, but now lives six miles distant from that place in Swannee County, Florida. Lewis Thornton Powell was the son of said George C. Powell (and Patience C. Powell), and was the eighth child of twelve children. The following is a correct transcript from the Family Bible record: "Lewis T. Powell, born April 23, 1844."
>
> There is no doubt that the so-called Lewis Payne, executed for the attempted murder of Secretary Seward, was the same Lewis T. Powell.
>
> I enclose herewith a copy of the letter sent by Payne's counsel, W. E. Doster, to the I enclose herewith a copy of the letter sent by Payne's counsel, W. E. Doster, to the father, Rev. George C. Powell. One of the boys was killed in the Battle of Murfreesboro. Another is at home wounded and maimed. The Powell family is said to be poor but industrious and respectable. The father, George C. Powell, is a Baptist preacher, and is a man of decided, positive qualities, who controls his feelings and bears up well under misfortune. The mother is a woman of fine personal appearance, and of strong maternal feeling, and judging from what I saw, she suffered intense mental agony.
>
> Capt. Adam C. Nutt
> Com'dg, Lake City, Fla

Captain Adam C. Nutt was directed to investigate further, and Brig. General I. Vogdes submitted the following information to General Hitchcock, undoubtedly for transmission to Eckert and or Stanton:

> Jacksonville, Fla.
> August 29, 1865
>
> General:
>
> Your note to General Gillmore, of the 2nd of August, having reference to a person named Powell, residing near Live Oak Station, said to be the father of the man Payne, who made the murderous assault on Secy. Seward on the night of the 14th of April last, has been referred to me for examination and report.
>
> I directed Capt. Nutt, 3rd U.S. Colored troops, to fully investigate the case, and report; he has done so, and the report has been forwarded through the proper military channel to you. As I am about to be relieved from command, I have taken the liberty to write to you, stating a few facts not mentioned in said report.

George W. Powell, the only surviving brother of Lewis T. Powell (courtesy Rufus Yent, great-grandnephew of Lewis Powell).

> 1st. Live Oak is a station on the railroad connecting Tallahassee with Jacksonville [and] is about 11 miles east of the Swannee River. During the war, the Rebel Authorities constructed a railroad from this point to join the road from Savannah to Thomasville, a line of great importance to them, as it served to connect Tallahassee and Florida by rail with Richmond. This road is still in good repair. It is not marked on any of the maps that I have seen.
>
> Sometime since, a man named Powell came to Jacksonville, as was reported to me, with the design of going to Washington to see his son, undergoing trial for the attempt to murder Mr. Seward. Learning in Jacksonville that his son had been executed, he returned to his home. I did not learn that he was here until after he left. There can be no doubt that he was the father of the young man tried under the name of Payne.
>
> Mr. Powell gave Capt. Nutt a letter from Payne's counsel to him, asking him to come to Washington. This letter is forwarded with the report.
>
> He also obtained a daguerreotype of young Powell from his mother, which I have directed to have copied and sent to you. Young Powell is represented as not being a bad boy, having some education, of strong will. He left the State with State troops, was captured at Gettysburg, and employed in the hospital, attending the wounded. From there he escaped to Baltimore.
>
> The article you enclose originally appeared in the *Jacksonville Herald*. The editor saw Mr. Powell and at my request has written the letter, giving an account of his interview with him.
>
> Brig. General I. Vogdes[4]

The Rev. Powell stated that he was kindly treated by the officers who interviewed him and was told that they would not molest him if he did not obstruct them in the investigative work that they had to perform. Mrs. Powell, already distraught by her youngest son's death, was further upset by Nutt's intrusive investigation and refused to remain in the same room with the Union captain.

An unnamed newspaper article carrying only the date 1888, describes the remarkably horrid cruelty of someone who troubled young Lewis' grieving father by sending him a series of "pictures from Washington, showing his son in every position occupied during the scene of execution.... A former neighbor of Mr. Powell's [stated] that he was equally loved and respected by white and black and that the rash conduct of his son in no manner altered the good opinion enjoyed by the old gentleman."

Eventually, the Rev. Powell pulled up stakes and moved with his family to Orange County, no doubt to escape the notoriety and the prying of Federal officers. Settling near Lake Jessup sometime in 1867, the minister buried himself in his mission and farm work, establishing several churches in the surrounding area. He and his family would make several moves before death claimed Mrs. Powell sometime around 1880. She is buried in a small plot in Geneva, Florida.

An old and broken man, the elder Powell was living with one of his daughters and son-in-law in 1880. One church record makes note of the fact that he was dismissed from the pastorship of one church for his "too strict discipline."[5] The Rev. George C. Powell died in November of 1881 at the age of 72. His burial place is unmarked.

After the executions at the old Arsenal prison, the four bodies were interred near the scaffold in the prison yard, enclosed by a whitewashed picket fence. In November 1865, Henry Wirz, commandant of Andersonville Prison, joined the conspirators' resting place after he was also hanged upon conviction of war crimes.

The bodies were disinterred on October 1, 1867, and reburied in Warehouse Number 1. The four pine boxes reposed in the Arsenal warehouse alongside the body of John Wilkes Booth. Stanton finally relented and released the remains to the various families in 1869.

The families of Surratt, Herold, and Atzerodt quickly claimed the remains of their kinsmen, leaving the unclaimed remains of Powell to lie in the warehouse a while longer and prompting the *New York Times* of February 25, 1869, to state that a "fund" was being established to defray the costs of reinterring Powell's body and giving him a decent burial. A check of subsequent press reports reveals nothing further in relation to such a "fund," as the incoming Grant administration took over most of the news coverage in the papers. Still there is the intriguing insinuation that someone, somewhere must have started the rumor of a fund drive. Who, besides the immediate family, would have conceived the idea, and why? There is the speculation that some people from Baltimore may have initiated the fund drive. Still unmarried and living at home in 1869, could Mary Branson have decided that enough time had passed to enable her to provide a decent burial for her lover of four years previous? (See Appendices K and S.)

The Powell family in Florida had moved a few times after Lewis's death and were apparently not notified that they could claim their kinsman's remains. Accordingly, Powell's body was disinterred a second time, subsequently removed to Graceland Cemetery and then, in the early 1880s moved to Holmead Cemetery, bounded by S and T streets and Nineteenth and Twentieth streets in the northwest section of the city. This graveyard was discontinued in 1879, but the cemetery was not converted to other use until the 1880s.[6] By this time, the cemetery was no longer being used as such, and it was decided to exhume the bodies and build on the lot. In the fall of 1884, the remains of Powell were exhumed from Holmead. An old article in the *National Republican,* September 25, 1884, makes reference to the fact that a large coffin was found which contained only a "small skull and a pair of broadcloth trousers ... there were no other bones in it. The coffin was tightly nailed, and the trousers, beyond a slight discoloration were excellently preserved."[7] (See Appendix S.)

The question remains, *did* the Powell family claim the body? One family legend states that the body was claimed by Reverend Powell who came to Washington to retrieve it accompanied by his surviving son, George W. The legend goes that on the way back home to Florida with the body, Reverend Mr. Powell was stricken with pneumonia somewhere in North Carolina. There the ailing clergyman was taken in by a family until he was well enough to travel on and the body was quietly buried on his host's property. Truth or fiction?

There certainly does not appear to be any truth in this story in light of recent findings. Somehow, on January 13, 1885, the cra-

Judge George W. Powell in later life (courtesy Rufus Yent, great-grandnephew of Lewis Powell).

nium or skull of Lewis Powell ended up as anatomical specimen number 2244 in the Army Medical Museum. At that time housed in Ford's Theater, the Seward assailant's skull was stored in company with the severed vertebra of John Wilkes Booth. That there was no evidence of the complete skeleton being transferred to the museum, it goes without saying that only the head was removed. The rest of the remains were reburied in Rock Creek Cemetery after exhumation from Holmead. It has now been determined that Undertaker Joseph Gawler removed the skull when the body was first exhumed from Warehouse 1 at the old Arsenal. (See Appendix S.)

The theory that the Powell family claimed the body is groundless in that there is no recorded receipt for the body listed in the records. Such is the case for the other three bodies of the deceased conspirators. The fact that the skull was given to the Army Medical Museum in 1885, a few months after the exhumation of the remains, discredits the belief that the family received the body.

Sometime in May 1898, the remains were turned over to the Smithsonian Anthropology Department. There they were stored away for approximately ninety-four years. Recently, while sorting through the remains of various Native American skulls in preparation for return to their respective tribes for burial, workers discovered the skull of a young white male. With the skull was documentation listing it as the "cranium of Payne hung [sic] in Washington, D.C. in 1865 for the attempted assassination of Secretary of State William H. Seward."[8]

That the skull is that of young Powell seems beyond doubt. The teeth are severely decayed. Lewis Edmonds Payne, whose family Powell boarded with while serving with Mosby's Rangers, recalled Powell's bad teeth, as did Marine Sgt. Seaton Monroe on board the ironclad *Montauk* when Powell was being photographed by Gardner.

Another interesting angle is the fact that at some time, Powell's lower left jaw had been broken. A molar was also lost as a result of the injury, which, according to anthropologists, probably occurred when Powell was a small child or young teenager. The injury healed over well enough but resulted in the left side of the jaw being more prominent than the right, another feature noticed by the medical personnel who examined Powell during the trial.

Recent findings have determined that Lewis, at the age of twelve, was kicked by a fractious mule while playing in his back yard in 1856. The resulting injury was a broken jaw and missing molar.[9] So at least part of the mystery has been solved.

Appendices

Appendix A

Record of U.S. Census, 1850, Stewart County, Georgia, lists House 193—the Reverend George C. Powell and family, with Lewis as six years of age. Census records of 1860 for Jasper or Hamilton County, Florida, do not carry the Powell family who could have been in transit to their new home at the time.

Page from Powell family Bible (courtesy Powell family).

U.S. Census 1850
Stewart County, Georgia

House Number	Name	Age	Sex	Occupation	Where Born
193	George C. Powell	40	Male	Baptist minister	Ga.
	Caroline Powell	39	Female	Housewife	Ga.
	Benjamin Powell	17	Male	Farmer	Ga.
	George Powell	13	Male		Ga.
	Oliver Powell	10	Male		Ala.
	James Newman	27	Male	Farmer	Ga.
	Mary Ann Newman	15	Female		Ga.
	Lydia Powell	8	Female		Ala.
	Lewis Powell	*6*	*Male*		*Ala.*
	Angeline Powell	4	Female		Ala.
	Minerva Powell	2	Female		Ala.
	Ann Powell	1	Female		Ala.

Appendix B

Records of Lewis Powell's enlistment in Hamilton Blues, Second Florida Infantry. Note that Powell gives his age upon enlistment as nineteen. He was in actuality seventeen—below the mandatory enlistment age.

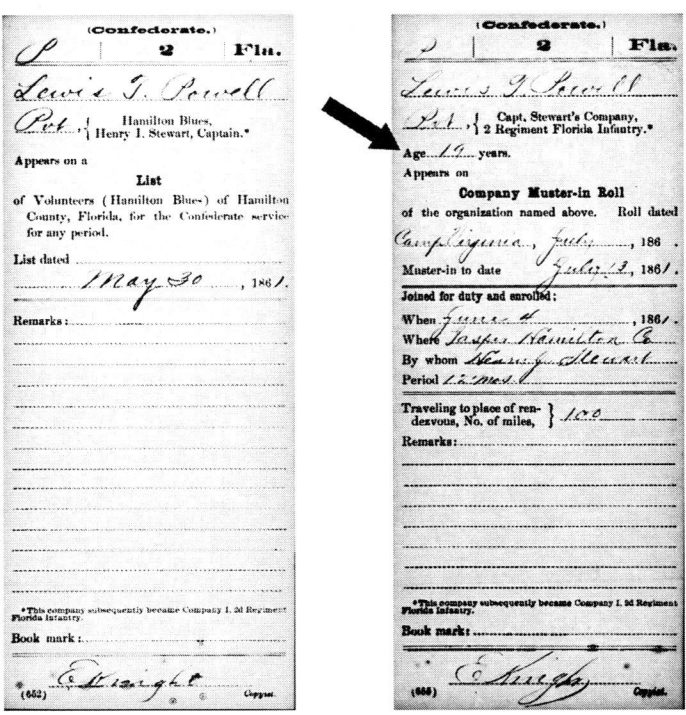

Lewis Powell's military records (Confederate Records, National Archives).

Appendix C

This lengthy article, written by Lewis Edmonds Payne, son of Dr. Albin S. Payne, recalls in romantic detail the partisan "career" of Lewis Powell. By reading between the lines and comparing the account with General W. H. Payne's recollections (Appendix D), a few pertinent facts may be brought to light concerning Powell and his affiliations with Col. John S. Mosby's Rangers. I have annotated this article with new findings.

LEWIS POWELL'S EXPLOITS

REMINISCENCES OF THE REMARKABLE YOUTH
WHO STABBED SECRETARY SEWARD

ADVENTURES AS A GUERRILLA

DARING ENTERPRISES, HAND TO HAND
FIGHTS AND HAIRBREDTH ESCAPES

IN THE COILS OF BOOTH

TRUE STORY OF THE ATTEMPTED ASSASSINATION
AND OF THE TRIAL OF POWELL

BY LEWIS PAYNE
FORMERLY U.S. ATTORNEY FOR WYOMING TERRITORY
WHOSE NAME THE ASSASSIN ASSUMED

Philadelphia Weekly Times, June 3, 1882

It was in the fall of 1863. Jackson had been killed at Chancellorsville; Pemberton had surrendered Vicksburg; Lee's army had been shattered and broken at Gettysburg. The Emancipation Proclamation had been issued. The Negroes, intoxicated by the first joys of freedom and liberty had gathered their bundles and baggage and left in squads of fifteen and twenty. The "quarters," as the long rows of log cabins, all single storied and built alike, were called, had been deserted. The fields were untilled and the crops had been destroyed where they were produced. The song of the "Shovel and the Hoe" and the merry jingle of the banjo had departed.

It was in the month of September, 1863 that my uncle John Scott Payne, who lived at *Granville Tract,* an old-fashioned Virginia homestead, some four miles from Warrenton, on the Waterloo Turnpike, came home from the Confederate Army on furlough. He was a prominent member of the famous "Black Horse Cavalry." While sitting on the porch with my uncle one evening, talking about the prospects of the Confederacy, a very young looking man, wearing the gray uniform, came sauntering across the lawn. This was the fist that any of us ha ever seen of him. I remember distinctly that the man wore no beard and I wondered to myself what such a boy was doing in the army anyhow. His arm was in a sling, bound with bandages and splints, as if it had been broken. His uniform was pretty well worn out. It was of the regulation Confederate gray and bore the stripes upon the collar which indicated his rank to be that of a first or second lieutenant. He was tall and well built, being particularly broad and robust about the chest and shoulders. He had one of those peculiar dark Southern complexions, blue eyes, dark hair and an imperfection in one of his front teeth. In short, there was nothing about the ordinary looking young man, as he strolled across the yard and asked to stay all night, to indicate the ferocity of his character. The closest student of human nature could not have looked in his pale face and imagined him the assassin of a few years later or seen the wild, defiant look in his eyes that they had all through the long days of that terrible trial or detected in his voice the fierce tones with which he uttered two memorable words, "I'm mad!" on that fateful night in April when he spilled the blood of Seward. The intensity of those words was graphically described at the trial and the whole court was filled with emotion when the prisoner was made to put on that slouch hat and repeat the words with the dagger in hand, "I'm mad!"

In conversation with my uncle, who seen returned to the army and is now dead, he told me that the young stranger's name was Lewis Powell; that he was the only son of a Baptist preacher in Florida, that his father was a Virginian and a relative of the late Dr. Powell of Alexandria.[1] The Powell family is one of great prominence and distinction in Virginia and the Powell, and not the Payne family, is clearly entitled to the questionable credit of having contributed this character to the annals of American history. It seems the young man had become fired with the excitement of secession; had run away from his home when quite young; been severely wounded at Gettysburg; had escaped from the hospital in Baltimore, and that he was then on his way to rejoin the armies around Richmond. That this was literally true, I afterwards learned from the father of this unfortunate man. After Powell had staid at my uncle's house long enough to get well, he disappeared and we had almost forgotten him until a body of Federal soldiers was dispatched to Warrenton to arrest the Payne family, "horse, foot and dragoons" for alleged complicity in the atrocious murder and assassination. I was at that time too young for the service, but from what I saw and know and have learned from the citizens and those who served as soldiers in the Piedmont region of Virginia which was known as "Mosby's Confederacy" during the war, it is evident that Powell was not more than twenty-four years old when he was hanged.[2]

His Strength and Horsemanship

Powell never returned to the regular army after the retreat from Gettysburg, but deserted and either attached himself to an independent body of Confederate cavalry operating in the Valley and Piedmont region of Virginia, or organized himself into a command of his own and went it alone.[3] In this section of the country, Powell soon became noted as the boldest of the bold and the rashest of the reckless. Powell afterwards became a member of Company B, Mosby's Battalion, and the rolls of that company, if preserved among the Confederate archives now at Washington, bear his name. I recollect seeing him on various occasions after he became a member of Mosby's command. He was a very reserved and silent, but restless man. He was what might be called a "prowler." He rode at night and was almost continually on the go from place to place. I saw him one day dismount from his horse, shoulder five newly-split chestnut rails, remount with the rails on his shoulder and ride a mile to my uncle's house and deposit the rails in the wood yard. At that time, the slaves had all gone, there was no wood to burn and no one to get any, hence, this feat of strength and horsemanship, which I doubt if there is any man in Virginia can perform today. General Turner

"The Terrible Lewis Powell"

In Scott's history of Mosby's Battalion, the writer, in describing the fight with Captain Blazer, who came to capture Mosby, but unfortunately got captured by him, in the Shenandoah Valley in 1864, says: "Captain Blazer, do thy speediest, for those are upon thy track who smite and spare not—Syd Ferguson, Cab Maddox and the terrible Lewis Powell."

This would indicate that Powell was acting with Mosby's command, if he was not a member of it, and it also shows that his reputation had an element of terror in it even at that day.[4] Powell as a good horseman and he knew all the byways and highways and shortcuts across the fields and through the woods, and he used to say he could travel from Warrenton to Winchester or from Fairfax Court House to Front Royal, in a third of the time by his own routs that it would take to travel the roads. He would go off alone, penetrate the lines of the enemy and come back with prisoners, horses and plunder. At one time, he had fifteen or twenty horses, all of them branded with "U.S." and the property of the Government at Washington. Powell was with Mosby's men all during the raiding in the rear of General Hunter's army in June 1864 when the celebrated "burning order" was being put into operation. During those raids very few prisoners were taken, but on the contrary, it was no uncommon sight to find a dead soldier almost anywhere in the Valley with a notice pinned to his back, "Shot for House Burning." A great many were, no doubt, shot who never saw a "house burning" under this pretext, which was gladly seized upon by the brutal and ruthless as an excuse for their atrocities.

His Narrow Escapes

Powell was also one of the men who made the celebrated calico raid in the Valley in the fall of 1864, when a train load of calico was captured and the calico strewn all over the country for miles around. In retaliation for shooting General Hunter's men, a soldier named Anderson and several others were captured and shot by the Federals at Front Royal. The speed of Powell's mare was all that saved his neck from being stretched on that occasion. He escaped with seventeen bullet holes thorough his clothing. On one occasion, the house in which Powell was stopping was surrounded by Federals, when Powell blacked his face with lampblack and walked out of the house. One of the soldiers remarked: "That is a damn tall Nigger" and let him pass on without molestation. I might give a great many incidents of this kind in the career and adventures of Powell, but it is unnecessary. Such things occur in the lives of many soldiers. Powell had the reputation of having killed a great many men, and when any desperate matter was to be undertaken he was selected.[5]

Incidents of Daring

Lieutenant Edward Thompson, a member of Mosby's command, recently related to me the following incident in the career of Powell. Thompson says he had charge of sixty men on the grade near Salem in Fauquier County, Virginia. A small body of Federal cavalry was in the town with pickets on all the roads leading to and from the place. Thompson had concealed his men in the woods and was waiting to capture the Federals at night, but fearing they would get information of his designs he determined to change his plans. He therefore called for two men who were willing to ride upon the picket line of the enemy and firing upon them, to retreat a certain distance down the road, so that he could attack the pursuers in the rear with his sixty men. Powell and a man named Shipley, now a prominent lawyer in Baltimore volunteered for the special duty of drawing the enemy into the trap.[6] Thompson says his orders were executed to the letter. Powell and Shipley galloped up the road in full view of the enemy, discharged their revolvers almost in their very faces, and turning their horses, sped down the road, followed by a volley of balls. The pursuit was almost instantaneous, and when the rear of the charging column of the enemy had passed on in pursuit of Powell and Shipley, rushed upon the enemy. In the meantime, Powell and Shipley turned in the road and charged the enemy from the front. The result was the capture by Thompson of almost the entire command of the enemy, who of course, thought they were entirely surrounded. To this reckless the testimony of John Grant and his wife of Warrenton, adduced at the Conspiracy trial, wherein they testified that Powell had saved the lives of two Union prisoners in front of their house about that time, forms an interesting sequel. It appears that a Confederate soldier named Keith had shot one prisoner without cause and was threatening to shoot the other when "Lieutenant" Powell, as he was then known, interceded and at the immediate risk of his own life, prevented the consummation of the deed. Some of the parties implicated in this affair are at present, prominent citizens of Fauquier and can attest to the truthfulness of this incident. One of the prisoners was lying dead in the road, pierced with bullets and the other two were begging for their lives covered by revolvers, when Powell came to their rescue. Mrs. Grant testified that they "wanted to bring the man who had been killed into he house, and they like to have scared her to death." These prisoners belonged to General Torbett's command, and had been captured during his celebrated raid through Piedmont, Virginia.[7]

A Stray Knight

On one occasion, Powell captured a sutler near Orlean with a wagon load of tin-cups and ginger cakes. After the war, the sutler, who name was Tomasen, settled in Fauquier. In describing his experiences with Powell, the old man used to say that he made him drive through the woods and up into the Cobbler Mountain, where a goat could hardly climb. There, they staid until the Union army moved away, when Powell distributed his goods and wares to the people in the neighborhood. For some time afterwards everybody was munching ginger cakes and every negro had a new tin-cup, a luxury, that they had not enjoyed "afore God, mass, since de war!" The old fellow never failed to wind up his narrative with "Mein Gott! Mein Gott! He was so clever mit my good, he gives 'em every tam bit away!" Powell's favorite mare was a blood bay. This animal had a habit of foaming at the mouth and exposing the whites of her eyes. Mounted on this mare, this strange man "rode fast and far to share war's fiercest perils." The people here in Virginia who remember Powell as he appeared twenty years ago, with his pale face, slouch hat and mysterious ways, mounted on that bay mare, dashing and splashing though the woods, across fields, over ditches and fences, by day, at night, and through all kinds of weather, almost believe that he must have been a stray knight from the Black Forest.

In the winter of 1863–64, John Cornwell, a native of this county and a member of Mosby's battalion, deserted and went through the lines to Washington. Cornwell had been a scout for Mosby and was thoroughly acquainted with the country and the habits and usages of the men belonging to his battalion. He undertook to lead an expedition to capture Mosby. Accordingly, the expedition appeared in "Mosby's Confederacy" dressed in gray uniform, with Cromwell at its head. Near Piedmont they surprised and captured Powell and a number of other soldiers who were dismounted and were grazing their horses along the road sides under the shade of some trees. When the expedition arrived in Paris, at Ashby's Gap, in the Blue Ridge Mountains, the Union soldiers with the gray uniforms on came suddenly upon some other Union soldiers in the regular blue uniforms. Powell took in the situation at once. He ordered a charge and dashed at the blue column, followed by the shouts and bullets of his captors. The apparent charge by the men in gray was of course, met by a counter movement on the part of the men in blue, who very naturally mistook those dressed in gray for Confederates. Quite a battle was fought between these two-bodies of Union soldiers before their mistake was discovered. In the confusion, Powell and his associates made good their escape. Several men were killed and many wounded. This little fight took place in the streets of Paris, and it shows in the mysterious economy of this life, upon what trivial things the mightiest events depend. Had Powell been taken to prison, both Mr. Lincoln and Mr. Seward might have been alive today, and the laurels around the brow of the republic might never have been stained with the red blood of an assassination.

Powell's Rhetoric

It was said at the time of the assassination trial that Powell could not write, but this was a mistake. He told Major Smith, who arrested him at Mrs. Surratt's that he could write and he told the truth. It is a matter of fact that Powell had a tolerably good education, as much perhaps as usually falls to the lot of southern youths living in the county, without special educational advantages, at his time of life. He undoubtedly possessed qualifications enough to have made a very useful citizen had they been employed in raising cotton and sugar cane instead of killing cabinets. However, much as we detest his crime, as all civilized people must abhor assassination, yet to give the devil his due, it must be said that Powell was not the illiterate creature he was represented to be. The following is a specimen of Powell's composition as found in his handwriting in an old docket of a Justice of the Peace, which was used by Powell as a sort of scrap book and diary, now in the possession of Miss Lily Bowie, who by the way, is no longer Miss Lily Bowie, she having married:

> In battle, in the fullness of pride and strength, little wrecks the soldier whether the hissing bullet sings his sudden requiem or the cords of life are severed by the sharp steel.
> L. Powell[8]

There was one incident in the strange and wayward life of Lewis Powell which I almost forgot to relate. An old man named Elias Corder became violently insane in upper Fauquier.

He is now in the asylum at Staunton and will probably never know how he got there. Powell had been on a raid, and returning late one stormy night, stopped at an old vacant church near Corder's house and spread down his blanket on the floor and was soon fast asleep. All of a sudden, he was awakened by a crash of thunder and saw by the flickering lightening an object standing near him. He got up and tried to find the door, but was either too excited or too little acquainted with the place to find it in the dark. The noise he made started old Corder into singing and shrieking. Powell did not know what to do. Another flash and he saw the figure coming towards him. He had lost his pistol in the darkness. There was no time to look for it. The maniac was advancing. Another flash of lightening and he found himself in a hand to hand encounter at midnight in a deserted church with a maniac. The noise made by Powell and old Corder, who had wandered off in his night clothes and was having his "devotions" all to himself, aroused some of the neighbors who, on going to the church, found that Powell had old Corder down and was sitting on him, and would occasionally give the old man's head a bump against the floor to subdue him. Powell was badly scratched and bitten, but with the assistance of the neighbors, Powell succeeded in tying the old man, and the next day he was delivered to the county authorities and placed in jail at Warrenton.[9]

When Powell Was Generous

Another incident will throw a gleam of pleasing light over the somber colors of his tragic career and show that after all, this terrible man was but a boy and that there were really some silvery threads running through the warp and woof of his misspent life. On the celebrated raid at Duffield's Depot, where a paymaster's train, freighted with greenbacks was captured, Powell took a prisoner named John Pratt, belonging to one of the New York regiments. Powell and John became great friends and their wearing apparel soon began to get mixed. In fact, it was hard to tell which was which for very often the prisoner would appear with a gray coat on and Powell with a blue blouse and breeches. Soon afterwards, Powell had to go into Winchester, the town being then occupied by the Union forces, to get some information which could not otherwise be gotten. What to do with his prisoner, he did not know. So, at last, he decided to trust to his honor, and told him if he would remain there until he returned, he would see that he was rewarded. The prisoner thought he was watched and did not make any attempt to escape. When Powell returned, to his surprise, he found the prisoner where he had left him. A few days afterwards, Powell mounted his prisoner on an old horse and sending him through the lines, told him to go, but if he ever showed his face in "Dixie" again, he meant to kill him.[10]

Powell's Romance

During the cannonading of Jackson and Banks across the Shenandoah River, a shell entered the gable end of a house on the Valley Pike, exploded, and chipped off the end of a bureau at which a young lady was dressing her hair in an upper room. It chipped off a large wedge-shaped piece of the bureau and drove it into her back under the right shoulder blade.

The same day, a young Confederate soldier was brought to the house by some of his companions, shot through the lungs. The name of the girl was Lily Bowie; the name of the soldier was Lewis Powell. Miss Bowie was the daughter of a gentleman from Alabama who married a Virginia lady. Under these singular circumstances, these two young southern people met in Virginia, wounded almost to their deaths, and formed an attachment for each other which only ended when the one breathed out the last of life upon the scaffold in Washington, and the other returned a broken-hearted woman to her far-away home in the south.[11]

Meeting with Booth

When Powell had recovered from his wound, he went to Richmond as a guard to some prisoners. While in Richmond, he attended the theatre for the first time in his life. John Wilkes Booth, who was in Richmond at that time appeared in the cast. Powell was so delighted with Booth's acting that he sought his acquaintance and gained it. At that time, Booth was engaged in his plan to abduct the President of the United States and his cabinet. He saw in Powell material to be used in his plot. As burr wound himself into the open heart of the unfortunate Blennerbassett by the elegance of his manners, the beauty of his conversation and the power of his eloquence, so Booth infused the venom of his own ambition into the credulous heart of this gawky and impressionable country boy and found him an easy conquest. Suavity of pretended friends over flowing bowls, jellies, ices and champagnes have turned older heads than Powell's and if he had no strength to resist the blandishments of John Wilkes Booth, he at least paid for his weakness with his life. Powell was a brave man, and it is a pity he was not brave enough to resist the wiles of his evil genius. But he was not; on the contrary, from the hour he first met Booth, he was his to do as he pleased with. Leaving Richmond, Powell returned to the Piedmont section a changed man. He seemed to be more grave and thoughtful than ever. He often spoke of his visit to Richmond and his intention soon to go to Baltimore to meet friends he had met in Richmond. He spoke of Booth with great warmth and admiration. Whenever anything was said about Mr. Lincoln or the conduct of the war, it was noticed that he would say quickly, "Seward is the man; he furnishes the brains. He's the power behind the throne, mightier than the throne itself." After his return from Richmond, he never went on any raid, but was continually talking about a visit or a raid into Maryland, and he and other soldiers would go off to the stables or woods and have long talks, and seem to be particularly anxious that no one should know what they were talking about.

Parting with His Sweetheart

Powell soon began to sell off his horses and dispose of his effects, saying that he would be gone for several months on his Maryland expedition. Among those who were to accompany him were William Sowers, John H. Coxe and others, of Norfolk, but when the time came to depart, all of them backed down except Powell. Whether these men knew anything as to the nature of the expedition, I will not pretend to say. I do know they were intimates with Powell, and I saw and overhead them talking about their "Maryland Expedition" just before Powell left the Piedmont section. Powell left Fauquier some time in January, 1865. Miss Lily Bowie quite naturally gives a feeling description of her parting with Powell, who promised to return within a few months. She never saw him again. The first imitation Miss Bowie had that Powell was one of the Lincoln conspirators was seeing his picture in the illustrated report of the trial. When we were told a man named Payne had stabbed Seward, it nearly frightened us to death. We all expected to be hanged. Miss Bowie went to Washington during the trial, but did not succeed in obtaining an interview with Powell. She wrote to him, but does not believe her letters were delivered as she received no response to her letters. She applied to Secretary Stanton, but he refused her permission to visit the jail, and as the Military Commission by which he was tried sat with closed doors, all efforts to see her lover were in vain.

Assuming the Name of Payne

After leaving Fauquier, Powell went to Noakesville, on the Virginia Midland Railroad, where he left his horse and exchanged his uniform for a suit of citizen's clothes. He then proceeded to walk down the railroad toward Alexandria. Near Alexandria, he met some Federal pickets, and representing himself as a refugee, was conveyed to Alexandria, where he took the Oath of Allegiance to the United States Government as "Lewis Payne, of Fauquier County, Virginia" and was allowed to pass through the lines. His reasons for assuming the name of "Payne" can only be accounted for upon the two-fold hypothesis; first that he wanted to hail from a section of the country with the people and geography of which he was familiar, and to select a name identified with that section of the country; second, he probably desired to take a name easily remembered, and one with the connection and relationship of which he was familiar. The information acquired during his brief stay with my uncle gave him this advantage, for the first thing a Virginian tells a stranger is who he is kin to and all about his family connections. In short, in case of arrest or surprise, it is reasonable to suppose Powell wanted to give a name easily remembered and one identified with the section of country from which he claimed to be a refugee, with the history of which and its people he was so familiar that he would not be liable to be caught by sharp questions. This is the only reason I can give for his appropriation of my name, which act upon the part of the assassin, came very near bringing serious trouble to all.

In Booth's Power

Powell proceeded by boat to Baltimore and thence by rail to Washington where he put up at the Herndon House. There may be some question in the public mind as to where this poor young man, serving as a subordinate officer (sic) in the Confederate Army got the money and means to travel around the country in the manner described.[12] This question may be answered by the fact that Powell had recently shared largely in the distribution of funds captured at Duffield's Depot. All during the months of January, February and March, 1865, Powell continued to live in Washington and John Wilkes Booth continued to wrap his coils tighter and tighter about him until at last he found himself mad as it were with a cord "too fine to be seen, but too strong to be broken."[13] It has been said that between the "acting of a dreadful thing" at the "first motion," all the interim is like a "hideous dream." What an awful moment it must have been in the life of this young man when he first made up his mind to join hands with Booth in the assassination. What a portentous secret these two men held between them. What "hideous dreams" by day and night Powell had between the "acting" of that dreadful deed and the "first action" may be never told by human tongue. Perhaps he thought of his mother, his home down by the sounding sea, of that pure, trusting girl he left, waiting for his return in the Valley of the Piedmont. Who knows? And, perhaps, under the influence of these tender thoughts, he would foreswear the crime he had promised to commit. And then, perhaps Booth would call again and the old influence would come over him and he would renew the bloody pledge that thoughts of mother, home and sweetheart had well nigh broken.

Powell's Pledge of Responsibility

There can be no intellectual comparison between Booth and Powell. I do not know that it was ever claimed for Booth that he possessed a great or profound intellect, but a vigorous and versatile mind he certainly had. He was mentally stronger than Powell, just as he was older in years and experience. While Powell was a romping lad in the orange groves of Florida, [undistinguishable] ... Booth was a man of the world, of the earth, earthy and knew all of life before and behind the scenes. His profession above all others, as an actor, enabled him to know human nature, emotion, weakness and impulse and gave him the power to use them as he wished. He found Powell plastic clay and fashioned him into an assassin with his own hands. That Powell was not a man of very great strength of mind is proved by the fact that he did not seem to see that Booth was using him and by his answer to Major Smith, who arrested him, telling him that he was from the south and had just arrived in the city, and by his going back to the house of Mrs. Surratt after the assassination with fine clothes on, yet pretending to be a laborer, calling at a late hour of the night to begin work in the morning.[14] These facts and admissions show that the young man was confused and are entirely at variance with the cool, calculating shrewdness with which he acted in the earlier part of the evening when endeavoring to gain admission to the residence of the Secretary of State. History and public opinion have already assigned Powell to the great tragedy, and it is evident from the surrounding conditions of the man, his intelligence and opportunities, that he has been placed in the proper position. That Powell did not have the ability for intrigue necessary to plan and execute so vast a plot as the assassination conspiracy is a fact about which there can be no dispute.

The Attempted Assassination

Precisely at the hour when these terrible scenes were being enacted in Ford's Theatre, on Tenth Street in Washington, when Booth had sent his fatal ball crashing through the brain of Abraham Lincoln and had leaped from the box to the stage brandishing a dagger and crying, "Sic Semper Tyrannis," and the whole audience was shocked, amazed and stunned and the wounded President clutched and gasped for life, Lewis Powell presented himself at the residence of Secretary Seward, who had been thrown from his buggy a few days before and was confined to his bed, and asked to be shown to the Secretary's room. He was met at the door by William H. Bell, a colored butler, who told Powell that he could not see the Secretary. Powell held a small vial of medicine in his left hand, with his right hand in his coat front. He wore a dark gray coat, black trousers, with a light overcoat and slouch felt hat bent down over his eye. He spoke in a firm, but low tone of voice, and said he had been sent by Doctor Verdi with the medicine, and with instructions to see the Secretary in person and tell him how it should be taken. After some hesitation, he was admitted by the butler and when he had ascended the stairs, he was met by Frederick Seward who demanded to know his business, when Powell felled him to the floor, cutting him twice in the head with a knife held with the blade down below his hand; he then turned upon Bell and disabled him severely.[15] He then proceeded to the room of the Secretary and was met at the door by Augustus Seward, whom he stabbed well nigh until death, cutting him five or six times. Pushing his way into the sick room, he was attacked by George F. Robinson, the nurse, and by E. W. Hansell. The former he wounded in the face and forehead with his knife and the latter he stabbed over the sixth rib to a depth of six or seven inches.[16] Forcing his way past the other attendants in the room, he went to the bedside of Mr. Seward and stabbed him three times, inflicting ghastly wounds in his jaw, neck and breast. In the struggle, the Secretary rolled out of bed and was lying on the floor in his blood when his physicians arrived, his attendants being utterly dazed by the sudden and terrible onslaught of this ferocious man.

The Capture

The only words uttered by the assassin during all this awful conflict were, "I'm mad!" and these were uttered in a "strangely intense, but not a strong voice," as described by the witnesses at the trial. As Powell left the dwelling of the Secretary and mounted his horse he slashed at the colored man who had held his horse, cutting him about the face severely.[17] He then threw the knife to the ground, and riding out Vermont Avenue slowly for a few squares, put spurs to his horse and rode out into the darkness and was seen no more until he was arrested in disguise at the house of Mrs. Surratt, No. 541 H. Street NW in Washington. When arrested, Powell had one of his trousers legs rolled up, a skull cap on his head and a pickaxe on his shoulder. He said he had come to dig a ditch for Mrs. Surratt, but she denied any knowledge of him. He was sent to the headquarters of General Augar and upon an examination of the boots he wore, one of them was found to contain the name of John Wilkes Booth.[18]

The Trial

At the trial, he was identified by Major Frederick Seward, Augustus Seward, George F. Robinson, William H. Bell, Robert Nelson and E. W. Hansell as the man who had made the attack upon the Secretary and upon them.[19] He was examined by Drs. Barnes, James C. Hall, Basil Norris and George L. Porter with reference to his sanity and legal responsibility, who found no signs of insanity whatever in his case. He was defended by William E. Doster.

His counsel claimed that in "the case of Lewis Payne there are three things to be admitted beyond dispute; first, that he is the person who attempted to take the life of Mr. Seward; second, that he does not come within the medical definition of insanity; third, that he believed what he did was right." Upon the last proposition, Mr. Doster based a powerful and ingenious argument, the objet of which was to show that his client was the victim of a misguided belief that he was doing right and was therefore not as fully responsible to the law as he might otherwise have been. Mr. Doster contended that to hang him would be to make a martyr out of him through all the future years, and that it would be better to let him eke out a miserable existence in prison than to canonize him by putting him to death. He also claimed that it would be a singular fact in the criminal jurisprudence to "take the life of this man who has taken the life of no one—it would be the anomaly of the victim surviving the condemned."

Sentenced to Be Hanged

The following is a copy of the judgment of the Military Commission before which he was tried:

After mature consideration of the evidence adduced in the case of the Accused, Lewis Payne, the Commission find him: of the specification Guilty, except combining, confederating and conspiring with Edman Spangler; of that Not Guilty. Of the charge, Guilty, and the Commission Do, therefore, sentence him, the said Lewis Payne, to be hanged by the Neck until he be dead, at such time and place as the President of the United States shall direct.

The same judgment was entered in the cases of Herold, Atzerodt and Mrs. Surratt. O'Laughlen, Spangler, Mudd and Arnold were sentenced to imprisonment for life at Dry Tortugas, Florida. The following is an extract from the proclamation of President Johnson made in pursuance of the findings of the Commission:

Executive Mansion, July 5, 1865
The foregoing sentences in the cases of David E. Herold, G. A. Atzerodt, Lewis Payne and Mary E. Surratt are hereby approved, and it is ordered that the sentences of the authority, under the direction of the Secretary of War, on the 7th day of July, 1865, between the hours of 10 O'clock AM and 2 p.m. of that day.

Accordingly, the persons named in the foregoing proclamation of the president were executed upon the grounds now known as the "Arsenal," at the foot of Four and a Half Street, Southwest, in Washington, on the banks of the Potomac River, July 7, 1865, within full view of the Virginia shores, which Powell had left just seven months before full of life and hope. They were buried near the scene of their execution, but the bodies have since been removed. Some have been taken to the cemeteries of their friends or relatives, but no kinsman or acquaintance of Powell has ever seen or sought his grave. Powell died boldly, and when Herold was almost prostrated with fear, slapped him upon the back and encouraged him to die like a man.[20]

Arrest of the Payne Family

The assuming of my name by Powell came very near getting the necks of several of my relatives, if not my own, stretched in a way "we most do despise." We had no more to do with the conspiracy than the man in the moon. During the trial, a body of troops were sent to Fauquier to "run us all in," under the impression that we knew something about it. General

William H. Payne, of Warrenton, brother of Captain John S. Payne, the Indian fighter, one being an officer in the Confederate and the other in the Federal Army, were arrested and came near being mobbed in Washington. Upon investigation he was discharged, after lying in prison some time; it having been ascertained that he had nothing to do with the conspiracy and that Powell was an adventurer who had assumed the name. When the mob made the attack upon General Payne, he was protected by Major Halleck, of the United States Army, who knew all the facts and General Payne undoubtedly owes his life to him.

In writing this article, I have not been actuated by any desire to defend the memory of the assassin, nor to charge up against him any crimes of which he was not guilty. I have endeavored to be the faithful chronicler of any events passing partially under my own observation, in my own time, to correct as far as lies within my power an important error in the history of my country and to wipe from a worthy name a blot with which it has been most unjustly smirched.

Appendix D

The following letter written by General William H. Payne to General Bradley T. Johnson presents Powell in an entirely different perspective as opposed to that presented at the conspiracy trial. General Payne and family knew Powell intimately during the latter's service with Mosby's Rangers.

September 6th, 1894
General Bradley T. Johnson
Pikesville, Md.
Dear General:
Since the receipt of your letter I have been partly in attendance upon Mrs. Payne, who has been very ill but I am happy to say appears to be convalescing, or engaged in this office or in private affairs to such an extent that I have not been able to answer it.

The "real name and story" of Louis [sic] Payne [Powell] is as follows:

He was born in Florida [sic]; was the son of a Baptist minister named Powell and came to the army of Virginia as a private in some infantry regiment. He got a transfer, by some means, to Mosby's command and served with credit as long as he was connected with it. You will probably remember that the county of Fauquier was called in the latter part of the war "Mosby's Confederacy," because it was the chief theater of his exploits and the rendezvous of his men; indeed, a very large proportion of his command was composed of the *boys* who were growing up in that section, who, too young to be received into the Confederate army nevertheless shared the enthusiasm and heroism of their fathers and brothers and could not brook to see the great fight going on without taking a hand in it. Some of them were children of 15 years. The command was without any rigid military organization. There was no camp or camp guards nor the usual military restrictions. They were like Fappenheimer's dragoons:

> "Their life was but a battle and a march, And, like the wind's blast, never resting, homeless, they stormed across the war-convulsed earth."

When off duty they lived around at different houses as the guests of their friends. When a raid was projected by Mosby, like Roderic Dhu, he sent Malise around with the burning brand. They met in the greenwoods,

> "Armed with banner, brand and bow,"

ready to follow their gallant leader wherever he chose to lead.

Powell had in some way become intimate with my people. When in the upper end of the county his home was with Dr. Alban S. Payne (General Lomax's father-in-law); when in the central part of the county it was at Granville, the home of my wife's uncle, Mr. Scott Payne and, indeed, of three generations of Paynes. His interest in the family, tradition says, extended to one of its daughters (a sister of Congressman Meredith), at least, she has his photograph given just before he disappeared from our country—but this is for nobody else but you.

He was a chivalrous, generous, gallant fellow, particularly fond of children. I am informed that my boys, who were then little fellows, were pets with him; and he rarely visited Warrenton that he did not bring them some little thing. Two or three of these children, now grown men, remember how he used to take them before him on his horse when he would come into town.

In the latter part of the fall of 1864, he disappeared from our country and the thread of his history is there broken. It is presumed that he met Booth somewhere and was fascinated by him as so many others seem to have been. From what I can learn of him he was not of more than ordinary brightness. The leading features of the man's character were courage, enthusiasm and loyalty which more than compensated.

It is now well known that as the days darkened around the Confederacy men's minds darkened too and, as the French say, they began to "see red." Hope from the government was waning and strange and *independent* thoughts and plans were stirring and working in the dispairing [sic] minds of many Confederates. Unauthorized plans, plans which a dignified and super-righteous government could not even look at, were projected. In their desperation men were resolving to venture desperate things upon their own hook, and among them was Booth's conception of recruiting the Confederate army with 50,000 *released* prisoners and renewing the war in the Spring of 1865 with revived hope and undiminished courage. He seems to have fancied that if he could abduct Mr. Lincoln he could force an exchange of prisoners. Possibly he may have been inspired by resentment at the recollection that it was the infamous duplicity of Lincoln that curious mixture of Satyr, Harlequin and Demagogue that had kept these 50,000 Confederate soldiers in prison; at any rate we know what he wanted to do and that he had the courage to attempt it.

Evidently Powell was a man made for his hand; fate brought the impassioned actor and the rude, uneducated boy from the Everglades [sic] together and they fitted like a knife into its sheath.

He remained out of sight of the people of Fauquier from November until April 15, 1865, when it was announced that Louis [sic] Payne [Powell] of Fauquier had been seized at Mrs. Surratt's house as an accomplice in the assassination of Lincoln and as the person to whom the killing of Seward was allotted. Of course, everybody was eager to know who Louis [sic] *Payne* was. There are three distinct families bearing that name in the county and they aggregate its most numerous voting force, they have never been able to trace relationship to each other. Each of the families no doubt ransacked their pedigrees and history but none had a *Louis* [sic].

The trial came on and if you recollect it you will recall that this man's bearing was exceptionally dignified and, without being offensive, was nevertheless daring. He declined counsel, confessed his purpose, regretted his failure, acknowledged that he had staked his life and lost, and seemed rather fatigued at the tedium and technicalities of a trial. On the scaffold he asked to walk next to Mrs. Surratt. Throughout the whole trying scene he was attempting to encourage her and pour some of his dauntless spirit into the poor woman's heart. The papers said that he died with absolute serenity.

The manner in which he was identified was in this wise:

The brutal court and prosecutor, not content with his confession and his defiant invitation to death, undertook to defame their intended victim. That much he resented. The charge was brutality and cruelty to prisoners. His answer was that his conduct was the reverse and he could prove it.

When Torbert returned from his raid upon Charlottesville in November, 1864, this man and a comrade captured six of his men near Warrenton. He left them in charge of somebody in the town while he rode up to greet some of his friends.

The men that he had captured were stragglers from Torbert's command who had been guilty of some gross and infamous brutality to Isham Keith (Judge Keith's brother) and his family. They sacked the house, piled the furniture and beds in the yard, and burned them. They insulted his old mother and his wife. Isham at the time was concealed in the woods. As soon as they left he came to his ruined home and heard the story. Mounting his horse he started in pursuit. Upon reaching Warrenton he found these men prisoners. He killed four of them. When the news was brought to Powell, with weapon in hand, he galloped to the place where he heard the pistol shots, stopped the massacre and was with difficulty prevented from killing Keith. He claimed the prisoners as his and announced his intention of saving their lives at the risk of his own.

This scene was witnessed by several citizens. Powell had them summoned. Alarmed and ignorant of what they were being taken to Washington for, they entered the court room, when to their astonishment they found that Louis Payne was *Powell,* and that they were unwitting witnesses in the assassination trial.

The story of the abandonment of Booth's original plan to abduct, the dispersion of all who were engaged in it except himself, Atzerodt, Harold [sic] and Payne, their capture and execution, is of course familiar to you. I cannot explain why he took our name except that it was endeared to him in some way. Certainly he did not mean to stain it, for his confession shows that he looked upon himself as a patriot discharging a patriotic duty and had no regrets except failure. Of course, much more of his history has been learned since but that is merely a matter of identification.

I believe, my dear General, this answers your inquiry. I repeat, do not mention my reference to my kinswoman; it is a painful one to the survivors—surpress Keith's also.

I am opposed to assassination in every form and under all circumstances, but eternity is too long to punish, and sometimes much may be forgiven for the motive. You will remember that our Lord forgave Mary Magdalen for having loved *too much* and *too promiscously* [sic]. Possibly this poor boy, for he was nothing but a boy, by this time at least "has crossed over the river and is now *resting* under the shade...."

Very faithfully, your friend,
William H. Payne

Appendix E

These Powell signatures are the only two currently known in existence. Both of them are in the National Archives. The formation of the various letters is enough to confirm beyond a doubt that they were written by the same hand.

1. Signature of L. T. Powell, page 9, Clothing Receipt Roll, 4th Quarter 1864, Mosby's Regt. of Va. Cavalry, War Dept. Collection of Confederate Records (Record Group 109). Original in National Archives.

2. Signature of "L. Paine" on original of Oath of Allegiance, File "W" RB (JAO) p. 31–1865, from Letters Received and Evidence of the Commission, Investigation and Trial Papers Relating to the Assassination of President Lincoln, Records of the Judge Advocate General's Office (Record Group 153). Original in National Archives.

Appendix F

In 1902, there appeared in a Nebraska paper, *The Columbus Journal*, Columbus, Nebraska,[1] two articles regarding the affair where Powell saved the lives of two Union soldiers. Recently discovered, one of these stories was contributed by a certain August Lockner. Lockner (enlisted under the name Lockwood) was born in Germany in 1844. A private in Company H, 21st New York Cavalry, Lockner gave full particulars of what happened the day he was saved from death by the young would-be Seward assassin.[2]

The affair took place on a snowy Christmas Eve, 1864. To quote Lockner:

> I had gone to a well to fill my canteen and returning to my horse was preparing to mount when two strangers, dressed in blue with rubber ponchos which covered their shoulders came to where I was standing. They held their revolvers under their ponchos in such a manner that the weapons were concealed ... one of the strangers said, "Come around the corner of the house quick, or we'll scatter your brains all over this dooryard." I sought to determine whether or not it was a joke. While I was deliberating, my revolver was jerked from my belt by one of the men, while the other took charge of my horse. Then I was rushed around the corner of the house out of sight. Here we all mounted and rode leisurely toward a small wood, my captors riding close to me. I was led a captive into the woods and searched for any valuables which I might have had. One of my captors then started toward the town with me. On the way he said that his comrades had been mingling with our men in the town and on the road. From his conversation, I was led to believe that they were Mosby's scouts or spies. As we rode back into town, I saw plenty of Mosby's troopers, dressed in blue and gray clothes.... In front of that leader's headquarters, I saw a number of prisoners surrounded by a crowd of people. These prisoners were compelled to exchange their good blue uniforms for the tattered garments which their captors had to offer. I did not escape and was soon garbed in an old black overcoat, pants and old boots. I was exceedingly grateful as I was left in possession of my shirt. A crowd of ugly drunken fellows threatened us shamefully and threatened to take our lives. Later, three of us were taken to the edge of town, stopping enroute at a house occupied by a family named Grant. While we were here, the drunken rabble from the town suddenly swooped down upon us, flourishing revolvers and sabers in the air, some more reckless than the others, shooting at the prisoners.

Both Lockner's recollection of the conflict as well as the later statement of General William H. Payne gives credence to what actually occurred during this particular skirmish. To quote Payne: "The men that he [Powell] had captured were stragglers from Torbert's command who had been guilty of some gross and infamous brutality to Isham Keith ...and his family. They sacked the house, piled the furniture and beds in the yard and burned them. They insulted his old mother and his wife. Isham at the time was concealed in the woods. As soon as they left he came to his ruined home and hard the story. Mounting his horse he started in pursuit. Upon reaching Warrenton, he found these men prisoners. He killed four of them. When the news was brought to Powell, with weapon in hand he galloped to the place where he heard the pistol shots, stopped the massacre and was with difficulty prevented from killing Keith. He claimed the prisoners as his and announced his intention of saving their lives at the risk of his own."[3]

Collaborated with the reference of General Payne, Lockner's description of the affair makes a sound backdrop for Mr. and Mrs. Grant's testimony given at the trial in 1865, although the Grants did not go into the same depth of detail. Lockner continues:

I looked inquiringly at my captor, whose name was Powell, and asked if the prisoners were to be shot. He replied by drawing his revolver and in strong language informed me that they were not. He succeeded in stopping the rush of the drunken mob from riding over us. While he was seeking to protect us, one of the pursuers shot a young prisoner from the Eighth New York Cavalry in the back. He fell mortally wounded, expiring a short time afterward.

That shot was an incentative for others and the ruffians commenced firing promiscuously at the prisoners. Unseen, I dropped from my horse, the animal serving as a barrier. The other prisoner, an old man from the Seventeenth Pennsylvania Regiment, was wounded in the hip. Guards and civilians rushed from the houses and shamed the attacking ruffians sufficiently so that they desisted in their hellish work. I was promised protection by one of Mosby's lieutenants and later buried the dead prisoners in an open grave in a cemetery which was in close proximity.

Powell was ordered to take me southward and turn me over to some Confederate command, and thence I was to be transported to prison. We commenced the journey toward Culpeper. Powell, who later proved to be the assassin of Secretary Seward, proved himself talkative and social, besides a brave man. He informed me that I was safe from all harm as long as I acted in good faith. Should I attempt to escape, he said, he would do his duty and shoot me. "If you try any of your blamed Yankee tricks on me, you know what to expect!"[4] To impress his words, he whipped out his revolver and sent three bullets whizzing in succession into a fence post also showing his unerring aim.

Powell and Lockner were the exact same age. Aside from being on opposite sides of the conflict, both boys aged 20 at the time, seemed to be rather congenial with each other: "We stopped at a farm house, where he [Powell] seemed to be somewhat acquainted and heartily ate of cornbread, bacon and corn coffee. After the meal, he asked one of the young women to play upon the piano for him, which request was granted."

It's apparent that besides possessing a hearty appetite, young Powell also had a strong music appreciation. At the Surratt boarding house three months later in March of 1865, he requested Anna Surratt to play the piano for him in pretty much the same manner as Lockner mentions here. One wonders if this piano-playing young lady was Lewis Powell's Northern Virginia girlfriend, Bettie Meredith. The 18-year-old Meredith was a cousin of General William H. Payne whose family young Powell boarded with during his tenure with Mosby's Rangers. Lewis Powell was second cousin to General John Brown Gordon and it was more than likely this illustrious family connection which had secured Powell a membership in Mosby's Rangers elite company, thereby opening doors into the homes of many of Northern Virginia's best families.

To continue Lockner's narrative:

We then resumed our journey, during which he became talkative and informed me that his father was a Baptist minister in Florida....

His conversation revealed to me that he was the most bitter secessionist I ever knew. When I intimated that the South could not hold out much longer, he uttered an oath and said that his cause had 300,000 men enlisted and that we would have to walk over their dead bodies. He also said that if necessary they would kill the head of our government. This remark did not cause any particular impression on me at the time as I considered it made during his rage.

Darkness finally overcame us while we were enroute. We stopped at a farm house, had lunch and then spread our blankets for the night, sleeping side by side.

Here the first article claims that "As night came on we came to a house where Powell seemed to be well acquainted. Our horses were put in the stable and we were assigned to the parlor on the first floor to sleep. We carried in our saddles and blankets...."[5]

The second article continues:

I noticed that he [Powell] kept his pistol in his coat bosom and also that the windows were not locked. I removed my boots and with my saddle I made a headrest. Our overcoats served as coverings. I was never more awake in my life. My guard acted as though he desired me to go to sleep first, so I held quiet and breathed heavy. About midnight I surmised that Powell was soundly sleeping. I raised myself slowly to a sitting posture, moving cautiously to determine if he would discover my actions. Taking my clothing, I reached the window and raised it cautiously. The moon shown between some clouds just at that moment and had Powell awakened, I would have made an excellent target as I clamored through the window. Once outside I escaped for the woods. I had noticed a road running in a westerly direction and this I chose, intending to reach the Blue Ridge, which I could follow to Harper's Ferry and friends.[6]

One is left to wonder why Lockner didn't take his horse. Or yet, his own horse and Powell's as well. We can only surmise that he was in a hurry to get away. His saddle was in the parlor with Powell and to make a quick getaway on horseback would require him to ride bareback. He may have been reluctant or uncomfortable riding in this manner, as it requires considerable skill. Besides, he would be a much easier target on horseback. One also wonders at the recriminations awaiting young Lew Powell when he had to report to his commanding officer that his prisoner had escaped; surely an embarrassment.

On January 13, Powell would slip through the lines at Alexandria, Virginia, sell his horse and sign an Oath of Allegiance. Next stop, the Branson Boarding House in Baltimore.

According to an article in the *Richmond Dispatch* for December 11, 1902, "They Knew Payne—Lincoln Conspiracy Recalled by Two of Mosby's Rangers," W. Ben Palmer, one of Mosby's top Rangers, was in the same unit as Powell; Captain Robert Walker's Company B. He remembered seeing Powell off the night before he left, claiming that Powell had sent for him to tell him goodbye. "The latter found the young man dressed in a badly fitting suit of citizen's clothes, with a black slouch hat pulled down over his eyes. He was in high spirits, and talked of his plans. This was the same dress which Powell wore when he turned up at the Branson House in early January 1865. "Powell said that they intended to kidnap Lincoln and bring him South." According to Palmer, "No mention was made of killing anyone. Palmer thought that Mosby knew *nothing* of Powell's plans." However, he did state that both General William H. Payne as well as Captain Walker had "intimate knowledge of certain incidents connected with the alleged conspiracy."

Appendix G

This unidentified and undated clipping clearly shows the mystery surrounding Powell and the straining attempts of the press to delve into his background. This ridiculous canard gained credibility at a time before Powell revealed his true identity to his counsel and is a good example of the yellow journalism of the times.

Another Curious Story About Payne—
Is He a Son of Jeff. Davis?

Decidedly the romance of crime receives a startling illustration in the person of Payne, the assassin of Secretary Seward. Payne is a perfect mystery; he is as imperturbable as the sphynx, as cool as an iceburg [sic]. His name is a misnomer, and he seems to have no comprehension of physical suffering. Nothing affects him; he bears his lot with stolid indifference, complains of nothing, and looks certain death in the face as quietly as though gazing into the eyes of a tender maiden. He has been a whole week at a time without eating since his incarceration and he was entirely constipated during thirty-four days. Yet his cheek has the flush of health and his respiration is easy and regular; he never changes color, and never manifests by any sign that he is affected by the evidence; that he would either deny or confirm it. He is not stupid; his piercing eye is bright with intelligence. But what is he? It is as difficult to answer this question as that other—Who is he? To solve this problem a good many sharp wits are at work; and already we have the most extraordinary stories in regard to him. It has been stated that he is a nephew of General Lee; but that report was quickly exploded. It has been affirmed that his name is Powell, and that he is one of the Florida family bearing that title; but no proof has been adduced in support of this assertion. Then we have been told that he is a Missourian, a Kentuckian, a Georgian, a Canadian; but there is no evidence of the truth of any of these statements. The latest story has decidedly more of the romantic features about it than any that have yet been told. To begin at the beginning, it is this: A young officer of the United States Army was sent, many years ago, to take command of the garrison at Fort Snelling, then the remotest military outpost of the far West. This officer was as gallant as all military men are said to be—too gallant as it proved, for the peace of mind of a buxom young daughter of a frontiersman, who, with his child, frequently visited the fort. The young lady—a rose in the wilderness—naturally attracted the attention of the officers, to whom, deprived of all feminine society, the sight of a sweet, fresh young face was a rare and indescribable pleasure. Among those who lavished peculiar attention upon this solitary flower was the young officer above mentioned, and in a short time, it became evident that his courtesy was not entirely lost. To shorten a long story, the devoted son of Mars succeeded in winning our damsel's heart. She—alas! that it should be told—loved him well, but all too unwisely. It is the old, old story. The officer was recalled to the East in time, and she, broken-hearted, followed him as far as St. Louis, where, through stress of circumstances, she was compelled to remain. Here, she gave birth to a child—a son—and here she gave the boy a common education. Shortly after the war with Mexico broke out, and the betrayer went to the land of the Montezumas as the colonel of a Mississippi regiment. When he returned he entered the field of politics, and was elected to the United States Senate. One day, while at Washington he was called upon by a woman, who presented to him a fine, hearty boy as his son. It was the western rose, grown old and faded, with the pledge of her affection. But the honorable senator refused to acknowledge paternity in the case, and the pair were shown out. It is said, however, that he secretly conveyed to the mother and child, from time to time, a certain stripend, sufficient to eke out their scanty income. Time passed on, and the great rebellion began. The senator became a prominent man in the Confederate government. As for the son, now grown to man's estate, the story does not say what became of him, but intimates that he entered the Rebel service. The grand crash came. The ex-lieutenant, ex-colonel, ex-senator and ex–Confederate leader, lies in a dungeon deep in the impregnable walls of Fortress Monroe. His name is Jefferson Davis. The son, in double irons is undergoing trial, the result of which will be death, in the penitentiary building at Washington. His name is Lewis Payne.

So much for the story. It certainly has an air of romance, if none of probability, about it and people who tell it say that members of the military commission are well aware of the relations between Davis and Payne; that Payne incorporated these statements in the confession he is alleged to have made; and that President Johnson was also made aware of the whole story before he issued his proclamation against the rebel chieftain. There are no resemblances between the two persons, however, save in one respect; it is well known that Davis' nervousness and irritability were heightened, if they did not proceed from irregularity in natural habits; and possibly Payne has inherited the peculiarity. The circumstances, however, are not worth much as evidence, and probably this "explanation" which only heightens the mystery, will be found as baseless as any of its predecessors.

Appendix H

Argument in Defense of Lewis Payne by W. E. Doster, Esq. May it please the Court:

I. There are three things in the case of the prisoner, Payne, which are admitted beyond civil or dispute:

1. That he is the person who attempted to take the life of the Secretary of State.
2. That he is not within the medical definition of insanity.
3. That he believed what he did was right and justifiable.

The question of his identity and the question of his sanity, are, therefore settled, and among the things of the past. The sole question that remains is, how far shall his conviction serve to mitigate his punishment? I use the word punishment deliberately, and with the consciousness that in so doing I admit that if he is a responsible being he ought to be punished. And I say it, because I can not allow my duties as counsel to interfere with my convictions as a man so far as to make me blind to the worth of the life of a distinguished citizen, and the awful consequences of an attempt to take it away. If, indeed, such an attempt be allowed to go without rebuke, than it seems to me the office is but a perilous exposure to violence; then the highest compensation for public services is the distinction which follows assassination, and then our public servants are but pitiable and defenseless offerings to sedition. And surely, if any public servant deserved to be excepted from that fate, it was he, the illustrious and sagacious statesman, who, during a long life of arduous services, has steadfastly checked all manner of facetious and public discontent; who, in the darkest days of discord, has prophesied the triumph of concord, and who at all times has been more ready to apply antidotes than the knife to the nation's wounds. How far, then, shall the conviction of the prisoner that he was doing right go in extenuation of his offense? That we may accurately, and as fully as the occasion demands understand the convictions of the prisoner, I invite your attention to a sketch of his life, the customs under which he was reared, and the education he received. Lewis Thornton Powell is the son of the Rev. George C. Powell, a Baptist minister, at present supposed to live at Live Oak Station, on the railroad between Jacksonville and Tallahassee, in the state of Florida, and was born in Alabama in the year 1845. Besides himself, his father had six daughters and two sons. He lived for some time in Worth and Stewart counties, Georgia, and in 1859 moved to Florida. At the outbreaking of the war, but four years ago, the prisoner was a lad of sixteen, engaged in superintending his father's plantation and a number of slaves. We may safely presume that, occupied in the innocent pursuits of country life, he daily heard the precepts of the Gospel from his father; that, in the society of his sisters, the hardy life of a planter was softened by the charms of a refined and religious circle, and that, in the natural course of events, he would be today as he was then, a farmer and an honest man. But in 1861, war broke out, war, the scourge and pestilence of the race. The signal, which spread like a fire, was not long in reaching Live Oak Station. His two brothers enlisted, and Lewis, though but sixteen, enlisted in Capt. Stuart's company, in the Second Florida Infantry, commanded by Colonel Ward, and was ordered to Richmond.

Let us pause a moment in this narrative, and consider what, in the eyes of this Florida boy, was the meaning of war, and what the thoughts that drove him from a pleasant home to the field of arms. At another time I might picture to you the scene, but too familiar, of his taking leave; a mother, like the mothers of Northern boys, shedding tears, less bitter, because she was dedicating a son to her country; sisters, whose sorrow, like the sorrow of the sisters of Northern boys, was alleviated with pride that they had a brother in the field; the father's blessing; the knapsack filled with tributes of affection, to be fondled by distant bivouac fires, and the heavy sigh, drowned in the rolling of the drum. But this is not a stage for effect. We know this was mistaken pride and sorrow in a mistaken cause, though the object of them was a son and brother, and we must not consider them, though the boy was but sixteen when he launched on the terrible sea of civil war.

In the state of Florida, were two separate races—one white and the other black—of which the one was slave to the other, and Lewis belonged to the race which was master. It was a custom of this State for masters to whip their slaves, sell them, kill them, and receive the constant homage which the oppressed offer to the powerful. It was the custom of this State to whip and burn men who preached against the custom. It was the custom to defend the institution in meeting-houses, at political gatherings, in family prayers. It was the custom to hunt fugitives with bloodhounds—even those who tried to help them to freedom.

In this custom the prisoner was bred; education made it a second nature; politicians had taught him to find it in the Constitution, preachers had taught him to find it in the Bible, the laws taught him to regard it as property, habit had made it a very part of his being. In the eyes of the lad, the war meant to abolish this custom and upheave society from its foundations. His inheritance was to be dissipated, his vassal equals, his laws invaded, his religion confounded, his politics a heresy, his habits criminal. Hereafter, to strike a slave was to be an assault, to sell one felony, to kill one murder. For this, then, the lad was going to fight—the defense of a social custom. That was the reason. It was a traditional political precept of the State in which the prisoner lived, that the State, like its elder sisters, had reserved the right of divorcing itself at pleasure from the Union, and that great as the duty of a citizen might be to the Union, his first duty was to Florida. Schoolmasters taught that the relative rights of the State and Nation had been left unsettled; politicians taught that the local power was greater than the central, and in support of it men were sent to Washington. The war, in the eyes of this boy, meant to reverse this, to subordinate the State to the Nation, the Governor to the President, Tallahassee to Washington City. And, therefore, he was going to fight; to defend State rights. That was the second reason.

It was a deep-seated conviction of the people in this State that their blood and breeding was better than the blood and breeding of Northerners; that they had more courage, more military prowess, and were by nature superiors. This conviction the war threatened to overthrow, this boast the war was to vindicate, this superiority was, by the war, intended to be proved. And this was the third reason he was going to fight—to show that he was a better man than Northerners.

There was a frantic delusion among these people that Northern men were usurping the Government, were coveting their plantations, were longing to pillage their homes, ravage their fields, and reduce them to subjection. The war was to defend mother, sister, home, soil and honor, and beat back an insolent invader. This was the fourth reason—to repel invasion. These were, in the mind of this lad, the incentives to war. Let us not pass unnoticed how he was schooled in the instincts and morals of war. Under the code of slavery we know that the murder of a companion with a bowie-knife or in a duel was an index of spirit; the torture of Negroes evidence of a commanding nature; concubinage with Negroes a delicate compliment [sic] to wives; spending wealth earned by other men in luxuriance, chivalric; gambling the sweet reprieve for confinement to plantations. Instead of morals had sprung up a code of honor—perhaps a false, but surely an exacting and imperious code, that kept bowie-knives in the belt and pistols in the pocket, and had no hesitation in using them, when slavery was assailed, and a code that remembered friends and never forgave enemies. These, then, were the morals and instinct of the lad—it is right to kill Negroes, right to kill abolitionists; it is only wrong to break promises, to forget a friend, or forgive an enemy, and to do right is to be ready with the bowie-knife and pistol.

Now let me ask whether in the world there is another school in which the prisoner could so well have been trained for assassination as in this slave aristocracy? The stealthiest Indian that ever shot from ambush was not so well instructed in the use of his knife; the deadliest Gherber that ever strangled his victim had not the animosity which comes from trading in and killing slaves. All the horrible accomplishments of assassination, which Machiavel says are three—"fierceness of nature, resolute undertakings, and having had one's hands formerly in blood," are his by religion, by politics, by law, by education, and by custom. And who is responsible for this training of the lad? Standing, as we do today, at the end of a four years war, having just heard again recited tales of prisoners starved, cities infected, cities burned, prisons undermined things that seem unparalleled in the barbarity of all ages—and all by men, who, four years ago, sat side by side with us, and seemed no different, we now know, what we never dreamt of, that this is the spirit of slavery, stripped of its disguise. In rebellion we now recognize the master never taught to obey; in arson of cities we see again the fagot and the stake; in Libby and Andersonville we see again the slave-pen; in capture the blood and the lash; in assassination the social bowie-knife and pistol; and in this prisoner the legitimate moral offspring of slavery, States Rights, chivalry and delusion.

But who is to blame that he, with five millions more, was so instructed, so demoralized, so educated to crime? Is it his father and mother? They found their precepts in the Bible; they gave their son but the customs they had themselves inherited. Is it the society of Florida? It was a society that ruled this country until within four years, and occupied the seats of Government. Is it the laws of Florida? They were but receipts of the Constitution. Is it the Constitution? That is but the creation of our forefathers. Who, then, is responsible that slavery was allowed to train assassins? I answer, it is we; we, the American people, who have cherished slavery, have compromised with it, for a hundred years have extended it, have pandered to it, and have at last, thanks be to God, destroyed it. Let us, then, not shrink from our responsibility. If there be any Southerner here who has sought to foster slavery, he is in part father of the assassin in this boy. If there be any Northerner here who has been content to live in slavery, he is also in part father of the assassin in this boy. If there be any American that has been content to be a citizen of a slaveholding republic, he is in part father of the assassin in this boy. Nay, all of us—such as he is we have made him—the murderous, ferocious, and vindictive child of by-gone American Constitution and laws. And what is to be the fate of our offspring? Let us see. That it is criminal, let us reform it; that it is deluded, let us instruct it. But let us not destroy it, for therein we punish others for our own crimes. Let the great American people rather speak thus; "for twenty years we have sent you to a wicked school, though we knew not the wickedness thereof, until our own child rebelled against us. Now we have torn down the schoolhouse and driven out the master. Hereafter you shall be taught in a better school, and we will not destroy you, because you learnt but as instructed."

II. But there is another school before him—the school of war. At Richmond his regiment joined the army of General Lee and was joined to A. P. Hill's corps; with it he shared the fate of the rebel army, pressed through the Peninsular Campaign, the battles of Chancellorsville and Antietam. Here he heard that his two brothers were killed at Murfreesboro. Finally, on the 3rd of July 1863, in the charge upon the Federal Center, at Gettysburg, he was wounded, taken prisoner, and detailed as a nurse in Pennsylvania College Hospital.

Let us pause again to consider the effect of two years campaigning as a private in the army of General Lee upon the moral nature of the accused. He was one of that army who made trinkets and cups out of the bones of Union soldiers—an army where it was customary to starve prisoners by lingering agonies, which supplied its wants by plundering the dead, which slew men after surrender, that was commanded by officers who had violated their sacred oaths to the United States, and who taught their subordinates that such violation was justifiable; an army who were taught by Jackson that God was the champion of their cause; an army that held the enemy in quest of "booty and beauty"; an army which believed that no means that helped the cause of Southern independence unjustifiable, but glorious; an army who for two years explained victory by the righteousness of the cause—finally, an army that held the person and Cabinet of the President in holy execration. Surely he could not pass through these two terrible years without being in his moral nature the same as the army of which he formed a part. He is now eighteen, and the last two years have formed his character. He also abhors the President of the Yankees; he also believes that victory comes because God is just; he also believes that nothing is bad so the South be free; he also regards a Federal as a ravisher and a robber; he also prays with Jackson to God for the victory. He further believes in Heaven and General Lee; dresses himself in the clothes of Union dead; stands guard over starving prisoners; also has his cup carved out of some Federal skull. Besides, he has learned the ordinary soldier's lessons to taste blood and like it; to brave death and care nothing for life; to hope for letters and get none; to hope for the end of the war and see none; to find in victory no more than the beginning of another march; to look for promotion and get none; to pass from death and danger to idleness and corruption; to ask for furloughs and get none, and finally, to despair, and hope for death to end his sufferings. The slave-driver is now become a butcher; the slave-holder, a pillager; he who found divine authority to support slavery in sermons now finds it in action; he who was led by fanatical politicians is now led by fanatical generals; and he who once had only the instincts, has now the practice and habit of shedding Northern blood.

These two years of carnage and suffering, from sixteen to eighteen when the character is mobile and pliable, and which he would naturally spend at college among poets and mythologies and tutors, are spent on picket, with fierce veterans, in drunken quarrels, with cards, with oaths, in delirious charges, amid shot and shell, amid moaning wounded and stinking dead, until, at eighteen he has the experience of a Cambronne, the ferocity of an Attilla, and the cruelty of a Tartar. This, gentlemen, is the horrible demoralization of civil war. It makes loyalty a farce, justifies perjury, dignifies murder, instills ferocity, scorns religion and enjoins assassination as a duty. And whose fault is it that he was so demoralized, and so educated in public vices, instead of public virtues, on the field of war? Let us be just and not shrink from the inquiry. Was it our forefathers who sowed the seed of discord in the character of Union? If so, then let their memories pay the penalty; but spare the fruit which has involuntarily ripened in the heart of this boy. Was it the southern leaders? Then let them pay the penalty; but spare their ignorant and misguided tool. Was it General Lee and Jackson and Hill, who were his immediate models and tutors in crime? Then punish them; but spare their pupil. Was it, perhaps, fanatical malcontents among the Northern men who first lighted the torch of war? Then extirpate them from the land, but spare the boy whose passions caught fire, and burnt until they consumed him. Rest then, the responsibility of this war with whom it will—with the living or dead, with the vicissitudes of things or in the invisible plans of God—it is not with this plastic boy who came into the world in the year of the annexation of Texas, has lived but four administrations, and is younger than the last compromise with slavery. He is the moral product of the war, and belongs to them who first begun it.

Now, I hear it said, true, that the boy has been a rebel soldier, and we can forgive him; but we can not forgive assassins. Let us, for a moment, compare a rebel soldier with the prisoner, and see wherein they differ. The best rebel soldiers are native southerners. So is he. The best rebel soldiers have for four years longed to capture Washington, and put its Government to the sword. So has he. The best rebel soldiers have fought on their own hook, after the fashion of the provincials during the Revolution, finding their own knives, their own horses, their own pistols. So has he. The best rebel soldiers have fired at Mr. Lincoln and Mr. Seward, have approached the city by stealth from Baltimore, and aimed to destroy the Government by a sudden blow. So has he. The best rebel soldiers have picked off high officers in the Government—Kearny, Stevens, Baker, Wadsworth, Lyon, Sedgwick. So has he.

What, then, has he done that every rebel soldier has not tried to do? Only this: He has shown a higher courage, a bitterer hate, and a more ready sacrifice; he has aimed at the head of a department, instead of the head of a corps; he has struck at the head of a nation, instead of at its limbs, he has struck in the day of his humiliation, when nothing was to be accomplished but revenge, and when he believed he was killing an oppressor. As Arnold Vinkelreid was braver than all the combined legions of Switzerland, when he

> Felt as though himself were he
> On whose sole arm hung victory.

As Leonidas, who thought himself in the gap of Thermopylae, was braver than all the Grecian hosts; as Mucius Seaevola was the bravest of the Roman youth when he approached Porsena with intent to assassinate, and said: "Hostis hostem occidere volui; nec ad mortem minus animi est, quam fuit ad coedem. Et facere et pati fortia, Romanum est"; so was this youth braver than all the rebel hosts when he came to offer up his life by killing the chief of the enemy.

As Harmedius and Aristogeton were more careless of their lives than the rest of the Athenian youth when they killed Hippias and Hipparchus, as Brutus said on the market place: "As I slew my best lover for the good of Rome, I have the same dagger for myself when it shall please my country to heed my death"; so was this boy more ready to offer up his life for what he believed to be the good of his country. And as Gerard was the bitterest Catholic of the Netherlands when he slew the Prince of Orange; Ravaillac the bitterest enemy of the Protestants when he slew Henry IV; as Jacques Clement was the bitterest Catholic when he killed Henry III; as Orsini was the most bitter Italian when he tried to kill Louis Napoleon, so this boy remembering his two slaughtered brothers, was the bitterest Southerner of all that defied the Government.

Courage, then martyrdom, inextinguishable hate for oppression, are his sins. Now, if courage be a crime, then have you and I, and all of us, who have braved death, been criminals? Then are the emblems of valor, which a grateful country has placed upon your shoulders and breasts, but marks of crime. Is readiness to be sacrificed for the common good a crime? Then are the millions of heroic youths, who have left the plow and girded the sword for four years, but criminals. Then is our banner but a flag of crime; then are our battlefields but loathsome scenes of general fraticidal murder. Is then, undying hatred for that which is believed to be oppression a crime? Then was our Revolution but successful crime. Then were the struggles of Tyrol of Hungary, of Venice, of Greece, but unsuccessful crimes. Then was Byron a traitor to Greece, Garibaldi a traitor to Austria, Kossuth a traitor to Austria, Hofer a traitor to Austria, and Washington a traitor to England. Mark, throughout the history of the world, there is no lesson taught in clearer language than that the noblest deed of men is to free the world of oppressors. But I hear students of history reply: True; but they must have been oppressors. Granted; but who is to be the judge? There can be no one but the assassin himself. It is he and he only, who takes the risk of becoming a deliverer, or a foul and parricidal murderer. Let us, then, see what these people were, against whom he aimed his blow, and what they appeared to him. In truth, if you seek for characters in history, you will find none further removed from the oppressors than our late President and the Secretary of State. The one was the Great Emancipator, the deliverer of a race from bondage, the great *salvator,* the deliverer of a nation from civil war. The other was the great pacificator, the savior from foreign war, the uniter of factions, the constant prophet and messenger of good will and peace. This is who they seemed to us; but such were they not in the eyes of this boy, or of five million of his fellow countrymen. To them, the one appeared as a usurper of power, a violator of laws, a cruel jester, an invader, a destroyer of life, liberty and property; the other a cunning time server, an adviser in oppression, and a slippery advocate of an irrepressible conflict. These Southern men had long borne power, and in their obscurity, felt the envy for greatness which once cried:

> Ye gods! It doth amaze us,
> A man of such a feeble temper should
> So get the start of the majestic world
> And bear the palm alone
> * * *
> Why man, he doth bestride the narrow world
> Like a Colossus, and we petty men
> Walk under his huge legs, and peep about
> To find ourselves dishonorable graves.

This was his idea of Mr. Lincoln and Mr. Seward. This was what he heard in Florida, among the village politicians. This was what he read in the Richmond papers, in the orders of the generals, in the gossip of the camp-fire, in the letters that he got from home. Every farmer by whose well he filled his canteen told him that; every Southern lass that waved her handkerchief toward him repeated it; his mother in mourning told it; every prisoner returned from Northern prisons told it; every wayside cripple but confirmed it. Lincoln, the oppressor, was in the air, it was in the echo of the drum, it was in the whizzing of the shell, it came on every breeze that floated from the North. Wonder was his terror; strange, indeed is it that charity and liberty should be thus misconstrued. Let us, then, remember that if he was wrong he erred on the side of courage, on the side of self-sacrifice, and on the side of hatred to what he believed to be oppression; that he differs from the Southern army simply because he surpassed it in courage; that he differed from a patriot and a martyr, simply because he was mistaken in his duty.

If then, you praise men because they kill such as they believe oppressors, you must praise him; if you praise men who are ready to die for their country, you will praise him; and if you applaud those who show any courage superior to the rest of mankind you will applaud him.

III. But there is a third school before him. From Gettysburg he was sent to West Buildings Hospital, Pratt Street, Baltimore, and remained until October 1863, when, seeing no hope of an exchange, he deserted for his regiment, and walking through Winchester, met a regiment of cavalry at Fauquier. Not being able to get through our lines, he was joined to this arm of the service, and remained in that service until January 1, 1865. On that day, we see by the narrative of Mrs. Grant, he saved the lives of two Union soldiers. About the same time he, like many of the Southern soldiers, began to despair of the Confederacy, came to Alexandria, sold his horse, gave his name as Payne, took the Oath of Allegiance as a refugee from Fauquier, went to Baltimore, took a room at the house of Mrs. Branson, the lady he had met at Gettysburg and resolved to wait for the return of peace. Now, let us see what he learned in the third school.

The rebel cavalry of Northern Virginia, as we now know, was considered, in the Southern Army, the elite of their horsemen. Dismounted cavalrymen of the Army of the Potomac were sent to Northern Virginia, remounted and then returned to their commands. In the spirit of war, however, they differed materially from the rest of the Southern forces. First, they came intimately in contact with the people of Loudon and Fauquier, who had suffered most from the war, and whose hatred of Northern troops was more bitter, so they fought rather from personal hate, and in individual contests, than from political sentiments, and in battle. Accordingly, whatever edge of acrimony was wanting in the temper of Powell he obtained at the houses of ruined slaveholders in Leesburg, Aldie, Middleburg, and Upperville. It was also the custom of these soldiers, and esteemed honorable from their standpoint, to capture quartermasters and paymasters, lie in wait for bearers of dispatches and important generals, and to make sudden attacks and hurried retreats. Accordingly, if he wanted a certain feline intrepidity in planning and escaping—a capacity to approach by stealth, execute with rapidity, and hurry off before his victims had recovered from their consternation—we may well believe that he learned it in this third school. And who is responsible for the third school? His Colonel? Then let him be punished. His Captain? He is now at liberty. General Lee? Then let him abide the consequences. Jefferson Davis who commissioned him? Then let the blow fall on him. This boy comes here with no marvellous spirit of fury, that we should wonder and say, where has he learned all this? Where among men are savages formed like this? He comes here fresh from Northern Virginia, with all its sorrow and all its bitterness. On the tablets of his memory are written curses of many a ruined master; in his ears are ringing the cries of women and children and the moans of dying men. Before his eyes are visions of burning barns, ravaged fields, a people prostrate, humble, starving, homeless—a land once beautiful, now a barren waste, peopled by famine, disease, and ruin—and these have brought him here to see a quick revenge. We know that we have done these things righteously, with malice toward none, for the salvation of the State, and for liberty. But the wail of woe and lamentation is not the less piercing; the thirst for a dire, bitter and consuming revenge, is not the less keen.... As the woes of Normandy brought Charlotte Corday to the Chamber of Murat, as the humiliations of France brought Louvel to the side of the Duke de Berri, as the ravages in Thuringia brought Stappa to Napoleon at Schonbronn, so is the prisoner at the bar the messenger of Virginia's sorrow and bitterness to the chamber of the Secretary of State. And how are we to meet this woe and bitterness and their deluded messenger? In anger? That were only to confess that we were wrong in inflicting them. No; rather let us say, "What we have done is more in love than in hate. Let us forget the past. For your sorrows there is sympathy—for your bitterness there is charity. From henceforward let there be peace, and let the great sacrifice which we have paid make us forever even."

IV. But there is a fourth school before him—the school of necessity.

Arrived at Baltimore and having taken up residence with Mrs. Branson, he looked around for something to do. He had no trade or profession. The period in which he would have learned one was spent in the army; and we know how abhorrent it was to men of the South to engage in manual labor; and as his hands attest, he has never engaged in any. Accordingly, in perplexity about his future—for the little money he got for his horse was fast going—he whiled away the time in reading medical books and brooding in his chamber. While in this condition, unable to get home, unable to see how he was to live at Baltimore, the fracas occurred by which he was arrested, brought before the Provost Marshal, and ordered North of Philidelphia.

Picture to yourself the condition of this unfortunate victim of Southern fanaticism, suddenly again cast into the street and exiled from Baltimore, a stranger, sundered from his only friends, in a strange land. He thinks of his own home in far-off Florida, but between him and it are a thousand miles and a rebel army on whose rolls he is a deserter. He thinks of rejoining that army, but between him and it are a Union army. He thinks of the unknown North into which he is banished, but his fingers refuse the spade; he thinks of a profession, but the very dream of one is now a mockery; he thinks of going where no one knows him but fears that after all the curse of secession will follow him; he thinks of eluding the authorities and staying at Baltimore, but then he is afraid of compromising his friends and leaves them. Everywhere the sky is dark. Among Northern men he is persecuted, for he is a rebel; among Southern men at Baltimore he is despised, for he is a recreant Southerner; among Southern men at home he is a by-word, for he is a deserter. The earth seems to reject him, and God and man to be against him.

Now, if there be any man in this Court who has ever wandered, penniless, homeless, friendless, in that worst of solitudes, the streets of a strange city, with hunger at his stomach, and a great sense of wrong at his heart, in rags, and these rags betraying him as a thing to be despised and spurned; afraid of meeting at every corner the piercing eye of a Government detective; too proud to beg, and when hunger overcame pride, rejected with a frown, that man will understand how the prisoner felt in the beginning of March 1865. If there be any man who has ever been hunted down by misery in his youth, and before much sorrow had made the burden easy, until he wondered why he was born, and hid his face in his hands praying to God to end his pain forever, he can, also understand how in the fulness of suffering, he has been brother to the accused.

Well, indeed, had it been for him if some angel of mercy had on that day, as he wandered a hungry specter through the streets of Baltimore, with flashing eyes and disordered hair, stretched forth her hand and said: "Here is bread; take, eat and live." A loaf of bread might have saved him; a single word of kindness might have saved him; the gracious lick of a friendly dog might have saved the glow of a once generous heart from going out forever. We have all, my friends, had the turning points in our lives, and we all reckon back to a time when we stood in the midst of gloom, and suddenly it was a glorious day, for we found a plank and reached the shore. His Creator, in His inscrutible [sic] wisdom, thought it good there should be no ray of light, no beckoning hand, no hope for the prisoner. Perhaps it had been better if he had dragged himself to the pier and ended his career in suicide. It was ordered that his very weariness should make him the prey of a human devil. We can already forsee the consequences. He is desperate, anxious for death, only he is a soldier, and he will not die ingloriously, after having faced death a hundred times. He is pursued by the Government in which he had confided, and for which he had deserted his own; pursued, tracked, followed like an outlaw among mankind. He will show that Northern Government that he is not a dog, and that Southern Government that he is not a traitor; and give him but a chance, and he will with one stroke, pay off the scores he owes abolitionists, restore himself in the eyes of his comrade in arms, and throw himself into the arms of a pitiful eternity.

And who is to blame that he was urged to desperation and consequent revenge? I answer, this civil war. The civil war took him from the magnolias and orange groves of Florida, and left him a waif upon the pavements of a Northern city. The civil war took the independent farmer from his fields, and left him a begger among strangers. The civil war took him from honest pursuits and professions and left him to make his living without any accomplishments than dexterity in murder. The civil war forbade him a home among Northern men, after it had taken him away from his home in the South. The civil war made him an outcast and a fugitive on the face of the earth; took the bread out of his mouth, and gave him the alternative of dying obscurely by his own hand or notoriously by the death of a public officer.

V. The education of our farmer's boy is now complete. He has been in four schools. Slavery has taught him to wink at murder, the Southern army has taught him to practice and justify murder, cavalry warfare has taught him to love murder, necessity has taught him resolution to commit murder. He needs no further education; his four terms are complete, and he graduates an assassin! And of this college, we the re-united people of the United States, have been the stern tutors, guides and professors. It needs now only that someone should employ him.

I need not pursue his dolorous history further. You know the rest. If you did not know it, you could infer it from what has gone before. That he should meet Booth at Barnum's Hotel, enter into his plans eagerly, and execute them willingly, are matters of course. That he should care nothing for money, but only for revenge; that he should hate the Lincoln

Government like a slaveholder; that he could enter the house of a cabinet officer like a guerrilla; that he should try to murder, and justify his murder like a Southern soldier; that he should then give himself up willingly, as one who exchanges the penalties of assassination for suicide, that he should sit here a statue, as one who fears no earthly terrors, and should tell the doctors, calmly and stoically, that he only did what he thought was right—all these things are certain to follow as use, education and employment necessity.

Now, in considering the condition of Powell at this crisis, I do not ask you to believe he was insane. That is a declaration of mental disease of which I am no judge. I only ask you to believe that he was human—a human being in the last stage of desperation, and obeying self-preservation, nature's first law. It is acknowledged by all that the possession of reason only makes man responsible for crime. Now, there are two ways in which reason is vanquished. One is when the passions make war against reason and drive her from the throne, which is called insanity. Another is when the necessities of the body overcome the suggestions of the mind, a state in which the reason is a helpless captive, and if you find that while his reason was so in captivity, he surrendered to temptation, I am sure you will not set it to the credit, not of reason, but of the body, whose wants were imperious while there was yet no reason in it, in childhood, and which will again exist without reason after death.

At the beginning of the war, Powell, one night, secured a pass and went to the theater at Richmond. It was the first play that Powell ever saw, and he was spellbound with that magical influence wielded by the stage over such, to whom its tinsel is reality. But he was chiefly attracted by the voice and manner of one of the actors. He was a young man of about twenty-five years, with large lustrous eyes, a graceful form, features classical and regular as a statue, and a rich voice that lingered in the ears of those who heard him. Although only a private soldier, Powell considered himself the equal of any man, and after the play was over, sought and gained an introduction to the actor. Never were two natures thrown together so different, yet so well calculated, the one to rule, the other to be ruled. The soldier was tall, awkward, rough, frank, generous and illiterate. The actor was delicate of mold, polished, graceful, subtle, with a brilliant fancy, and an abundant stock of reading. Each was what the other was not, and each found in the other an admirer of the other's qualities. The actor was pleased to have a follower so powerful in his muscles, and Powell was irresistibly drawn to follow a man so wondrously fascinating and intellectual. They saw enough of one another to form a close intimacy and confirm the control of the actor over Powell, and parted, not to meet for nearly four years.

In the twilight of that memorable day in March, which I have described, Powell was dragging himself slowly along the street past Barnum's Hotel—a poor creature overcome by destiny. Suddenly a familiar voice hailed him. Looking up the steps he saw the face of the Richmond actor. The actor on his side expressed astonishment to find Powell in such a plight—for the light in the eyes of a desperate man needs no translation—and in that distant city. Powell answered him in a few words: "Booth! I want bread—I am starving!" In ordinary circumstances, I do not doubt that Booth would have said, "Come in and eat"; he did not tell him to go and die, but he seized with eagerness upon this poor man's hunger to wind about him his accursed toils, saying, "I will give you as much money as you want, but first you must swear to stick by me. It is in the oil business." An empty stomach is not captious of oaths, and Powell then swore that fatal oath, binding his soul as firmly to Booth as Faust to Mephistopheles, and went in and feasted. Next morning, Booth gave him money enough to buy a change of clothing and keep him for a week. Powell now became anxious to know what plan it was that was to make him rich, but Booth answered evasively that it was in the oil business. He knew well enough that he had to do with a desperate man, but he knew, also, that any proposition of a guilty character might yet be rejected. He must get full control of this desperate tool, and instill into his nature all the subtle monomania of his own. Accordingly he proceeded to secure every thought and emotion of Powell. With a master pencil he painted before the eyes of this boy the injuries of the South and the guilt of her oppressors. He reminded him of devastated homes, Negroes freed, women ravished, the graves of his brothers on a thousand hillsides. He reminded him that he was a traitor to the Southern cause and that it was necessary he should regain the favor of his country. He pointed out to him his desperate condition—a fugitive from his friends, and an exile among strangers. He touched him upon his pride, and showed him how he was born a gentleman, and ought to live like a gentleman. He touched upon his helplessness, and showed him that there was no hope for him, in peace or war, in heaven or earth, except by rendering a great service to the South. He touched upon his melancholy and said if he must die, he should offer up his life in a manner that would bequeath his name as a blessing to posterity. Powell now awoke from the depth of despair to the highest pinnacle of agonized excitement. It was as if he had been breathing that subtle Eastern poison, wherein the victim sees swimming before his eyes a vision of more than celestial felicity, but far off and unattainable. What wonder he swam in dreams of delicious pain! Instead of that former melancholy, he felt an eager desire to live. Instead of that long torpor, he felt all the old wounds bleeding again, and burned to avenge the South. Instead of laboring like a Negro, he saw a vague vision of rolling in boundless wealth. Instead of being cursed by his kinsmen, he was fired with zeal to be cherished as one of her chief martyrs. Instead of being the toy of fortune, he dreamed of being her conqueror. But yet he saw no avenue to all this, and spell-bound as he was, turned to his tormentor, who held him as firmly as ever Genii did their fabled imps, for the explanation, for the means and quick road to happiness. Booth saw his victim was ready, and hastened to impart his mysterious plans. The first plan was to go to Washington, take a ride with confederates on horseback, to the Soldier's Home, capture the President, and deliver him to the Rebel authorities. This failed. The second plan was to kill the heads of the State—a plan first broached to Payne on the evening of the 14th of April, at eight o'clock.

Booth, on the evening of the 14th, at eight o'clock told him the hour had struck; placed in his hands the knife, the revolver and the bogus package of medicine; told him to do his duty, and gave him a horse with directions to meet beyond the Anacostia Bridge; and he went and did the deed. I have asked why he did it. His only answer is: "Because I believed it my duty."

VI. Now let us not be deceived by the special name of assassination and confound it with the conscientious killing of what is believed to be an oppressor. When we read of assassination we involuntarily bring to mind examples of men hired by statesmen to make away with princes. There is the Italian perfumer, Rogeri, of Catherine of Medici; there is Orloff of Catherine, and Alexander of Russia; we think of the tools used by Tiberius, by Richard III, Philip the II, Mary of Scotland, by Louis XI, and our minds are filled with associations with State murders accomplished by tigers in human shape killing for gold.

But there is another type of assassination and of so-called assassins. That comes to pass when a fanatic, religious or political, deems it his duty to offer up his life in exchange for the life he believes to be a public enemy. This is the hand of Kotzebue, the Corday of Murat, the Count Ankerstroem of Gustavus III, the Brutus of Caesar, the Gerard of Orange, the Ravaillac of Henry IV—men who may ally themselves with others, but who receive their orders immediately, as they believe, from God Himself.

The first order kills for money, it is hired by princes, it would for money kill its employers, it uses concealment, it is ashamed, it strikes in masks and dominoes, and when caught gives way to despair. Not so the second order. It glories in its deed, it goes joyfully to its own death, it has commandments from Heaven, it stabs without changing its dress, it makes no effort to escape, it gladly delivers itself up; on trial it is composed as on the eve of triumph, it justifies its crime, it makes no defense, and longs for death, saying in the words of Corday, "Tomorrow I hope to meet Brutus and the other patriots in Elysium."

It needs no argument to show to which class the prisoner belongs. He did, indeed consort with others, but he lent his ear only, as one would say:

> What is that you would impart to me?
> If it aught toward the general good
> Set honor in one eye and death in the other,
> And I will look on both indifferently;
> For, let the gods so speed me, as I love
> The name of honor more than I fear death.

You have not shown that any gold has soiled his motive. You have shown that he gained from others plans, made with them agreements of time and place; but the motive, the spirit, the self-sacrifice, the courage, the justification, the longing for death is all his own. He alone says he thought it was his duty.

I say he is the fanatic, and not the hired tool; the soldier who derived his orders from conscience, and who, in the applause of that tribunal, smiles at all earthly trials. How else do you explain his bearing? He smiles at all that you can do against him. To him, the clanking of these chains is the sweet music of his triumph. The efforts of the prosecution and its bitter witness to convict him are but the confirmation of his glory. The power and majesty of the Government brought upon his head seem but clear and pleasant praises for his deed. He lives in that land of imagination where it seems to him legions of the souls of Southern soldiers wait to crown him as their chief commander. He sits here like a conqueror; for four weeks he has held his head erect when all others have quailed; he meets the stare of curiosity like a king might face his subjects; he keeps his state even in his cell, and the very keepers, in admiration, acknowledge him their master. Now, I dare not call him mad—the doctors have forbidden it. I might say that if ever men fell within that definition of Chief Justice Shaw of insanity, "A very common instance is where a person fully believes the act he is doing is done by the immediate command of God, and he acts under the delusive but sincere belief that what he is doing is by command of a superior power, which supercedes [sic] all human laws and the laws of nature," this is the man. But the doctors have said he is not insane, and though he fills the legal definition he does not fill the medical, and, therefore, I cannot hope that you will hold him insane.

But I appeal from medical definitions and from legal definitions to your good sense, and I ask you to explain to me the riddle of this man's conduct in any other way that he is a political fanatic; a monomaniac on the subject of his duty—call him sane or insane—yet one who is responsible only to that God from which he derives his commandments. Before another tribunal, where all his previous life might be inquired into, and where time would be given for all this mystery to be unraveled, I do not hesitate to say I could convince the judges beyond a doubt that he is no more responsible for what he has done to the laws of the United States than a Chinaman whom custom and religion give the right to strangle his daughters. You have not the time, and I must end this inquiry. But as you are sworn to try this man on your consciences, so I charge you to give him the benefit of his.

Gentlemen, when I look at the prisoner, and see (as it has been my duty for four weeks to see) the calm composure with which he has gone through the horrors of this trial; the cheerful and firm fortitude with which he has listened to the evidence against him, and with which he has endured the gaze of the public, as well as the ignominy of the fetters; the frank and honest way in which he speaks of his crime, as a thing revolting in itself, but due to a cause which he thinks holy; and more than all, the settled conviction, which robs the trial of all terrors, that he has but obeyed the voice of custom, of education, and conscience; and the calm serenity with which he retards all pains that man can inflict upon him as contemptible, and part of his duty to endure, I can not help being proud—though blood is on his hands—that such fortitude, unparalleled that throughout the coming vicissitudes of life, in all perplexities and doubts, on all occasions of right and wrong, in all misconstructions and trials, I may have so cheering, so brave so earnest a conviction that I have done my duty.

And what is that duty? What is this doing right? Ask the Indian, as he returns to his wigwam, laden with the dripping scalps of the dispossessors of the soil, why he has done it, and he will answer you, with a flourish of his tomahawk and his face turned toward Heaven, that he is doing right—the Great Spirit has commanded it. Ask the Hindoo, as he disembowels some English officer by the Ganges, and riots in his blood, the reason for his crime, and he will tell you it is his duty, he is doing right—the Brahmins have decreed it. Consult the records of the Vendee, and see why Charlette and Gastou murdered the Republican soldiery in ambuscades and thickets, and you will find they entered, at the bar of the Parisian Court, the plea that they were doing right; it was their duty. Now go to the devastated South; speak with a few of the five millions, and ask them why they have thirsted for and taken Northern blood in secret places, murdered stragglers, waylaid orderlies, and killed by stealth, and they will answer you, pointing to the charred remains of some ancestral home and some neighboring hill dotted with graves. Because it was their duty; because we felt bound in conscience to do it.

Let us not undervalue the force of the conscience. It is man's sole dictator, his highest judge, his last resort. Without it he is but an erring wanderer, tossed by every kind of passion, interest, and caprice. With it, his course is as certain and regular as the stars. In labor it cheers him; in pleasure it restrains him; to all manner of good things it prompts him; from all manner of evil it defends him. In peace it teaches him to labor; in war to fight; for religion it tells him to fear God; for his country it says, protect and defend it; for himself it says, thy country, thy home, thy friends first, and thyself last. It is this spark of heavenly fire which has supported martyrs at the stake; which has sustained good men on the scaffold; which brought liberty and preserved it in this land for you and me and all of us. Let us, then, respect it, even when it speaks in a voice which we can not understand. Let us honor it as the same voice which directs us, even when it directs others to a grievous fault. We are but men. The same God who created us all, may reconcile all that, and find in our difference but ignorance on the one side and ignorance on the other. And if we dare to judge the dictates of conscience, do we not arrogate to ourselves the prerogatives of the sovereign Lawgiver of the Universe, who gave the rule, "Judge not, that ye be not judged?" Therefore, considering that we have the limit set, and that we can not go beyond without becoming in turn transgressors, let us leave that cause with Him who measures the conduct of men by no standard of success, but by obedience to the invariable dictates of conscience. For us it is enough that we are weak judges of weak men. If we were beasts, unconscious of the sacred limits of right and wrong, we might excuse him, if we were Gods and superior to destiny, we might destroy him; but as we are men who know our duties, but also our weaknesses, often seek good but do evil, therefore let us do the work of man to man—punish and reform him.

VII. Gentlemen, I have done with a narrative and reflections. We now know that this Florida boy is not a fiend, but an object rather of compassion. We now know that slavery made him immoral, that war made him a murderer, and that necessity, revenge, and delusion made him an assassin. We now know that in all regards he is like us, only, that he was taught to believe right when we were taught to believe wrong; and that if we had been taught in his school, we would be like him, and if he had been taught in ours, he would be like us. We know, that from his point of view, he justifies the murder of the Secretary of State; we know that, from our standpoint, we would gladly have seen, for four years, the death of the rebel Secretary of State. We know that we were on the side of the Government, because we were born North; we know that he was against it because he was born South; and that had we been born South we would have been in his place, and had he been born North, he would be in ours. We know, also, that all the enemy desired the death of the President, and that he surpassed them only in courage; and that if we forgive them who killed our brothers, we must, in consistency, forgive him who tried to kill Mr. Seward, because he thought Mr. Seward guilty of murdering his brothers.

We know further, that this man desires to die, in order to gain the full crown of martyrdom; and that, therefore, if we gratify him, he will triumph over us; but if we spare him, we will triumph over him. We know, also, that the public can gain nothing by his death from the example; for if he dies as he lived, they will be more anxious to emulate his bravery, as Adam Luc, a deputy from Mentz, who on the death of Corday, fired with admiration, wrote to the tribunal requesting to die like Charlotte Corday, while the multitude exclaimed: "She is greater than Brutus." But if he is suffered to live, he will receive the worst punishment—obscurity—and the public will have nothing to admire. We also know, and we can not consider it too much, that he has killed no man, and that if he be put to death we shall have the anomaly of the victim surviving the murderer; and that under the law, this man can be punished only for assault and battery with intent to kill and therefore, imprisoned. We know, also, that we are at the end of a civil war, a time when it is desirable there should be no further mention or remembrance of fraternal strife. If we put this man to death, he will live forever in the hearts of his comrades, and his memory will forever keep our brethren from us. If, moreover, we put him to death, we will show that war is still in our hearts, and that we are only content to live with them because we have subdued them.

Finally, we know that if we let him live and teach him better, we show the whole world that this war was carried on to undeceive a deluded people and to maintain the supremacy of the laws, so that now the laws are supreme, we may begin with reform; but if we put him to death we show only that we are vindictive, and use our victory only to gratify our anger. Let him, then live. His youth asks it, fraternity asks it, the laws ask it, our own sins ask it, the public good demands it. Because you and I taught him the code of assassination in slavery;

because you and I brought about a civil war, which practiced him in assassination and made him justify it; because you and I spurned him from us when he sought revenge with us, and bade him destroy himself, ignobly by his own hand, or grandly by assassination; because, in short, you and I have made this boy what he is, lest we who are really ourselves guilty of this attempt at murder, should perpetrate a real murder, let him live, if not for his sake, for our own. Take from the refugee his desperation, and you have the cavalryman; take from the cavalryman his hate, and you have the soldier of Hill; take from the soldier his marital habits, and you have the slave-holder; take from the slave-holder his slavery and you have again the pure and simple child, who four years ago, went singing in innocence over the land.

Before I close, one word from myself. I have heretofore spoken of the prisoner as his counsel; I may also speak of him in my character as a man; and I can testify that in the four weeks' acquaintance I have had, hearing him converse with freedom and explain all his secret thoughts, in spite of the odious crime with which he is charged, I have formed an estimate of him little short of admiration, for his honesty of purpose, freedom from deception and malice, and courageous resolution to abide by the principles to which he was reared. I find in him none of that obstinacy which perseveres in crime because it is committed, and hopes to secure admiration in a feigned consistency. Neither is there about him a false desire for notoriety, nor a cowardly effort to screen himself from punishment; only one prominent anxiety—that is, lest people should think him a hired assassin or a brute; an aversion to being made a public spectacle of, and a desire to be tried at the hands of his fellow-citizens. Altogether, I think we may safely apply to him, without spurious sympathy or exaggeration, the words which were said of Brutus—

> This was the noblest Roman of them all
> All the conspirators, save only he
> Did that they did in envy of great Caesar;
> He only, in a general honest thought,
> And common good to all, made one of them.
> His life was gentle, and the elements
> So mixed in him, that nature might stand up
> And say to all the world, "This was a man!"

I commit him, then—without hesitation to your charge. You have fought on the same fields, and as you have never been wanting in mercy to the defeated, so I know you will not be wanting in mercy to him. You have all commanded private soldiers, and as you could estimate the enthusiasm of your own men, so you will know how to estimate the enthusiasm of those who fought against you. The lives of all of you have shown that you were guided in all perplexities by the stern and infallible dictates of conscience and duty, and I know that you will understand and weigh in your judgment of the prisoner, dictates and duties so kindred to your own.

(Lewis Payne)

Appendix I

Following are the Rev. Dr. Abram Dunn Gillette's recollections of young Powell's last hours in the death cell and on the gallows as written by the clergyman's son, Daniel Gillette. This is perhaps the most revealing of Powell's so-called confessions.

Appendix I

The Last Days of Payne

An Interesting Contribution to the History of the Assassination
THE ASSAILANT OF SEWARD WAS THE SON OF A BAPTIST
MINISTER HIS STORY AS TOLD TO THE FATHER OF A
FEDERAL SOLDIER—REPENTANT AND PERFECTLY PREPARED
FOR DEATH—THE ASSASSIN'S OWN FATHER—SOME PATHETIC LETTERS
WRITTEN AFTER THE HANGING—WHAT PAYNE SAID OF MRS. SURRATT
TO THE EDITOR OF THE *WORLD:*

There lies before me the original death warrant of Lewis Thornton Powell, alias Payne, the boy who made a shambles of the house of Secretary Seward on the night of April 14, 1865, leaving behind him as he fled, the mangled and prostrate bodies of five victims of his awful rage—the Secretary and the four who attempted the rescue of their master.

The warrant bears the date of July 5, 1865, and is in the hand of Assistant Adjt. General H. D. Townsend. Accompanying it is a printed copy of the charge and specifications against all the conspirators, including the names of the President of the Confederate States and his Cabinet—who were presumably tried and convicted under the same indictment. On the official envelope enclosing both documents, I found the following indorsement in the microscopic characters of General Hancock:

To be delivered in person by Major-General Hartranft, Mil. Gov., Mil. Prison.
Wm. S. Hancock, Major-Gen., U.S. Vols., Commanding M. M. Division
Washington Arsenal, June 6, 1865, 11 o'clock A.M.

Even the battle-tested nerves of Gen. Hancock were stirred by the excitement of the moment—as he has written June for July 6—the President's approval of the findings and sentences of the Military Commission having been made public July 5, a month later than the General's endorsement would seem to indicate.

On the reverse of the envelope, my father had written in pencil:

This death warrant was given me by Payne less than an hour before his execution. I was in his cell and with him at the last moment of his life.
A. D. Gillette

In the Lincoln history, I find Payne variously characterized. First as a "disbanded rebel soldier from Florida," then "a brutal, stalwart, cruel simple-minded boy from Florida," and lastly "a deserter from a Confederate Florida regiment."

I am neither prepared to dispute nor disposed to qualify any or either of these indictments, yet one might easily suggest that a "disbanded soldier" and a "deserter" were scarcely interchangable terms, even in Confederate military ethics. As for the man himself, his character and his right to a somewhat less horrible distinction, I have thought that a glimpse of his home and his hitherto unuttered plea for himself might have some interest to those who now can look calmly back upon the wretched days that made his motive and his crime possible.

What I venture to relate came to me from the lips of my venerated father, who from the time of the death of Payne and his companions, had been determined upon by the authorities, scarcely ever left his side.

Payne had himself designated Dr. Gillette as his spiritual advisor, to which call the

Doctor responded in total ignorance of the young man or any part of his history. To the solemn functions of such an office were soon added a new tenderness and pathos when Payne admitted his identity as Powell and the son of a Baptist clergyman.

Three or four days before the execution, Dr. Gillette received notice from the War Department that Payne had requested his services. The notice was accompanied by a safe conduct admitting him to the military prison at all times. As before stated, Dr. Gillette knew nothing of the young man and therefore was much concerned to learn why he had chosen him, a loyalist in preference to other clergymen of his own faith who were in admitted sympathy with the Southern Cause.

In the course of the explanation much of the story leading up to the crime was revealed. There was but one controlling reason for his choice, Payne said, and that was that he had heard my father preach not long before.

"Do you remember," he asked, "a bitter, sleety Sunday last Febuary, when you preached in the Rev. Dr. Fuller's church in Baltimore? It was then I heard you. I sat with two ladies in one of the end pews to the right of the pulpit. There were scarcely more than a score of people in the church as the walking was so icy and dangerous. My companions and myself were the only occupants of the end pews on either side of the chancel. I had hoped that perhaps you might remember the circumstances, as you frequently turned towards us as though addressing us."

In the course of their subsequent meetings, Payne related that he was a guest in the house of a Baltimore family to which the ladies belonged, and they had invited him to accompany them to service. The head of the house was a party to the scheme then in contemplation, the abduction of Mr. Lincoln. Powell insisted that he was a Confederate soldier, and for months previous, while in the Secret Service of the Confederacy, he had journeyed back and forth from Richmond to Washington and Baltimore in conference with prominent men in the latter city, whom of course, he did not name.

These gentlemen had kept him in funds, encouraging him in many ways and especially with dreams of glory and the lasting gratitude of the Southern people.

Until the morning of the fatal day, no crime more serious than the abduction had been contemplated. It was early in that day that he was instructed as to what was expected of him, a bottle of medicine given to him and the pretext outlined by which he was to gain access to the Secretary's apartment.

Of the actual occurrences in the house of the Secretary that night, he had only confused memories. The moment, the consummation of months of anxious contemplation, determination, lost opportunities, chances and changes had come, and he believed that its frenzy would have prevailed over many more obstacles than there opposed him. He had, however, no sooner mounted his horse and begun his flight than the revulsion came. He saw his crime in its real light and as a crime merely. With this consciousness, an indifference to his fate overwhelmed him. Riding to the boundaries of the city, he abandoned his horse and took shelter in the branches of a tree in which concealment he learned the fate of the President from a troop of cavalry riding by. Daylight found him an aimless wanderer, and hunger drove him back to the city. In the knowledge of the result of the night's work, except the death of Mr. Lincoln, he betook himself to the fatal rendezvous the house of Mrs. Surratt, the only refuge he knew.

Concerning the fate of Mrs. Surratt, Payne spoke with great feeling. Of a prior knowledge of their later deeds he declared her innocent, but did not, of course, deny her interest in their original actions and plans. He never ceased to upbraid himself for seeking the shelter of her home, as in that lay the misfortune of her doom. He hoped, fervently, that she might be spared.

"She at least," he exclaimed, "does not deserve to die with us. If I had no other reason, Doctor, she is a woman, and men do not make war on women."

At the very last, he asked if no respite had come to her and the pitiless fate of the woman seemed his chiefest regret. As for himself, without the least arrogance, brag or mock heroism, he still maintained that his deed made for him a duty when under the spell of its motive. He did not know that he had ever shed human blood before. The powerful and secret friends of the Confederacy within the Northern lines had played upon his imagination with visions of triumph for the Southern Cause and immortal fame for himself. He had been their honored guest in palatial homes and with means which they had supplied, he had come and gone at their bidding.

As for his doom—if he did not welcome it in the form it came to him—he never uttered a word of protest or expressed a pang except as it left the cruel iron in the hearts at home. He said to my father:

"My course is run. I know now how foolish, vain and wholly useless it is and must have been, and were I set at liberty this morning, I should hope to be dead by sunset, as all men must hereafter point at me as a murderer."

This is the same cry his leader is said to have uttered, "Vain—all is vain!" when he fully realized that even had it been worthy, it came all too late to effect the result and torture of tortures—those who had urged it fled in terror from the thought, while those for whom it was ventured had for it only scorn and loathing.

Upon the scaffold, there was no scene—no theatrics. Bound about the arms and ankles, Powell sat awaiting the final preparations, my father shielding him with an umbrella from the fierce rays of a July sun. Some movement dislodged the doomed man's hat and Dr. Gillette replaced it upon his head. Powell turned and looking up in his friend's face, whispered: "Thank you, Doctor. I shall not need it much longer." A few minutes later and he was dangling with his three companions in crime.

It was a dishonored death for a most unsoldierly deed. At least Payne gave to it something of dignity by calmness, modesty and silence.

Of the spiritual results of Dr. Gillette's mission to young Powell, my father seemed never willing to speak, possibly under a promise to Powell, perchance a concession to the public mind at that time, which was dead to sentiment or to the conditions of the crime, which would have thrown contempt upon the slightest display of religious feeling. That there was some turning to the dear paths from which his wayward feet had wandered so wide and far is shown in the three letters from his father which I find enclosed with the official papers and from which I may be permitted to quote:

Live Oak, E. Fla., Aug. 21, 1865

Rev. Dr. Gillette:
Dear Sir:
 After my best respects, I beg leave to address you a few lines and assure you that it is with the purest intentions I do so, having heard that you were a Baptist Minister; and I being a minister of that branch of the Christian Church. I hope you will please pardon the intrusion.

I ascertained from newspaper extracts—which I presume to be true—that you were with my dear, though unfortunate son, Lewis Thornton Powell, during his last moments on this vain earth. If so, permit me to request you to give me a full statement of his confession in regard to the offense of which he was charged and more especially would I be pleased to hear of his prospects for future life—for I assure you that he received all the moral training and advice it was possible to give and I do hope that his future prospects were such as to ensure an eternal felicity beyond the grave.

I make this request, not for show or from any deleterious motive, but solely for the gratification of myself and family, as you may well know that we, as members of the Baptist Church, are very anxious indeed in reference to the future welfare of our son and brother.

That such a statement was sent the following letter, bearing the date of November 7, 1865, shows. Dr. Gillette kept no copy of his, and no one of his family or friends ever saw the original.

Rev. Dr. Gillette:
Dear Brother:
Your kind favor of the 12th of September last was duly received, and I assure you the contents were read with great interest by myself and family.

Pray accept, my dear brother, my most sincere thanks and my humble gratitude for the many kind services and faithful religious instructions to my dear son, Lewis Thornton. Such acts of kindness, my dear brother, will ever be remembered with heartfelt gratitude by myself and family.

You will confer a favor by presenting my kind regards to Major Eckert, and return him my thanks for his kindness and good will towards our son, Lewis Thornton; also to all others who were kind enough to assist my son. To those I shall ever remain under a debt of gratitude.

Lewis left home to enlist in the war much against the wish of all the family. Previous to and up to the time of his leaving home, he was very pious and consistent, was much respected by all of his associates, and took great interest in the young men's prayer meetings and all other religious services.

His favorite hymn, which he often sang to the family, commenced:
> Farewell, farewell to all below
> My Savior calls ...

Please write as early as possible ... as everything in reference to my son is very interesting to us.

The last of these series is dated March 4, 1866. I read therein:

You state that my son left his Bible, autograph, and other articles with you; also a few articles with some money, which were in the hands of the Assistant Secretary of War....

Please inform me if it is possible I would be permitted to get and remove the remains of my son from Washington, D. C. to my home in Florida? And if so, would I be safe in so doing, and what would be the best plan to remove him? I would not make any effort to remove his remains unless it was perfectly agreeable with the Government authorities...

"Short and simple annals," these fireside touches of a Christian home, to which had come more than a common sorrow. But I look in vain for resentment, protest, or a disposition to know more than the manner of a beloved son's death, and the hope he had of heavenly pardon. Remembering the bitterness, the awful passions that were then beating along the shores of human life, wrecking souls and tearing hearts asunder, I am myself rebuked by the restful calm of this voice and the tender dignity of his prayer. I must doubt, also, if blood-hardened butchers have ever sprung from or dwelt within the influence of souls so purified and sweetened.

Violent deaths meant little to most of us in those times and Dr. Gillette was no stranger to them. The effects, however, of his association with this execution were most lamentable. For days he seemed wholly incapable of duty, while his nights were passed in restless tossings. Frequently would he bury his face in his hands, as though to shut out the sight, exclaiming, "Horrible! Horrible! Horrible!" Nor could he bring himself to the task of telling the miserable story to the stricken family for more than a month after his sad duty had ended.

I stood in the crowd that waited all through the night in front of the house where Mr. Lincoln lay dying, and when for the slightest levity, men were savagely warned of their life. I had just been released from a long captivity in a Confederate stockade. I was not then and am not now in any mood to extenuate the wretched deeds of these more wretched men. It may be possible that there are those who will begrudge the memory of Powell this feeble plea for the world's judgment made to the last friend he knew on earth, but I claim the right to here record it and to say that I, for one, am glad so black a picture is now without relief.

Daniel Gillette.

New York, March 31

Appendix J

Louis Paine ... or Lewis Powell?

In 1965, Vaughn Shelton's book *Mask for Treason* appeared on the Lincoln assassination research scene. This work, dedicated to Otto Eisenschiml, an early chemist turned historian, attempted to provide a new key to the motives behind the assassination. The "key" was in the person of Lewis Powell (Paine).

With laborious detail, Shelton attempts to convince his reader through a nightmare of historical research that "Lewis Paine" did not attempt to assassinate Secretary of State William H. Seward—did not even know Booth and had nothing whatsoever to do with the conspiracy. Indeed the reader is encouraged to believe that "Hugh Louis Paine" and Lewis Thornton Powell (alias Payne/Paine) were two *separate individuals*.

Paine, claims Shelton, was Powell's third cousin—a kinsman with remarkable family resemblance. As a double agent, the villainous Powell assaulted the secretary of state on the night of April 14 and escaped to Canada, leaving his naively innocent cousin "Paine" to suffer the consequences of capital punishment.

Shelton's theory falls flat by comparison of the signatures on Paine's Oath of Allegiance and the signature of L. T. Powell on a quartermaster's clothing receipt for Mosby's Forty-third Battalion.

Discovered by James O. Hall, the signature on the clothing receipt, when compared with that of L. Paine on the Oath of Allegience, bears enough resemblance in the formation of the letters "L" and "P" and in the general appearance or slant of the two signatures to prove beyond a shadow of a doubt that both were written by the same hand.

Beyond the complex absurdity of Shelton's hypothesis, we also have the identity of Powell/Paine by at least two separate individuals who gave particulars concerning an outstanding facial characteristic. Young Lewis Edmonds Payne, son of Dr. Albin S. Payne, with whose family the young Confederate boarded during his stint with Mosby, remembered Powell as having "an imperfection in one of his front teeth." This same characteristic was also noted by Seaton Munroe, a District of Columbia attorney who was present at the inquest of John Wilkes Booth's body and also happened to be on board the *Montauk* when Powell was photographed. Munroe speaks of Powell's "bad teeth" in an article he wrote for the *North American Review,* March 1896. It would seem strange indeed for two men to look so much alike so as to be indistinguishable even down to the very teeth!

And then there was Powell's voice, "small and thin, inclined to tenor." Certainly Mrs. Surratt knew Powell's voice the night of his arrest—and previously. The other boarders had no trouble distinguishing "Wood" from "Payne" or Powell!

Whether or not others were skeptical—Munroe was not:

> Of the truth of the so-called Payne's statements regarding his name and origin, I had abundant evidence to satisfy me within two months after his execution. There is at present residing in Washington a well-known and successful lawyer, a native and Confederate soldier of Florida, who in the early autumn of 1865 became an intimate of my home on his first visit to the North. During one of our strolls about the city, and without disclosing my object, I took him into Gardner's gallery on Seventh Street, where were to be seen photographs of the conspirators. We examined them all casually, and I then called his attention to that of Payne, asking if he perceived in it a likeness to any one. He gave it a closer scrutiny, and then said it "looked like a youngster named Powell." He said that the boy was the son of a minister in Florida. He had not belonged to Powell's company, and had not known him well; but making allowance for the changes that five years might have wrought in his face and form, he felt confident in the recognition of the individual he had known. These and other items I gleaned from my friend, who had never read Colonel Doster's plea, with which, on comparison, I found his statements to coincide.

Nevertheless, there are those who continue to swallow the whole gullible fishbait of Shelton's *Mask* hook, line and sinker in view of recent logical findings by which "Hugh Louis Paine" is unmasked in actuality as Lewis Thornton Powell.

Appendix K

Those Elusive Branson Ladies:
Lewis Powell and His Baltimore Lady Loves

They are, and have been for years, as elusive and as shadowy as ghosts; inscrutable figures in hoop skirts who have glided in and out of the Lincoln assassination story. The Branson sisters of Baltimore are nebulous figures on the periphery. Very little was revealed regarding them at the time and there are still cover ups to unveil; after all, a Victorian lady was not supposed to be placed in the limelight. Her name was to appear in print only twice in her lifetime—at her marriage and at her death—with nothing in between.

Ghostly and fraught with mystery, even their fashionable boarding house at 16 North Eutaw Street has disappeared with time—now in its place is an 1880s red sandstone bank structure, cold, impersonal and solid. Even photographic images of the ladies and their family have failed to make an appearance.

Who and what association did these women have in relation to the Lincoln assassination? They have continued to people the outskirts of the story, fraught with mystery and speculation. One of these ladies held the key to much mystery regarding young Lincoln conspirator Lewis Thornton Powell, alias "Paine." The head of the Branson household, Captain

Joseph Branson, was also "in on the abduction plot" as Powell reiterated to Reverend Dr. Abram Dunn Gillette, his spiritual advisor in the death cell and on the gallows. Just how involved Branson was in the plot has never been determined. The fact that the Branson patriarch was referred to by the title of "Captain" may have had some bearing on his inception into the plot. Captain Branson, a Baltimorean, born in 1796, was a War of 1812 veteran as well as being one of the founding members of the Baltimore chapter of the Improved Order of Red Men; a secret patriotic society which was founded long before the Revolution. It was this particular society which organized the Boston Tea Party in 1773. According to one account, "Joseph Branson was a hatter in the year 1827 at 182 Market Street. He was the son of William Branson, who was engaged in the same business from 1796 to 1817. According to one account, Joseph Branson ranked as the fashionable hatter of that time in Baltimore. He was a man of considerable military distinction in the state of Maryland. He raised and commanded the famous Marion Rifles, a superb military organization of the city to which was accorded the honor of receiving General Lafayette upon his visit to Baltimore in 1824. Mr. Branson is said to have been the first to introduce a thorough system of military tactics in the Monument City. He served several terms in the City Council and was an active, enterprising citizen. In the year 1831 he went out of business and took the position of inspector in the custom house."[1] Branson married Mary Ann Dukehart in Baltimore on November 14, 1826.

Thus the Branson family was one of apparent longstanding and prominence within the city of Baltimore. In 1855, the family was living on Paca Street, but soon relocated to 16 N. Eutaw Street in 1858 and opened what has been described as a "fashionable boarding house."[2] From the one or two photographs which do exist, as well as a bird's eye view lithographed map, the house was an imposing three-story brick Federal style structure with a "stair-step" roof.

Like most Baltimoreans, when the Civil War broke out in 1861, the Branson family was seemingly pro–Confederate. However, recent findings indicate that Captain Branson was playing "both sides" of the conflict.

Recently uncovered documents state that apparently Branson was selling goods (hay and cord wood) from a farm in the country, the owners of whom were related to his wife. Branson was therefore supplying both the Confederacy and the Union—and making a profit on both.[3]

Sisters Maggie and Mary Branson, in 1861, respectively 30 and 28 years old, long past the age when most girls married, volunteered their services as nurses as well as aiding Confederate POWs held in Union prison camps. At least one reference to the girls described them as being "handsome."[4] Unfortunately, a thorough search has refused to turn up any photographic image of either woman. Both ladies had confessed to sending provisions to Confederate prisoners at Forts McHenry and Delaware, Johnson's Island, Camp Chase and Elmira.[5] While both ladies appeared to be ardently "Secesh," Mary seems to have been the spunkier of the two; confessing to Lieutenant H. B. Smith, Chief of Detectives and Assistant Provost Marshal General of Baltimore that "I have *always* been a rebel sympathizer," a fact that her sister Maggie denied to Federal authorities. Both ladies devoted their time to nursing, primarily concerned with the Confederate wounded. In July of 1863, while Mary worked at the notorious Wests Buildings Hospital in Baltimore, Maggie, accompanied by an elderly aunt, Mrs. Du Bois Egerton, journeyed the 54 miles to Gettysburg to

Branson Boarding House highlighted in Sachse's Bird's Eye View of the City of Baltimore, circa 1869 (Library of Congress).

work in the Federal Hospital then located in Old Dorm. Miss Branson was strongly under suspicion as a Confederate sympathizer there and she appears in the memoirs of some of the other Confederate lady nurses at Gettysburg.[6] According to one account, "A unique bond was forged between the female nurses and their sick or wounded patients during the Civil War.... The close human connection between nurse and patient was often deep and lasting and sometimes extended to their respective families."[7]

Indeed, the women referred to their wounded compatriots as "honorary cousins" as did the wounded themselves in reference to their nurses. Both Maggie and Mary Branson would later refer to Lewis Powell by the same euphemism of "cousin," and Mary Branson would later admit to authorities after Powell's arrest for the attack on Seward, "He is not my cousin."[8]

Ardently pro–Confederate, these ladies, particularly Maggie, attracted the attention of Samuel S. Bond, a Hospital Steward.

> Washington City, June 5, 1865
>
> Colonel,
>   I perceive by reading the proceedings of the trial on the 5th inst. that a Miss Margaret Branson was a witness for the defense.
>   Desiring that all evidence adduced shall tend to the conviction of the guilty, and acquittal of the innocents, I feel it my duty to inform you as one of the prosecuting officers in the trial, that Miss Branson while a female nurse in the General Hospital at Gettysburg together with several others was always considered a strong sympathizer with the rebellion, coming to the hospital with the sole purpose of caring for the wounds of the rebel wounded therein; about the time of her departure from the hospital, or a day or two previous, a first Sergt of the rebel army who was nearly recovered from his wounds, a man of unusual intelligence and one of the most unyielding of all the rebels we had, in company with some 8 or 9 others made their escape from the hospital and were never heard from afterwards; it was the general belief that they were assisted in their escape by this Miss Branson, and another of the same stripe who left about or at the same time; this lady was always considered as devoted to the interest and success of the rebel cause and associated only with those of the same proclivities....[9]

Maggie Branson describes in a letter to a wounded prisoner, Captain Thomas Houston, whom she nursed at College Hospital, Old Dorm and who was subsequently sent to imprisonment at Johnson's Island how she and another nurse, Henrietta McCrea, known as "Rhettie," and an assortment of other nurses journeyed a year later in 1864 back to Gettysburg, located the grave of their former patients' brother and had the body transferred back to be interred in Baltimore's esteemed Green Mount Cemetery.[10]

> Baltimore, July 18, 1864
> My Dear Cousin,
>   Many, many thanks for your beautiful gift. It has been greatly admired, and pronounced to be as fine a piece of work, as that imported from France and I assure you, much more highly prized by me. Cousin Rettie called early this morning and after breakfasting with me, we went to "Greenmount, that lovely city of the dead." Mrs. Gibson, your cousin Miss "S," and a little daughter with Cousin Rettie and I were the small flock that surrounded the grave which was to rest your great beloved brother. Think not though his spirit has fled to its eternal home twelve months no tears were shed. Yes, many fell, both for the living and the dead and though it was the fist sod broken in the lot, he will not sleep alone; tomorrow three of his comrades will lie by his side. It will ever be Rettie's and my sad, but pleasant task, to twine flowers and evergreens over and around the grave, of our cousin brother. It will not be a grave of a stranger, but ever fondly watched over and loved. I culled there little flowers from a vine overhanging the head of your brother; while standing there, I could think of nothing save our glorious resurrection, when all would be again reunited. I have not forgotten the conversation I had with a friend at the back of his tent, one lovely summer morning, in which he told me he was inclined to be skeptical. I hope he will not always think as he did then.
>   You cannot imagine how much I would love to see you all. I hope Lieut. Palas is quite well. I received his kind letter and will answer very soon. I have just received letters from friend Robinson and Bartley. They are both well but don't like their new abode very much—Kind regards to Col. Locket—On Monday Rettie and I had a delightful sail down the river. We wished very much for our Cousins. My Papa was one of the party. He has been very ill, and is still looking wretchedly. He spoke of you often and sends much love—it is exceedingly warm today. I suppose you never suffer from heat. I have named Cousin R, our "guardian angel." I wish you could see her decked out in all her charms and trinkets. I expected to see quite a fright on my arrival at church on Sunday, but am happy to say was disappointed. Thanks and

regards to all my old friends—May God bless you my dear cousin and make you his own child is the prayers of your Cousin,

Maggie Branson

Maggie Branson

Maggie Branson Signature, Houston Letter (courtesy Thomas Dix Houston Papers, Rockbridge Historical Society Collection, Special Collections and Archives, Washington and Lee University).

Maggie made the acquaintance of the wounded Powell shortly after the Battle of Gettysburg, where he was in her ward and she noted that he was "kind to the sick and wounded."[11] When Powell was transferred to West's Buildings Hospital in September of 1863, precluding possible deportation to Johnson's Island Prison Camp, Maggie decided to offer her nursing services at West's also. An apparent relationship of some sort had developed between the then 30-year-old spinster and the 19-year-old Powell. She recalled at the 1865 Conspiracy Trial that Powell was referred to by the name of "Doctor" or "Doc" while incarcerated at Gettysburg. "Doc" was in actuality Powell's childhood nickname. The question remains however, did Maggie Branson assist Lewis Powell in his escape from the hellish West's Buildings Hospital shortly after his arrival in the first week of September 1863? All indications seem to point in the right direction. One source stated that a young lady (Maggie Branson?) managed to convey to Powell a Federal uniform as well as a ten dollar note baked in a cake with which he bribed the guard and secured his freedom.[12]

Whatever actually occurred, shortly thereafter, Powell turned up on the Bransons' doorstep in Federal uniform. Odd that he would seek the Branson House out of the blue, especially since he had apparently never before been to Baltimore.

While paying a "quiet call," the teenage Powell was subsequently introduced to Maggie's 32-year-old sister, Mary, for the first time. Spending at least two hours with the ladies in the parlor, he told them in the course of conversation that he was "going south."[13]

It would be two years later in January of 1865 before Powell would once again ring the doorbell of the fashionable Eutaw Street boarding house in Baltimore. Dressed this time in "black citizen's dress," Powell "called as soon as he came to the city," according to Mary Branson. She claimed that he spent a pleasant evening in the parlor with the ladies, conversing on a wide variety of subjects, including his exploits with Mosby.[14] When Powell, who at this time had just acquired rooms at Miller's Hotel, inquired about boarding at the Branson res-

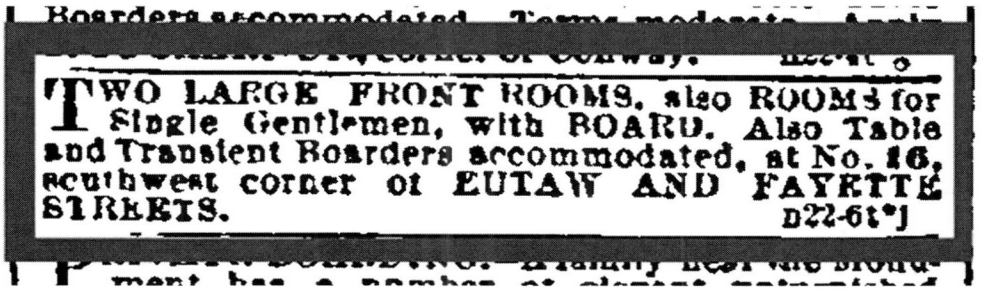

Advertisement for boarders at 16 N. Eutaw Street, *Baltimore Sun*, November 11, 1867.

idence, the ladies regretfully informed their handsome guest that he could not be accommodated at the time.[15]

The 20-year-old Powell, meanwhile, continued to pursue his interest in the ladies—particularly the 32-year-old Mary, in whom he apparently confided to some degree. His relationship with Mary Branson would continue to grow. Two weeks after his arrival, arrangements were finally made for young Mr. Powell to board at 16 North Eutaw Street.

Miller's Hotel advertisement, *Woods Baltimore City Directory for 1865.*

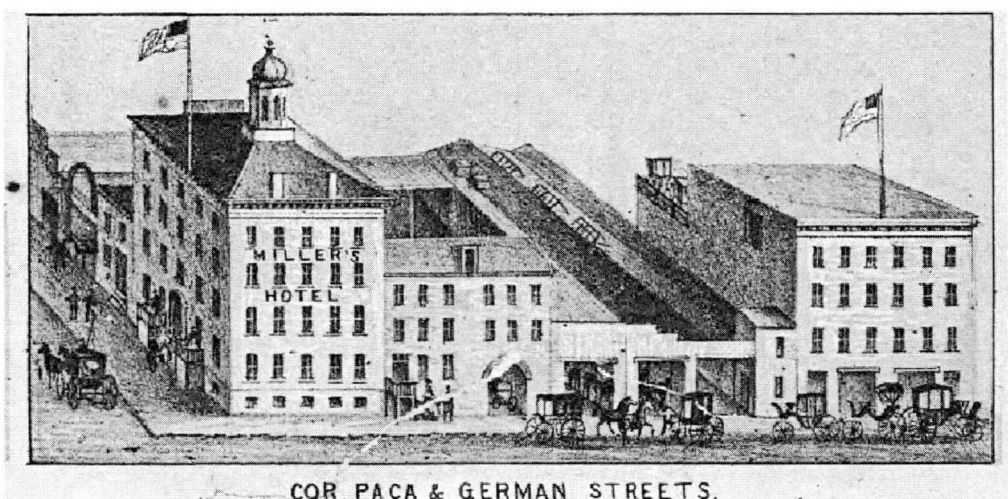

Miller's Hotel 1869 lithograph, E. Sachse and Company, Baltimore Bird's Eye View Map (Library of Congress).

This was about January 17, 1865. He would remain at the Branson house for the next three months, until March 14. Thus, Mary Branson proceeded to introduce him to the other boarders as "Mr. Paine, from Frederick County, Maryland."[16] Another source, however, states that he was registered at the Branson House as "Mr. Ferguson."[17]

One sees a thread running through Powell's aliases including conspirator George Atzerodt's nickname for his young associate, *Mosby.*

Kincheloe, and *Ferguson* ... these were names affiliated with Mosby's Rangers; however, as far as is known concerning the alias of Wood, there does not seem to be a "Wood" listed in any roster of Mosby's Rangers.[18] "Paine" of course was a variant spelling of the name of his host in Northern Virginia, General William H. Payne's family. At the Branson house, Lewis Powell would acquire another nickname to add to this string of pseudonyms; because of his 6'1½" height, the likeable young man was playfully known by his fellow boarders as "Longfellow."[19]

One wonders at all of Powell's various aliases. Surely he was not afraid of Federal officials seeking him out as a missing POW after two years had elapsed. The Branson house had a shadowy gray tinge not unlike that of a certain boarding house located on H Street in Washington, D.C. Both the Surratt Boarding House as well as that of the Bransons appear to have been classed as Confederate safe houses; a hotbed of spies and Confederate operatives. We do know that the Branson household was under the continued watchful surveillance of the Provost Marshal's office in Baltimore, as was many another home in the Monument City at the time.

Although Mary went to great lengths to hide Powell's identity from the rest of the boarders at her residence, she was not averse to revealing the truth of his real identity to her aunt, a Mrs. Mentz, on whom they occasionally called. To her aunt, Mary revealed that Powell "was from Virginia." Both Maggie and Mary also revealed that Powell was on "speaking terms" with all of the boarders and he would also occasionally socialize with them, playing chess in the parlor and even going to the theatre. One later account stated that the

St. Barnabas Episcopal Church (courtesy Episcopal Diocese of Maryland Archives).

youth was extremely congenial, and that "his demeanor while in Baltimore was such as to gain the esteem of all who made his acquaintance."[20] Powell would also occasionally speak with Mr. Joseph Thomas who boarded at 16 N Eutaw with his family. This affiliation with Powell was of much speculation when Thomas committed suicide shortly after Powell's arrest in April of 1865.[21]

That Powell was a thorough church going youth appears to have been verified by the Reverend Augustus Stryker, who stated that the young man attended service "morning and evening," with and without the ladies. He also attended the Reverend Dr. Fuller's Seventh Baptist Church and there met Dr. Abram Dunn Gillette, in company of the Branson ladies about February 12, 1865, on a bitter, sleety Sunday.[22] As the son of a Baptist minister, Powell was acting on how he was raised; and he was raised in a strict, religious environment.

The fact that Mary and Powell were romantically involved seems beyond a doubt. The spirited 34-year-old spinster held an apparent fascination for the 20-year-old Powell. That she was about fifteen years older didn't seem to bother the youth in the least and recent findings state that "a strong attachment sprung up between Payne and Mary Branson ... and it is said that they were engaged to be married."[23]

Mary Branson signature (Fold3.com, Provost Marshal File, Confederate Pay Receipts National Archives).

As bold as proverbial brass, Mary boasted that she spent "considerable time" with him and confirmed, "I think I was with him more than any other party in the house, even my sister. I walked out with him very often."[24] Oscar D. Ladley, an Ohio soldier who boarded at the Bransons' establishment a year after the assassination, recounted that in conversation with the dining room maid, Margaret Kaighn, he was told "the daughter of Mrs. Branson would get up at midnight and serve Powell his meals and pay all kinds of attention to him."[25] This was not by any means the proper behavior of a young Victorian single lady. One also wonders at the "attention" paid to Powell by his lady love. One does not have to read between the lines to guess that more possibly went on between Powell and Mary than that spirited miss would ever reveal to her parents or the authorities, notwithstanding Lieutenant H.B. Smith's assertions that she and Powell shared a "remarkable intimacy even under ordinary circumstances."[26]

One wonders just what was the extent of their intimacy; particularly the late night visitations to Powell's bedroom. Certainly it was unconventional. Could Powell have gotten Mary pregnant? Later developments may seem somewhat valid. Maggie stated that although sociable and well liked at the boarding house, Powell was seemingly depressed in spirits and spent a great deal of time in his room "reading medical books."

Although speculation, this could signify several things:

1. Powell was "depressed" because he had gotten Mary pregnant and knew it—or he was afraid that he had gotten her pregnant. He realized that he must do the honorable thing and marry her.
2. Powell was very young and had no job other than working with the Confederate government/secret service. This would end soon and he realized that he did not have the means to support a wife. He "complained" about his education. Before entering the army, he wanted to be, like his father, a preacher. He was also interested in medicine. Did he want to become a doctor? He had no college or even high school education or training. His education, while good, was basically equivalent of an elementary school education at best.
3. Powell more than likely discussed marriage with Mary; i.e., proposed. The proper thing for him to do would be to talk to Mary's father, the formidable Captain Branson; who was also one of Powell's superiors. Mary's father could have possibly been against the marriage, as the boy was extremely young and had no "prospects," i.e., job training or skills other than farming. The Branson family was one of upper middle class standing and was considered rather "well to do." Powell, although from middle class roots, was simply a poor country boy without formal education or means in a large city. Mary's mother and Maggie may have supported the match; after all, Mary was certainly not getting any younger. With most marriageable young men dead or injured, there was not much chance of a match to be had, and a handsome besotted youngster was better than no suitor at all! This could have caused dissention within the household.
4. Lastly, Powell could have been discovered in a compromising situation with the much older Mary; the last thing he would have wanted to happen. The boy therefore was being forced by Captain Branson to marry Mary.

At any rate, when Lewis Powell beat up an African American maid, Annie Ward, on March 13, 1865, because she gave him impudence over cleaning his room, it is to be surmised that perhaps Annie knew more than was let on regarding Mary's midnight visits to Powell's room. This was more than likely thrown up into Powell's face, along with threats to tell Mary's parents. The usually taciturn and gentlemanly Powell exploded in a fit of rage and "whipped" her, to use the youth's own euphemism. Annie marched straight to the Provost Marshal's office and promptly had him arrested. Strangely enough, he was held on a charge of being a spy and not on assault and battery.

Annie Ward (colored) was also subpoenaed as a witness at the conspiracy trial according to this LAS file.[27] She was never called. One wonders why. Doster, Powell's attorney, when attempting to bring up the incident during the trial was stopped by Bingham with a "You do not have to state what happened between that man [Powell] and that woman." Again one wonders why.

The spunky Mary immediately followed, stressing to Lieutenant Smith that the maid was "impudent," that Powell was her cousin and that he should be released. Later, she recanted her story and admitted that she wished to "shield him from harm."[28] Although she was much older than Powell, it seems strange that this spitfire would feel a need to "shield" such a large, muscular youth. Released two days later after being held on the charge of "Spy" and administered the Oath of Allegiance, Powell returned to the Branson house, ate dinner, gathered his belongings and left, with his next residence being the Surratt House in Washington for a few days as the kidnapping plot was finalized.

After that venture failed, John Wilkes Booth and Powell went on to New York, where the hapless youth lost no time in corresponding with his supposed *fiancée*, writing her from the Revere House in Manhattan and requesting that she reciprocate. According to Mary, she wrote him one letter and subsequently never heard from him again.[29]

One questions the validity of this considering the arrest of the entire Branson household after the assassination.[30] Although the boarders and domestics were released the next day, the entire family was incarcerated under house arrest by Colonel Woolsey under orders from Secretary of War Edwin M. Stanton, until the beginning of the conspiracy trial in the early part of May 1865.[31] They would then be taken to the Old Capitol Prison in Washington, D.C., where they were incarcerated until about the first of June. Recent findings, however, seem to clarify that the Branson ladies were not housed in the Old Capitol Prison—even though records from the same file state as such. A letter included in the file claims that the Branson ladies "have not now nor have ever been housed in the Old Capitol."[32] Mrs. Branson and Maggie gave testimony at the trial in Powell's defense to no avail.[33] Mary did not testify. Why?

According to Mrs. Branson's obituary, dated March 27, 1883, Mary became ill after the entire family was put under house arrest in late April of 1865.[34] Apparently this could have signified the beginnings of her fatal bout with uterine cancer. One report stated that Mary was "greatly shocked" when her young erstwhile lover, Lewis Powell, was arrested for attempted assassination and her "health failed rapidly after the execution."[35] Another article reiterates that Mary Branson was very ill right before and during the execution.[36]

One is left to wonder if perhaps Mary was under such emotional and mental duress that she was not considered a good witness by the defense. Could she have been pregnant?

Opposite: Persons subpoenaed from the Branson Boarding House, May 1865. "Annie Ward (Colored)" was called but never testified (LAS File, Fold3.com).

Appendix K

Witnesses for Payne.

	#	Name	Address		Date	Date
	1	Mrs Mary Branson	15 Eutaw St Baltimore		May 23	June 2
	2	Miss Mary Branson	"	"	" 23	" 2
✓	3	" Maggie Branson	"	"	" 23	" 2
	4	Calvin Shriver	"	"	" 23	May 29
	5	Henry D. Shriver	"	"	" 23	" 29
	6	Hall	"	"		
	7	Chas. H. Morgan	"	"	" 23	" 29
	8	Sam! T. Morgan	"	"	" 23	" 29
✓	9	Anne Ward (col)	"	"		
✓	10	Mary Keagle / Margaret Kaighn	"	"	" 23	" 29
	11	Josephine Hall	"	"		
26	12	Ella Turner	Washington			
26	13	Gifford	" Fords Theatre			
✓26	14	Miss Anna E. Surratt				
26	15	" Surratt				
27	16	Edwin Booth	New York			
27	17	Rev. Geo Powell	Belleville Va			
29	18	Mrs Lucy Ann Grant	Warrenton Va		June 12	June 12
29	19	Dolly Richards	Uppperville Va			
✓29	20	Dr Chas. Nichols	Supt Insane Asylum			
31	21	Junius Brutus Booth	Old Capitol Washington			
	22	John N. Grant	Warrenton Va		June 12	June 12

If so, she would more or less have not been allowed to go out in public—trial or no. She could very possibly have had a miscarriage which would most certainly have pulled her health down. If carried full term, would Mary have gone away from Baltimore to bear her illegitimate baby? Mary's child, if indeed she did have one, would have been born in November or December of 1865. Likewise, if the beginnings of her fatal cancerous tumor were in the makings, she could have been on opiates or morphine for pain and therefore not considered lucid enough to give good testimony.

Sister Maggie married boarder Charles E. Barnett on December 16, 1867, in St Barnabas Episcopal Church with Reverend Augustus Stryker officiating at the ceremony. She and her husband shortly thereafter moved to Brooklyn, New York. That Mary had property is defined by the fact that she owned a large lot and two houses which she attempted to dispose of in a sale in November of 1867. Could Mary have intended to move into this property upon her marriage to Powell? Or was she planning to gift it to her sister Maggie upon her impending marriage?

Likewise, listed in the Maryland Court of Appeals dated June 1869, two years before her death, a Will with Vested Interest to the effect that Mary gave the "rents, issues and profits of her whole estate" to her sister during her life, and then bequeathed as follows:

"And it is my will and desire, that after the death of my said sister, I give and bequeath to C. E. B and M. E. B., children of my nephew J. B., *or the survivor of them,* the moiety or half part of my whole *estate to them and their heirs forever. Item.* And it is further my will, that after the death of my sister aforesaid, I give and bequeath the other moiety or half part of my estate to D. A. M. and W. H. M., children of my niece S. M., or the survivor of them, their heirs and assigns forever. *Item.* It is further my will and desire, that if all the above-named legatees should die before they arrive at age, and without lawful issue, then and in that case I give and bequeath the property aforesaid to the surviving children of my nephew J. B., and my niece S. M., to them and their heirs forever, share and share alike. And I do further order and direct that after the death of my said sister, that the rents, issues and profits of my estate be deposited in the Savings Institution at Interest, and there to remain until the youngest of the first named legatees should arrive at full age, when a dividend will be made and the property given to them."[37] Mary Branson was a well propertied young lady. According to 19th century law, the majority of her financial or other holdings upon her marriage would revert to her husband. Powell therefore would, upon his marriage to her, have become a wealthy young man. Could Captain Branson have been against this; wanting to keep the holdings within the family itself under the Branson name?

At any rate, Mary Branson, age 40 years old, died of uterine cancer at her sister Maggie's home (13 2nd Place Brooklyn, New York) on January 14, 1871. Mary's body was shipped home to Baltimore where she was buried in the Branson vault in Old Saint Paul's Cemetery, with Reverend Augustus Stryker officiating at the funeral. One wonders why the funeral took place at the home of her aunt, A. Du Bois Egerton, 230 North Howard Street and not her own home on Eutaw Street.

Subsequently, the Branson patriarch would lose all in the end and die in dire financial straits; too poor to be removed to his beloved Baltimore for burial. The illustrious Captain Branson passed away the following year on October 29, 1872, and also breathed his last at

Maggie's Brooklyn home. The elder Branson was buried in Brooklyn's illustrious Green-Wood Cemetery, alone in the Barnett plot; his grave unmarked.[38] Recent findings indicate that a year after Mary died, Mrs. Branson was so poverty stricken that she could not afford to pay for her husband's burial and funeral arrangements. She was desperate, and with Maggie's help, attempted to file for Mr. Branson's 1812 military pension as subsistence.[39]

Mr. Branson's obituary in the *Brooklyn Eagle* states "Baltimore papers please copy," but no notice ever appeared in the *Baltimore Sun*. This is somewhat strange considering the apparent esteem and high regard with which Mr. Branson had once been held in the Monument City. Were the Bransons so desperately poor that they could not afford to place an obituary in the Baltimore papers?

It therefore appears that the Branson family lost their home and moved to New York to live with Maggie and her husband sometime in 1870. This was a severe blow to a family who, during the war, had appeared financially sound. It would get worse. After the war, many southern homes were seized by the U.S. government, leaving the owners in dire straits. Due to the Bransons' affiliations with the Confederacy and the assassination, this could also have been their fate. Likewise, after Mary's death, the entire Branson family resigned their membership from St. Barnabas Church—more than likely upon their move to Brooklyn, New York.

St. Barnabas Episcopal Church Communicants, 1871. "Miss Mary Branson—Dead; Miss Margaret Branson, Removed December 1867; Mrs. Joseph Branson, Removed 1871" (courtesy Episcopal Diocese of Maryland Archives).

One also wonders if there could have been some sort of possible estrangement/strained relations between Mary and her parents. Was it possible that there had been a family argument over Powell's remains, exhumed in 1870? It was stated in the papers at the time that Powell's remains were to be "claimed by his friends and a fund set up for his reburial"—just where the burial was to be was never stated. Could Mary have wished her errant fiancé's remains buried in the Branson family vault in Old Saint Paul's Cemetery—an idea which would have possibly inflamed the proud Branson patriarch?

Maggie remained active all through her life with the Henry Ward Children's Aid Society and the Baltimore Friends of the Homeless, as well as supporting remembrances for the Confederate Cause. In the early 1880s, the Barnetts—Maggie, husband Charles and daughter Elizabeth—returned to Baltimore to live. With them came the elderly Mrs. Branson, who on March 24, 1883, died of "old age," so bereft of funds that she died and was buried from the Henry Ward Children's Home where the elderly lady lived and worked alongside daughter Maggie who was at the time matron of the home. Mrs. Branson was buried alongside daugh-

Mary Branson's Death Certificate, January 14, 1871 (Brooklyn New York Vital Statistics).

Opposite, *top:* William Branson plot, Old Saint Paul's Cemetery, Baltimore, Maryland, Plot 89 (author's collection).
  Bottom: Death Certificate for Margaret Branson Barnett, State of Maryland, Towson, Baltimore, Maryland, May 29, 1914 (Maryland State Archives).

WILLIAM BRANSON PLOT
MARY E. BRANSON AND
MRS. MARY A. BRANSON
BURIED HERE. PLOT 89

ter Mary in Old Saint Paul's Cemetery in the old William Branson plot. By the 1890s however, the Barnetts' fortunes had turned towards the better. Living in the Baltimore suburb of Towson, Maggie's husband, Charles E. Barnett, opened and operated a successful business college.

Maggie Branson Barnett would precede her husband in death. On May 29, 1914, Maggie died at age 81, three days after suffering a stroke and falling down the stairs in her home. She is buried in Towson's Woodlawn Cemetery. As late as 1920, Charles Barnett, Maggie's widower, was living with their daughter Elizabeth Chapman, her husband and their three children.

It was upon the death of old Mrs. Branson that it was brought out in the newspapers that her daughter Mary had been engaged to be married to the notorious "Payne the Assassin."[40]

URIOUS BITS OF NEWS.

An interesting incident in the tragic death of President Lincoln and the attempted assassination of Secretary Seward was revived the other day in the death of Mrs. Mary Branson, a venerable woman who, about the time of the tragedy, kept a large boarding house. Payn, one of the conspirators who was convicted and executed, boarded at her house under the name of Ferguson, and, on account of his tall, ungainly figure, was nicknamed "Longfellow." A strong attachment sprung up between him and Mary Branson, the pretty daughter of his landlady, and they were engaged to be married. When the detectives were hunting Payn they visited the boarding house, but he had left there before the assassination. Miss Branson was greatly shocked at the arrest of Payn, her health failed rapidly after the execution, and she died in a few years. Mrs. Branson was one of the witnesses in the trial of the conspirators.

Mary Branson's Reaction to Lewis Powell's Arrest, "A Curious Bit of News," *New Plain Dealer,* Ohio, March 30, 1883.

Appendix L

One of Powell's most highly prized possessions upon his capture and incarceration was a little embroidered pincushion—apparently made by his mother for his soldier's "housewife" sewing kit upon his enlistment in May of 1861. This cushion would remain with him up until his capture—when it was taken away as evidence. According to Colonel H.H. Wells, Powell, upon being incarcerated aboard the monitor *Saugus,* begged to have the pincushion returned. Apparently he was so vocal about this that Wells complied. The pincushion was again taken away when Powell was transferred to the Arsenal prison and utilized as "Evidence No. 13." Supposedly it was returned to him upon notification of his death sentence.

THE ST. PAUL DAILY GLOBE.
WEDNESDAY MORNING. APRIL 9, 1884.

CAPTURING LINCOLN'S ASSASSINS
New Facts of the old Story Told by Ex-Provost Marshal Wells.
Philadelphia Times.

Ex-Gov. H. H. Wells, who was provost marshal in the district of Columbia following the assassination of President Lincoln, gave last night in the course of a lecture at North Road street Presbyterian church some interesting reminiscences of that exciting period and the circumstances connected with the conspiracy and its sequel.

When Payne, with his arms in an iron bar and a ball and chain on his leg, was ten feet under water on a monitor, and when everything had been taken from him and he realized what was in store, he asked for one favor, which was granted him—the return of a little embroidered pin cushion.

Appendix M

An article, "Billy Williams' Good Works," written after the death of Captain William Williams in June of 1898 and copied from the *Washington Post*, reiterates the story of Williams' detective work and his supposed friendship with Lewis Powell. Whether or not there is validity to this report remains to be seen. Lewis Powell's "letters" to Williams have never surfaced.

Booth's Detective Friend
The Deseret Weekly Utah
July 2, 1898

"Of the personal bravery of the assassins, Capt. Williams spoke in terms of contempt save one, Lewis Powell Payne, who made the desperate attempt on the life of Secretary Seward. He was but a boy, but a powerful specimen of physical manhood. The calm courage with which he met death on the scaffold commanded Capt. Williams' highest admiration. 'That boy,' he was wont to say, 'would have made a great man if he had only been started right in life.' Payne formed a warm attachment for Capt. Williams and wrote him several letters, which the captain prized highly. For some time after his arrest, Payne begged Capt. Williams, who knew his real name, not to disclose it, as it would distress his mother to know that her son was hanged as an assassin. So for quite a time he was known as Lewis Powell [sic], and it was only near the day of the execution that his identity was discovered."

Detective William Williams, from *Reminiscences and Souvenirs of the Assassination of Abraham Lincoln* by John Edward Buckingham, Press of Rufus H. Darby, 1894.

Appendix N

An article published in the *Portsmouth Literary and Political Journal*, July 15, 1865, after the executions presented a different perspective on Lewis Powell's character.

After giving the details, the *Newburyport Herald* gives the following sketch of the convicts:

> As to their guilt, Mrs. Surratt's case alone admits of doubts. She denied to the last all complicity in the affair, and the others do not charge her with being a partaker in the crime. But she neither denies, nor is any one for her, a full knowledge of the plot before the fact; and it made clear through the words of Payne and others, that her son John H. Surratt, now in Canada, was as deeply implicated as Booth. While therefore, we exceedingly doubt whether in a court of justice there would have been sufficient evidence to have united a jury in conviction, we have no doubt that she was fully involved in the whole affair; that it was in her house the conspirators met to arrange their plans; that she—a mad woman, who is equal to a frenzied devil—gave to it countenance, and aided in the escape of Booth. Some persons will be shocked at the hanging of a woman; we are always shocked at the hanging of anybody, and hope that in the progress of the age, sometime we shall be able to do better with the vilest criminals; but the distinction asked between male and female conspirators and assassins is founded upon a sentiment and not justice. In an ordinary murder it might be yielded to; but this was an extraordinary offence—a crime not against a single law, but against all the laws of the nation;—a crime not against a single life, but against the national life—a crime against order to induce anarchy—a crime against liberty, that would have affected the world.
>
> Our sympathies went out much more for Payne, who has never denied his guilt, than for the woman. He seemed a man—bold and courageous in action, and not hardened, but tender, frank and generous. We do not know that the mystery thrown over his character has been fully cleared up. He first gave his name as Lewis Payne; but no one knew who he was or where he came from. We have been told since that he was Lewis Thornton Powell, the son of a Baptist minister in Florida. It is evident that he intended, if he had friends, to shield them from suffering and cover them from disgrace on his account. He seems to have sent them no word and to have left none for them; and if it proves that there is no such Baptist minister in Florida, we shall not be surprised. Payne was a Baptist—a member of the church, and was educated to a Christian life. It is not known that he had any bad habits, or that he had ever before committed a crime, but it was known that he was kind and generous. Had he not been fascinated by Booth, and thinking, as he said, that he was performing a duty to his country, he never would have lifted the assassin's knife upon Mr. Seward or any other person. He was young, scarcely arrived to manhood and though physically developed to noble proportions, his flesh was as soft as a woman's, and his chin as smooth as a boy's. But Payne had within terrible energy of purpose accompanying his great physical force, and a power of endurance that was very great. He went through the terrible trial, and death itself, without shrinking. Most of all he blamed himself that he went to the house of Mrs. Surratt; thereby involving her; and of his companions he only censured John H. Surratt, who after being a leader with Booth, ran away instead of remaining to die with his mother. While Payne was fearless, there was nothing light or trifling in his character; and while he was frank, there was nothing of bravado in his conversation. Payne, under other circumstances, might have made a man to be admired and loved. Misled and deceived he had become useless for the world, and his life being justly forfeited, he has passed on.
>
> The other two were of little consequence—Harold was weak, simple and unmanly. He was the moth that flitted about the brilliant light of Booth, to be drawn into the flame and die. He was not a Southern soldier and had no justification to draw blood, nor had he the capacity of an enthusiast to conceive that he was venturing upon the defense of great principles. He was of the material that curb stone loafers are made of, and could never have risen above that.
>
> Atzerodt was a pitiable coward. When within the ring he did not dare to refuse to act; he did not dare to act when he agreed to; he wilted when he was arrested, and showed not one manly trait when convicted. The fact that he and Harold were in the conspiracy shows how blind Booth was to human character.
>
> The parties convicted do not seem to implicate others, and they probably formed the whole party.

Appendix O

Payne the Assassin—A Strange Character

An interesting assumption on Powell's character, taken from the *Weekly Rocky Mountain News* for August 9, 1865.

(Washington Correspondent of the *Cincinnati Commercial*)

Lewis Thornton Powell, who of his own choice, goes into the wonderous history of these times as Lewis Payne, was worthy of a better fate than this he has met. Very strong men of good impulses, noble ambitions, and earnest convictions of duty are not so numerous that the world can afford to lose them. This man was no common, bloodthirsty villain hired for a price and only anxious to earn his money. If through the deed of that dread evening of April 14, 1865, the South had gained a national independence as the Confederate States of America, this Lewis Thornton Powell, and not that John Wilkes Booth, would have been its idol and hero. He was a true child of the South—simple, direct, frank, honest, passionate. He was moreover, reserved, self-composed, and very self introspective. He had no religion, and but a very crude conception of God, but he was naturally religious, and believed that Providence ordered and sanctioned the very deed he attempted at Mr. Seward's.[1] He affected no concealment and no mystery, but his daily bearing was a mystery, and his real life, however and wherever he had lived, would have been mostly concealed.

He was in a very special sense, of a dual nature—vigorous in conception, strong in execution and every way fitted for a leader; yet giving to inward musings, strange longings and all the pomp and paraphernalia of morbid imagination. That the promise of his life and the possibility of his manhood were ruined by slavery, is true—sadly and cruelly true; but therein was no ground for a desire that he should be pardoned or respited. There never was a being more richly deserved hanging; he himself admitted that there was no punishment for his crime but death. The natural expression of his eye was kindly; the intonation of his voice was pleasant to the ear. He was courteous, but awkward. He spoke readily and happily with his guards and attendants. He made no complaints and gave no trouble and often thanked the officers for their kindness. He had no braggadocio, and did not even know such a word as fear. He had no aggressive self assertion, but he counted himself the natural equal of any man. He was one of the best of the thousands upon thousands of young men whom slavery has devoured.

On the scaffold, he manifested neither assumption nor indifference. Remembering his crime, there was righteous joy in seeing him hung—seeing his youth and possibilities, there was increased and intensified hate of that villainy whereby have come the war and all our woes.

ANDREW

Appendix P

The Daily National Republican for May 15, 1865, gives details regarding the court reporters assigned to the trial from the various newspapers.

"The Court met to-day at 11 a.m., all the members present and the prisoners with their counsel. The proceedings of the court on Saturday were read by Mr. Murphy, one of the phonographers of the court. At the green table used for the reporters were seated

L. A. Gobright and F. H. Smith of the *Associated Press*; C.H. Noyes and James Croggon, of the *Star;* Messers. Shaw and Painter of the *Philadelphia Inquirer*; John H. Woods of the *Boston Daily Advertiser*; A. H. Carauran of the *Washington Chronicle*; W.A. Croffuth of the *New York Tribune*; W. W. Warden of the *New York Times* and R. F. Boiseau of the *Republican.*"

Appendix Q

Saving Seward

Various accounts abounded in the 1870s and 1880s that by stabbing Seward, Lewis Powell actually saved his life—one instance stating that Powell's knife attack opened a "pus filled" sack in his jaw that doctors had actually been afraid to tackle. This particular report claims that Powell saved Seward from the ill effects of an ulcer in his throat. There is no basis in any of these accounts—but they do make interesting reading:

> When Payne reached over to strike Mr. Seward the first thoughts of the latter was "What handsome cloth that coat was made of," and when he got a view of Payne's face, the only thought he had was what a handsome man he was. Payne saved Mr. Seward's life by opening an ulcer inside of the throat.

Appendix R

Episcopal Prayer Book:
Prayer for Condemned Persons

Interestingly enough, there is a prayer for condemned persons in the 1865 Episcopal Prayer Book. Reverend Stryker probably read this, or something much like it, to Lewis Powell in the death cell before he walked to the gallows on July 7.

Prayers for Persons under sentence of death.

When a Criminal is under sentence of death, the Minister shall proceed, immediately after the Collect, *Oh God, who repent,* &c., to exhort him after this form, or other like.

Dearly beloved, it hath pleased Almighty God, in his justice, to bring you under the sentence and condemnation of the law. You are shortly to suffer death in such a manner, that others, warned by your example, may be the more afraid to offend; and we pray God, that you may make such use of your punishments in this world, that your soul may be saved in the world to come.

Wherefore we come to you in the bowels of compassion; and, being desirous that you should avoid presumption on the one hand, and despair on the other, shall plainly lay before you the wretchedness of your condition, and declare how far you ought to depend on the mercies of God, and the merits of our Saviour. Consider then seriously with yourself, in all appearance the time of your dissolution draweth near; your sins have laid fast hold upon you; you are soon to be removed from among men by a violent death; and you shall fade away suddenly like the grass, which in the morning is green and groweth up, but in the evening is cut down, dried up, and withered. After you have thus finished the course of a sinful and miserable life, you shall appear before the Judge of all flesh; who, as he pronounces blessings on the righteous, shall likewise say, with a terrible voice of most just judgment, to the wicked, Go, ye accursed, into the fire everlasting, prepared for the devil and his angels.

Your sins have brought you too near this dreadful sentence: it is therefore your part and duty, my brother, humbly to confess and bewail your great and manifold offences, and to repent you truly of your sins, as you tender the eternal salvation of your soul.

Be not deceived with a vain and presumptuous expectation of God's favour, nor say within yourself, Peace, peace, where there is no peace; for there is no peace, saith my God, to the wicked. God is not mocked; he is of purer eyes than to behold iniquity; and without holiness no man shall see the Lord. On the other hand, despair not of God's mercy, though trouble is on every side; for God shutteth not up his mercies for ever in displeasure: But if we confess our sins, he is faithful and just to forgive us our sins, and to cleanse us from all unrighteousness. Do not either way abuse the goodness of God, who calleth us mercifully to amendment, and of his endless pity promiseth us forgiveness of that which is past, if with a perfect and a true heart we return unto him.

Since therefore you are soon to pass into an endless and unchangeable state, and your future happiness or misery depends upon the few moments which are left you, I require you strictly to examine yourself, and your estate both towards God and towards man; and let no worldly consideration hinder you from making a true and full confession of your sins, and giving all the satisfaction which is in your power to every one whom you have wronged or injured; that you may find mercy at your heavenly Father's hand, for Chirst's sake, and not be condemned in the dreadful day of judgment.

Lastly, beloved, submit yourself with Christian resignation to the just judgment of God, which your own crimes have brought upon you, and be in charity with all men; being ready sincerely to forgive all such as have offended you, not excepting those who have prosecuted you even unto death; and, though this may seem a hard saying, yet know assuredly, that without it your charity is not yet perfect. And fail not earnestly to endeavour and pray for this blessed temper and composure of mind. So may you cast yourself with an entire dependence upon the mercies of God, through the merits of our Saviour and Redeemer Jesus Christ.

Appendix S

And Now, the Rest of the Story:
The Search for the Rest of the Remains of Lewis "Paine" Powell

When the bodies of the Lincoln conspirators were let down from the gallows on July 7, 1865, at the Old Arsenal, four darkened holes beside the scaffold waited in the scorching hot sun to receive them. The bodies of Mary E. Surratt, Lewis Thornton Powell *alias* Paine, David Herold and George Atzerodt were hurriedly examined and thrust into the rough pine gun boxes which served in lieu of coffins. There they would remain for the next two years. Eventually a small white picket fence would be placed around them accompanied by a wooden headboard upon which the scrawled name of each "resident" marked the grave. Four months later, the four conspirators were joined by Captain Henry Wirtz, the executed commandant of Andersonville prison. They would remain side by side until 1867. Unknown to the general populace, in April 1865, the body of John Wilkes Booth had been interred under the brick and dirt flooring of what was known as the "wardroom" of the Penitentiary building which was used as a "dwelling by the Warden, and the prison proper."[1] On October 1, 1867, the bodies of the four convicted conspirators as well as Wirtz were instructed to be moved to the Number 1 warehouse:

> Laborers were at once set to work and soon accomplished the work, taking them from the graves before mentioned and carrying them to No 1 warehouse, where a trench was dug a few feet from the north wall. Into this trench the bodies were placed, and as secrecy had been enjoined, but few persons were aware that the removal had been made. Notwithstanding the length of time that the bodies have been buried, the boxes containing them were so heavy and the odor from them so offensive as to indicate that decomposition had taken place very slowly, a fact due probably, to the nature of the soil.
>
> It would seem from this action that the Government does not intend to give up the bodies to the relatives. The bodies of Booth, Payne, Herold, Atzerodt, Wirtz and Mrs. Surratt now rest in a common grave, where their ashes will be mingled.[2]

This "trench" was described in the *Brooklyn Daily Eagle* as being "five feet deep, fifteen feet long and six feet wide."[3]

In February 1869, it was stated in the *Jersey Journal*, "The President yesterday granted the required permission to remove the bodies of Booth and Atzerodt, but the necessary orders were not issued by the Secretary of War until late in the afternoon. A little before dark, the bodies were disinterred. Atzerodt was buried in Glenwood Cemetery [sic], in the presence of his mother, brother and a few other relatives. Booth's body was taken to Baltimore to be deposited in Green Mount Cemetery, near the grave of his father, Junius Brutus Booth, the elder."[4] The bodies of Mrs. Surratt and Herold had already been given up to their respective families by this time. Powell's body was the only one which still remained in the trench alongside that of Wirtz. As an interesting side note in 1869, it was thought that Powell's "friends" would soon remove his body.[5] One wonders about the "friends." Who, aside from the Branson ladies would these friends be? Powell's family knew previously that they could not acquire his remains. They did not try again. So, unfortunately when young Mr. Powell's remains were not claimed, they remained there under the flooring of the No. 1 Wardroom Arsenal warehouse for yet another year. Finally in February of 1870, it was considered time enough to move Powell's remains. "The trench from which the remains of the other conspirators, together with those of Wirtz, had been removed, was found open and the box containing the bones and dust which constituted all that was left of the body of Mr. Payne was raised and given in charge of the undertaker, and was quietly taken out of the grounds, the officer of the guard not even knowing the fact. The undertaker was instructed to be very quiet in relation to the affair, and has followed his instructions. This is the last of the conspirators buried at the arsenal."[6] The *National Daily Republican* for February 23, 1870, reported that Powell was "interred in a lot in *Glenwood Cemetery*," while the *Harrisburg Morning Patriot* of the same date stated that the remains were "buried secretly in one of the district cemeteries. There is no headstone to mark the spot, but the number of the lot was taken, so that if at any future time any relative shall desire their removal to any other locality, their resting place may be accurately known. The bones were crumbling to dust, as was ascertained on opening the coffin." The undertaker was none other than Joseph Gawler, who stated that the young conspirator's "family and friends could find his grave by contacting him as he had a record of where he is buried."[7] It could very well be at this time that Powell's skull was removed by Gawler and given to the Army Medical Museum where it resided along with the piece of John Wilkes Booth's spinal column.

Powell would remain in either Glenwood or Graceland Cemetery for the next ten years or so. According to one paper, Powell's remains were moved in late in 1884 to Holmead Cemetery. "About the last interment made there was Lewis A. Paine [sic], convicted as one of the conspirators in the assassination of President Lincoln. His body rested here but a few months, as shortly

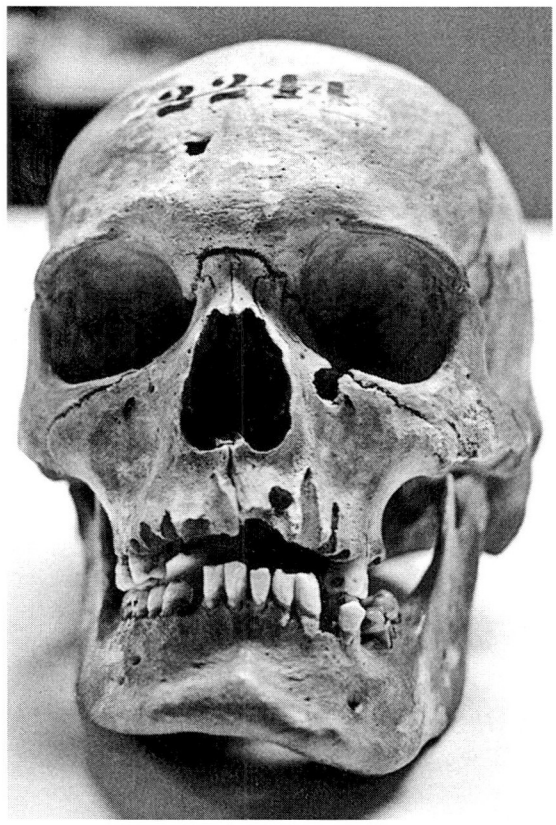

Powell's skull (author's collection).

after its interment, all the unclaimed bodies were removed to Rock Creek cemetery."[8] If this article is to be believed, Lewis Powell's remains apparently rested in Holmead for only a short period of time before exhumation December of 1884.

Holmead had been considered a health menace, and the bodies were exhumed and totally removed by January of 1885. According to a report in the *San Francisco Bulletin* for December 29, 1884, "The skeleton was buried in a box four feet long and in it was placed a glass bottle containing a piece of paper on which was written *his name, brief statement of his crime, execution, etc.* but the paper was not to be found when the box was opened." The *Macon Telegraph* also reported: "The skeleton was buried in a box four feet long, and in it was placed a small glass bottle containing a piece of paper on which was written his name, brief statement of his crime, execution, etc., but the paper was not to be found when the box was opened." According to another report in the *Critical Record* (D.C.), for the same date of December 29, 1884, "The remains were exhumed recently but the bottle was found empty, only some remains of insects that had eaten through the cork stopper and consumed the paper being left." This gives verification as to the fact that more than just the condemned conspirators' names were written on the papers contained in the vials upon the initial burial—not only their names were included, but also a statement of their crimes, and the reason and date of their execution. Lewis Powell's remains were removed

190 APPENDIX S

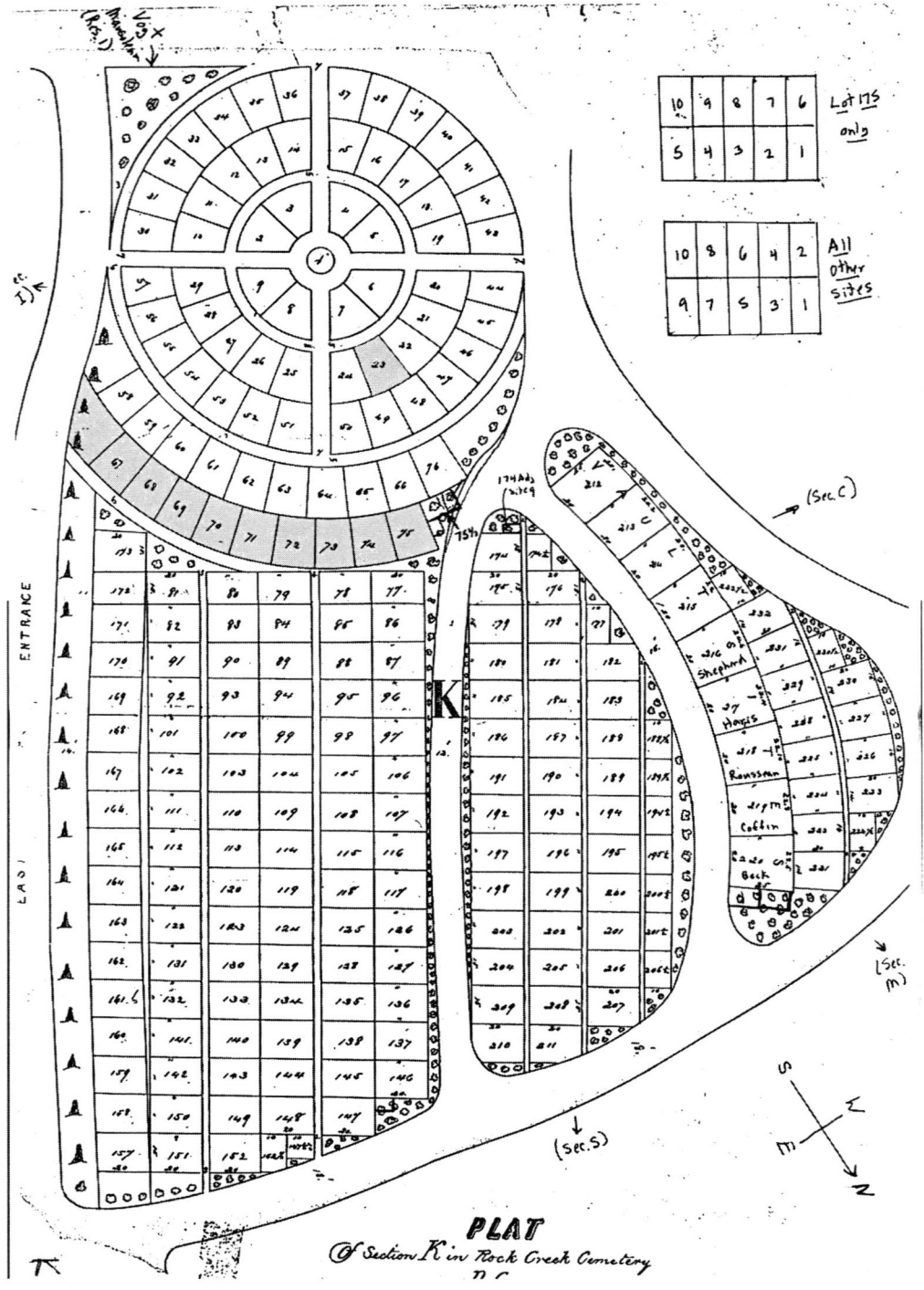

Where the rest of Lewis Powell's remains more than likely rest: Rock Creek Cemetery, Section K, Lot 23, *Rock Creek Record Book, 1823–1893*, List for 1884.

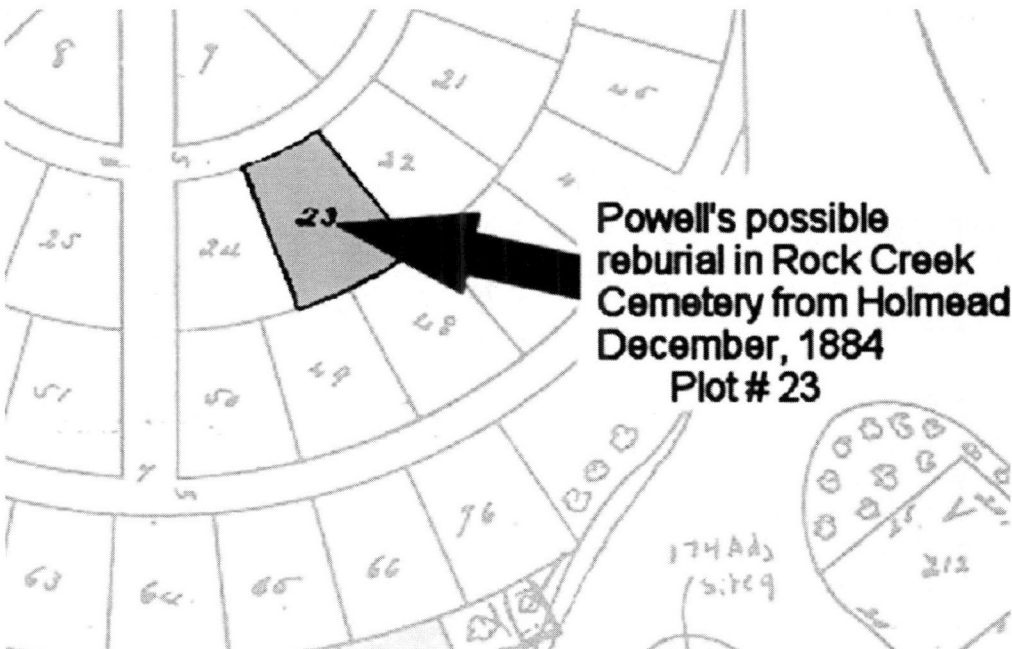

Detail of Section 23, where the rest of Lewis Powell's remains more than likely rest, Rock Creek Cemetery.

from Holmead Cemetery to that of Rock Creek with other bodies between December 21 and 29, 1884.

In research conducted at Rock Creek this past spring and summer, I went though their record books for 1884 (listings 1737–1740) and concluded that there are numerous listings of bodies, about 1,200 total, posted as "Unknown—Removed from Holmead " with Jos. Gawler as "Undertaker." These bodies are all buried in Section K, Lots, 21, 22 and 23 with the predominance of bodies interred in Lot 23. As far as I can ascertain from following the period paper trail of accounts and records, the rest of young Mr. Powell's remains is more or less interred in Rock Creek Cemetery, Section K, Lot 23.

Appendix T

General Lew Wallace and the Portrait of a Conspirator: "Lew Wallace meets Lew Powell"

General Lewis Wallace, one of the Commission members chosen to sit before the court during the conspiracy trial was obviously intrigued by the appearance of those whose fate he was to decide. During testimony, Wallace sketched away creating the only life portraits of the alleged conspirators. General Hartranft would not allow a sketch artist into the courtroom during the trial, so the only real sketches extant at the time were the portraits made by Wallace, and the only prisoner whom he did not sketch was Mrs. Surratt. This was more or less because she wore a heavy veil over her face for most of the duration of the trial. Wallace would later, post-war, incorporate his courtroom sketches into a large portrait of the conspirators (including Booth and John Surratt). The painting suggests their attendance at Lincoln's Second Inauguration in March of 1865 and shows the group trodding on building material for the completion of the Capitol dome. This is perhaps meant to be an allegory of the Confederacy attempting to trod on the Union.

Lewis Powell (Payne/Paine) drawn from life by General Lew Wallace while Powell was on trial seated in the prisoner's dock (Indiana Historical Society, M0292).

General Lew Wallace's large-scale painting, "The Conspirators," which incorporated his earlier courtroom life sketches (courtesy General Lew Wallace Study and Museum, Crawfordsville, Indiana).

Chapter Notes

Chapter 1

1. Annice Flack and Shyrl Littleton, *Powell Family Genealogy* (privately published), p. 6.
2. Shyrl Littleton, fourth cousin to Lewis Thornton Powell, letter to Betty J. Ownsbey, June 9, 1979.
3. Records of county clerk, Talbot County Courthouse, Talbot County, Georgia; Marriage Book "A," p. 9.
4. U.S. Census of 1850, Stewart County, Georgia, house number 193; George C. Powell family Bible in possession of Powell family.
5. Vaughn Shelton, *Mask for Treason* (Harrisburg, Pa.: Stackpole Books, 1965), p. 214.
6. Shyrl Littleton letter to Betty J. Ownsbey, June 9, 1979.
7. "Interesting Facts About the Late Assassins: Sixteen Hours in the Cells," *Daily Morning Chronicle*, Washington, D.C., July 10, 1865.
8. "Trial of the Conspirators: Proof Against the Prisoners," *Boston Daily Advertiser*, May 31, 1865.
9. Georgia Baptist Church Records, Reels 196 and 339/1 (negative), Microfiche (negative) and Box CH 36: CB, 1837–1865 (photocopy) [SAM/MU 19/1] [MU].
10. Leon Pryor, "Lewis Payne: Pawn of John Wilkes Booth," *Florida Historical Quarterly*, June 1965, p. 2.
11. *Fanning's Illustrated Gazetteer of the United States*, p. 143.
12. Barrows, *American Baptist Register*, p. 54.
13. *Minutes of Fort Early Baptist Church* (now Warwick First Baptist Church), Warwick, Worth County, Georgia, 1837–1865, Entries No. 153 and 163, http://www.genrecords.net/emailregistry/vols/00031.html#0007649 (file contributed for use in USGenWeb Archives by Gary Posey).
14. Shyrl Littleton, letter to Betty J. Ownsbey, June 9, 1979; interview with Jewell Powell Fillmon, grandniece of Lewis Thornton Powell, October 1992.
15. Fillmon interview.
16. George C. Powell, letter to Colonel William E. Doster, September 30, 1865, Amy Gillette Bassett Papers, Manuscript Division, Library of Congress; Fillmon interview.
17. G. C. Powell letter to Doster.
18. Fillmon interview.
19. "Lewis Payne: Seward's Would-be Assassin," *Saundersville Herald*, Georgia, February 24, 1887, David Rankin Barbee Papers, Georgetown University.
20. "Booth's Conspiracy: The Desperado of the Party," *Washington Star*, December 3, 1887.
21. Joshua Hoyet Frier II, *Reminiscences of the War Between the States by a Boy in the Far South at Home and in the Ranks of the Confederate Militia*, M76–134, Florida State Archives. (The author wishes to thank Michael W. Kauffman for bringing this article to her attention.)
22. Fillmon interview.
23. George C. Powell, letter to the Rev. Dr. Abram Dunn Gillette, November 7, 1865, Amy Gillette Bassett Papers, Manuscript Division, Library of Congress.
24. Fillmon interview.

Chapter 2

1. "Lewis Payne: Seward's Would-Be Assassin," *Saundersville Herald*, Georgia, February 24, 1887.
2. General Services Administration, National Archives, Confederate Army Records, Company Muster Roll, Florida.
3. Ibid.
4. "Capturing Lincoln's Assassins—New Facts of the Old Story Told by Ex-Provost Marshal Wells," *St. Paul Daily Globe*, April 9, 1884.
5. Ibid.; Fillmon interview, October 1992.
6. Fillmon interview. Young Lewis wrote home frequently while serving in the infantry. His niece, Ida, daughter of George W., claimed that Lewis complained in his letters of being homesick.
7. "Booth's Conspiracy—The Desperado of the Party: Lewis T. Powell Alias Payne," *Washington Star*, December 3, 1887.
8. Ibid.
9. General Services Administration, National Archives, Confederate Army Records, Company Muster Roll, Florida.
10. Shyrl Littleton letter to the author, June 9, 1979; Fillmon interview. After the war, George W. returned to Florida, farmed and raised his large brood of children. A son named Lewis T. was born in 1860. George suffered the loss of a leg, which can clearly be seen in photographs taken of him after the war. He studied law and was later appointed judge of Lee County, Florida, in addition to being an ordained Baptist minister. He died in 1923, a highly respected official.
11. H. B. Smith, *Between the Lines: Secret Service Stories Told Fifty Years Afterwards* (New York: Booz Brothers, 1911), p. 307; statement of Mary Branson, LAS File, M-599, R3, National Archives.

Chapter 3

1. Benn Pitman, *The Assassination of President Lincoln and the Trial of the Conspirators* (Cincinnati: Moore,

Wilstach and Baldwin, 1865), testimony of Margaret Branson, June 2, 1865, p. 160.

2. Smith, *Between the Lines,* p. 306; statement of Margaret Branson, LAS File, M-599, R3, National Archives.

3. David Homer Bates, *Lincoln in the Telegraph Office* (New York: Century, 1907), p. 377.

4. Eileen Conklin, *Exile to Sweet Dixie: The Story of Euphemia Goldsborough, Confederate Nurse and Smuggler,* pp. 17–20.

5. Henry Elliott Shepherd, *Narrative of Prison Life in Baltimore and Johnson's Island, Ohio,* pp. 5–9

6. National Archives, LAS File, Samuel S. Bond to Colonel John A. Foster, June 3, 1865, M-599, R3.

7. Smith, *Between the Lines,* pp. 306, 307; statement of Margaret Branson, LAS File, M-599, R3, National Archives.

8. "Booth's Conspiracy—The Desperado of the Party: Lewis T. Powell Alias Payne," *Washington Star,* December 3, 1887.

9. "Lewis Payne: Seward's Would-be Assassin," *Saundersville Herald,* Georgia, February 24, 1887.

10. Statement of Mary Branson, LAS File, M-599, R3, National Archives.

Much as been made that Margaret L. Branson, "Maggie," was the elder sister and Mary E. Branson the younger of the two. Granted, as with most Victorian ladies, they gave apparent "white lies" to various census takers over the years in regards to their true ages. The Death Certificates of both seemingly tell the truth. Mary's age at death on January 14, 1871, is given as 40, making her birth year 1831. Maggie's age at death on May 29, 1914, is given as 80, with her birthday given as August 16, 1833. This would therefore make Maggie the *Younger* sister and Mary the *Elder* sister; not the reverse as has been thought in the past.

Chapter 4

1. Lewis E. Payne, "Lewis Powell's Exploits: Reminiscences of the Remarkable Youth Who Stabbed Secretary Seward," *Philadelphia Weekly Times,* June 3, 1882. (See Appendix C.) Surprisingly, young Lewis E. Payne remembered that Powell had an "imperfection in one of his front teeth." Seaton Monroe, a Washington, D.C., lawyer whose brother was on board the monitor *Montauk* also noted Powell's "bad teeth," a feature which would confirm the identity of the soldier who stayed with the Payne family in northern Virginia and thereby clear up some of the absurd "double identity" stories concerning Lewis Powell. (See Appendix J.)

2. Ibid.

3. "The Guerrilla War," *Civil War Times Illustrated Special Issue,* October 1974, p. 9.

4. Statement of Mary Branson, LAS File, M-599, R3, National Archives.

5. John W. Munson, *Reminiscences of a Mosby Guerrilla* (New York: Moffat, Yard, 1906), p. 231.

6. B. Curtis Chappelear, Esq., *Maps and Notes Pertaining to the Upper Section of Fauquier County, Virginia* (Warrenton, Va.: Warrenton Antiquarian Society, Publishers, 1954), p. 84. n. 44.

7. Letter, General William H. Payne to General Bradley T. Johnson, September 6, 1894, Eppa Hunton Papers, Virginia Historical Society.

8. Ibid., James O. Hall Research.

9. Ronald Ray Turner, Prince William County, Virginia, 1900–1930 Obituaries (1996), pp. 162–163. In 1869, Bettie Meredith would wed Robert H. Hooe, a Confederate veteran from Prince William County who had lost an arm at the Battle of Cold Harbor. Hooe later became, in addition to a prosperous farmer, a well-known name in local political and government circles. Bettie died on January 17, 1906, and her husband followed in 1913. Upon her death, her sons found that she still had in her possession Powell's diary and photograph. These artifacts remain to be found.

10. Jeffry D. Wert, "In One Deadly Encounter," *Civil War Times Illustrated,* November 1980, pp. 12–19.

11. Edwards and Steers, *The Lincoln Assassination: The Evidence,* p. 1363.

12. John C. Brennan, "The Confederate Plan to Abduct President Lincoln," *Surratt Society News,* Laurie Verge, ed., March 1981, p. 5; *Chronicles of Saint Mary's,* St. Mary's, County Historical Society, November-December 1974.

13. Ibid.

14. *Trial of the Assassins and Conspirators for the Murder of Abraham Lincoln* (Philadelphia: Barclay and Company, 1865; reissued by James L. Barbour, Port Tobacco, Md., 1981), p. 100.

15. Daniel Gillette, "The Last Days of Payne," *New York World,* April 3, 1892.

16. Ben Perley Poore, *The Conspiracy Trial for the Murder of the President* (Boston: J. E. Tilton and Company, 1866), vol. 3, pp. 503–6.

17. Smith, *Between the Lines,* p. 258.

Chapter 5

1. Statement of Mary Branson, LAS File, M-599, R 3, National Archives.

2. Ibid.

3. "Lincoln's Death—The Great Tragedy of 1865 Revived in Baltimore by the Demise of Payne's Landlady—The Conspirator's Habits," *The Cleveland Leader,* March 27, 1883.

4. Smith, *Between the Lines,* p. 258.

5. Ibid., p. 303.

6. Edwards and Steers, *The Lincoln Assassination,* p. 1359.

7. "Lincoln's Death—The Great Tragedy of 1865 Revived in Baltimore by the Demise of Payne's Landlady—The Conspirator's Habits," *The Cleveland Leader,* March 27, 1883

8. Letter, H. B. Smith to Maj. W. H. Wigel, April 21, 1865, National Archives.

9. "Lincoln's Death—The Great Tragedy of 1865 Revived in Baltimore by the Demise of Payne's Landlady—The Conspirator's Habits," *The Cleveland Leader,* March 27, 1883

10. Pitman, p. 312, Argument in Defense of Lewis Payne by W. E. Doster, Esq. (See Appendix H.)

11. Statement of Mary Branson, LAS File, M-599, R 3, National Archives.

12. Asia Booth Clarke, *The Unlocked Book: A Memoir of John Wilkes Booth by His Sister, Asia Booth Clarke* (New York: G. P. Putnam's Sons, 1938), pp. 115–16.
13. Ibid., pp. 115–16
14. Statement of D. Preston Parr, LAS File, M-158, R 5, National Archives.
15. Ibid., LAS File, M-157, R 5, National Archives.
16. William A. Tidwell, James O. Hall, and David Gaddy, *Come Retribution* (Jackson: University Press of Mississippi, 1988), pp. 339–40; *Surratt Trial*, Vol. 1, p. 373.
17. Osborn H. Oldroyd, *The Assassination of Abraham Lincoln* (Washington D.C., privately printed, 1901), p. 167.
18. Ibid., p. 167.

Chapter 6

1. Statement of D. Preston Parr, LAS File, National Archives.
2. Ibid.
3. Dorthy Meserve and Philip B. Kunhardt, *Twenty Days* (New York: Harper and Row, 1965), pp. 30–35. The interesting photos taken during the second inaugural propose to show the alleged conspirators in attendance at the inauguration. Although the speculation is tempting, there is little evidence to support the claim that the photos are indeed of the persons whom they are supposed to be. Most historians remain unconvinced.
4. Smith, *Between the Lines*, p. 257.
5. Pitman, Testimony of Margaret Kaighn for the Defense, June 2, 1865, p. 161.
6. *The Trial of the Assassins and Conspirators for the Murder of President Lincoln* (Philadelphia: T. B. Peterson and Brothers, 1865) pp. 124–25, testimony of Miss Margaret Branson.
7. LAS File—Witnesses for Payne, National Archives, Fold3, http://www.fold3.com/.
8. Ladley Manuscript Collection, Manuscript Number 138, Wright State University, Dayton Ohio. (The author is indebted to Michael W. Kauffman, and to Dawne Dewey, archivist, Archives and Special Collections, Wright State University, for bringing these intriguing letters to her attention.)
9. "Local Matters" column, *Baltimore Sun*, March 15, 1865, p. 1.
10. Eighth Army Corps Papers, RG 93, Register 125, p. 411, National Archives.
11. Smith, *Between the Lines*, p. 257.
12. Ibid., p. 258.
13. Statement of Mary Branson, LAS File, M-599, R 3, National Archives.
14. Smith, *Between the Lines*, p. 258.
15. D. Preston Parr Statement, Roll 3, Frame 1044, LAS File, National Archives.
16. Imaginary dialogue based on Parr statement.

Chapter 7

1. Louis J. Weichmann, *A True History of the Assassination and of the Conspiracy of 1865*, Floyd A. Risvold, ed. (New York: Alfred A. Knopf, 1975), p. 97.
2. Pitman, p. 115, Testimony of Louis J. Weichmann for the Prosecution, May 13, 1865.
3. Ibid., p. 115.
4. Peterson, p. 63, Testimony of Louis J. Weichmann.
5. Weichmann, *A True History*, p. 97.
6. Pitman, pp. 116–17, Testimony of Louis J. Weichmann.
7. Weichmann, *A True History*, p. 97.
8. Pitman, p. 118, Testimony of Louis J. Weichmann.
9. Theodore Roscoe, *The Web of Conspiracy* (Englewood Cliffs, N. J.: Prentice Hall, 1959), p. 68.
10. Statement of David E. Herold, LAS File, M-599, R4, National Archives.
11. *Washington Evening Star*, Classified Section, November 30, December 7 and December 27, 1864.
12. Statement of Mrs. Mary E. Surratt, LAS File, M-599, R 6, National Archives.
13. Weichmann, *A True History*, p. 97.
14. Ibid., pp. 97, 98.
15. Statement of Samuel Bland Arnold, LAS File, M-599, R 6, National Archives.
16. Ibid.
17. *Web of Conspiracy*, p. 84.

Chapter 8

1. Samuel Bland Arnold, *Defense and Prison Experiences of a Lincoln Conspirator* (Hattiesburg, Miss.: The Bookfarm, 1943), p. 31.
2. Ibid., p. 31.
3. *Surratt Trial* (Washington, D.C.: Government Printing Office, 1867) Vol. 1, p. 430, Testimony of Louis Weichmann.
4. "The Last Days of Payne," *New York World*, April 3, 1892.
5. Lincoln Obsequies File, James 0. Hall Research.
6. Arnold, *Defense and Prison Experiences*, p. 47.
7. Ibid., pp. 23–24.
8. LAS File—Witnesses for Payne, National Archives, Fold3, http://www.fold3.com/.
9. Weichmann, *A True History*, p. 101.
10. "City Hotels," New York Evening Express, November 11, 1875.
11. Weichmann, *A True History*, p. 101.
12. Ibid., p. 120.
13. Statement of Mary Branson, LAS File, M-599, R 3, National Archives.
14. H. H. Wells to John Young, May 11, 1865, LAS File, M-599, LAS 1, p. 36, James 0. Hall Research.
15. Pitman, p. 24, Testimony of Richard Montgomery.
16. Ibid.
17. *Surratt Trial*, Vol. 1, p. 315, Testimony of William E. Wheeler.

Chapter 9

1. Peterson, p. 131, Testimony of Miss Anna Ward.
2. Weichmann, *A True History*, p. 121.
3. Ibid., p. 122.
4. *Surratt Trial*, p. 246–47, Testimony of Mrs. Martha Murray.
5. Weldon Petz, *In the Presence of Abraham Lincoln*

(Harrogate, Tenn.: Lincoln Memorial University Press, 1973), p. 81.

6. George J. Olszewski, *The Restoration of Ford's Theatre* (Washington D.C.: National Park Service Publication, 1963), p. 33–39, 122.

7. Weichmann, *A True History,* pp. 121, 122. See also *Surratt Trial,* Vol. 1, p. 375, Testimony of Louis J. Weichmann.

8. Bates, *Lincoln in the Telegraph Office,* p. 384.

9. Ibid., p. 385, 386, 387.

10. Ben Perley Poore, *The Conspiracy Trial for the Murder of the President,* Statement of Maggie Branson, Volume, III, pp. 75–81.

11. Weichmann, *A True History,* pp. 127

Chapter 10

1. "Last Days of Payne," *New York World,* April 3, 1892.

2. Edwards and Steers, *The Lincoln Assassination: The Evidence,* p.1111; information also from James O. Hall research.

3. Statement of Sgt. George F. Robinson, LAS File.

4. "Last Days of Payne," *New York World,* April 3, 1892.

5. Michael Davis, *The Image of Lincoln in the South* (Knoxville: University of Tennessee Press, 1971), pp. 48–56.

6. Pitman, p. 19, Charges and Specification.

7. "Last Days of Payne," *New York World,* April 3, 1892.

8. William Hanchett, *The Lincoln Murder Conspiracies* (Urbana: University of Illinois Press, 1983), p. 53.

9. Statement of M. P. Pope, LAS File, M599, Reel 4, Frames 0511–13, National Archives.

10. Edwards and Steers, *The Lincoln Assassination: The Evidence,* pp. 1072–1073.

11. *Surratt Trial,* Vol. 1, pp. 240, 241, 242, 243, 244, 245, Testimony of Benjamin W. Vanderpoel.

12. Statement of Julia Ross, LAS File, M599, Reel 6, Frames 0107–110, National Archives, James O. Hall Research.

13. Recent findings may turn up yet another picture. Gen. W. M. Gardner, C.S.A. had a cousin named Mary E. Gardner, according to J. B. Jones, *A Rebel War Clerk's Diary,* p. 315, entry dated October 26, 1864, Vol. 2, James O. Hall Research.

14. *Surratt Trial,* Vol. 1, pp. 246–47, Testimony of Martha Murray.

15. LAS File—Statement of William Bell, National Archives, Fold3, http://www.fold3.com/.

16. "The Assault at Gov. Seward's," *National Intelligencer,* April 16, 1865; "The Assassination," *Daily National Republican,* April 18, 1865.

17. Rio Grande Camp Knife, Sheffield, England, Huntington Library, San Marino, CA.

Chapter 11

1. *Surratt Trial,* Vol. 1, Testimony of William Bell, pp. 247–49.

2. Poore, p. 474; Pitman, p. 154.

3. Poore, p. 474; Pitman, p. 154.

4. Pitman, Testimony of William Bell, p. 155.

5. National Archives, War Department Records, File "B," Evd. B.P. 4, JAO.

6. Poore, Testimony of William Bell, p. 475.

7. *American Heritage,* Patricia Carley Johnson, "I Have Supped Full on Horrors: The Diary of Fanny Seward," October 1959, pp. 64–101.

8. Dialogue based on testimony given at the Surratt trial. See *Surratt Trial,* Vol. 1, p. 251.

9. Lattimer, *Kennedy and Lincoln,* pp. 102, 103, 104. Michael W. Kauffman, a highly proficient assassination scholar is quite correct in his assertion that Powell probably panicked at the Seward residence. See *Lincoln Herald,* summer issue, 1982, p. 134.

10. "Diary of Fanny Seward," pp. 64–101.

11. "Death of Miss Seward," Obituary, *Baltimore Sun,* October 31, 1866.

12. Lattimer, *Kennedy and Lincoln,* p. 102. Dr. Lattimer's impressive research refutes the fallacy of a "protective collar" being worn by Secretary Seward, as opposed to the metal bedrest upon which the Secretary was lying.

13. Pitman, Testimony of George F. Robinson, pp. 262–63.

14. *Surratt Trial,* Vol. 1, Testimony of George F. Robinson, pp. 262–63.

15. Pitman, Testimony of Robert Nelson, p. 158. Nelson testified that he found the knife on the morning of April 15 and subsequently gave it to an officer at the door of Seward's house and then later to Dr. John Wilson, surgeon, who turned it over to the government as an exhibit at the Surratt trial.

16. Statement of Alfred Cloughey, National Archives, M619, R 458, F 456; Maxwell Whiteman, *While Lincoln Lay Dying* (Union League, Philadelphia, 1968).

17. "The Last Days of Payne," *New York World,* April 3, 1892.

18. Dr. A. D. Gillette, "Interesting Facts About the Late Assassins," *Washington Constitutional Union,* July 10, 1865."The Execution," *Boston Post,* July 8, 1865.

19. "The Assassins Executed," *Boston Daily Advertiser,* July 8, 1865. In his novel of the assassination, *Katy of Catoctin,* George Alfred Townsend (Gath), portrays a frightened and repentant Powell hiding out in a cemetery.

20. "Judgement," *Washington Morning Chronicle,* July 8, 1865.

21. *Daily National Republican*—"Sketch of Payne," May 23, 1865; Cauchon and Ellliott, *A Peek Inside the Walls: The Final Days of the Lincoln Conspirators,* pp. 14–15.

22. Edwards and Steers, *The Lincoln Assassination: The Evidence,* p. 532.

23. Ibid., p. 536.

24. Research by Dr. Blaine Houmes, Betty Ownsbey, John Elliott and Barry Cauchon, *Inside the Walls, the Final Days of the Lincoln Conspirators, 13 Days Aboard the Monitors,* pp.14–15.

25. "Judgement" *Washington Morning Chronicle,* July 8 1865

26. "The Trial of Mrs. Surratt," by J. W. Clampitt, *North American Review,* September 1880, pp. 223–40.

27. Ibid.

Chapter 12

1. *Surratt Trial,* Vol. 1, Testimony of Richard C. Morgan, p. 340.
2. Statement of C. H. Rosch, National Archives, LAS Series, M-599, Reel 6, Frames 0091–93.
3. *Surratt Trial,* Vol. 1, Testimony of H. W. Smith, p. 332.
4. Ibid., Testimony of William W. Wermerskirch, p. 485.
5. Ibid., Testimony of R. C. Morgan, p. 341.
6. Ibid., Testimony of H. W. Smith, p. 334.
7. Ibid., p. 335.
8. Ibid., Testimony of Richard C. Morgan, p. 332. The spelling of the name on the oath was "Paine"; however, during the trial, Lewis's actual name of Powell was unknown and an attempt was made to prove him one of the Payne brothers of Kentucky who had participated in the Saint Alban's Raid in Vermont in October 1864. Thus the spelling of the name. The paper found on Powell after his arrest at Mrs. Surratt's house was not the original oath, as has been stated, but a confirmation copy of the signed paper. After his capture, the original oath, signed by Powell as "L. Paine," and on file in Baltimore, was sent to Washington (James O. Hall Research).
9. Dialogue taken verbatim from the statement of Detective Officer Thomas Sampson, National Archives, LAS File, M-599, Reel 2, Frames 1077–84.
10. Lists of Powell's personal effects taken from the statements of C. H. Rosch, Ely DeVoe, Thomas Sampson, National Archives LAS Files, M-619, Reel 456, Frames 0340–44; M-599, Reel 2, Frames 1077–84; LAS Files, M-599, Reel 6, Frames 0091–93.
11. "How the Game Was Bagged," *New York Tribune,* April 19, 1865.
12. Statement of Detective Officer Thomas Sampson, National Archives, LAS File, M-599, Reel 2, Frames 1077–84.
13. "The Assassins," *New York Herald,* April 19, 1865.
14. Poore, Testimony of C. H. Rosch, Vol. 2, p. 25.
15. Sampson Statement, LAS File, M-599, Reel 2, Frames 1077–84.
16. Peterson, p. 73, Testimony of William Bell.

Chapter 13

1. Pitman, Testimony of Major Augustus Seward, pp. 156, 157.
2. "The Assassination of the Sewards," *Juniata Sentinel,* June, 25, 1873 .
3. Bates, *Lincoln in the Telegraph Office,* p. 380.
4. Poore, Testimony of H. H. Wells, pp. 45–46.
5. Ibid.
6. "Booth's Captors—Distribution of the Reward Money. Other Interesting Facts," *National Tribune,* October 23, 1885.
7. John Peddicord, "About John Wilkes Booth," *Roanoke Evening News,* June 6, 1903.
8. National Archives, LG File, Military Telegram, G. V. Fox, Assistant Secretary of the Navy Department to Commander J. B. Montgomery, Commandant, Navy Yard.
9. "About John Wilkes Booth," *Roanoke Evening News,* June 6, 1903.
10. Ibid.
11. Surratt would escape Federal justice for the next two years. In Elmira, N.Y., at the time of the assassination, he would scurry to Canada and then to England to escape the dragnet and from England proceed to Italy, where he served in the Papal Zouaves. His identity discovered, he made a daring escape and fled Italy, subsequently seeking refuge in Alexandria, Egypt. United States authorities finally cornered him there in November 1867. Brought back to the U.S. for a sensational civil trial which ended in a hung jury, he was set free on bond and never convicted or retried. He lived out his life as a reclusive auditor for the Old Bay Steamship Line, dying at the age of seventy-two in 1916.
12. "Attempted Suicide of Payne," *Philadelphia Press,* April 26, 1865.
13. Bates, *Lincoln in the Telegraph Office,* p. 381.
14. Ibid.
15. Arnold, *Defense and Prison Experiences,* p. 51.
16. Bates, *Lincoln in the Telegraph Office,* pp. 382–83.
17. "Fort Lesley McNair and the Lincoln Conspirators," Michael Kauffman, *Lincoln Herald,* winter issue, 1978.

Chapter 14

1. Oldroyd, *Assassination of Lincoln,* pp. 117–19.
2. Col. Julian Raymond, *History of Fort Lesley J. McNair* (unpublished manuscript, Washington, D.C., 1901), pp. 50, 51.
3. Ibid.
4. *The Hartranft Letterbooks,* Logs kept pertaining to the imprisonment of the Lincoln conspirators at the old Arsenal; April July 1865, Collection of Gettysburg College, Gettysburg, Pa., p. 2.
5. *Judiciary House Committee, House of Representatives: The Impeachment Committee Investigation* (Washington, D.C.: Government Printing Office, 1867), Testimony of Major Thomas T. Eckert, pp. 673–75.
6. *Hartranft Letterbooks,* p. 4.
7. Ibid., p. 11.
8. Arnold, *Defense and Prison Experiences,* pp. 59–60.
9. "The Plot: Counsel of the Assassins," *Philadelphia Inquirer,* May 3, 1865.
10. John B. Jones, *A Rebel War Clerk's Diary* (Philadelphia: J. B. Lippincott, 1866), Vol. 2, p. 315, entry for October 26, 1864.
11. Ladley Manuscript Collection, Manuscript Number 138, Wright State University, Dayton, Ohio. (The author is indebted to Michael W. Kauffman, and to Dawne Dewey, archivist, Archives and Special Collections, Wright State University, for bringing these intriguing letters to her attention.)
12. Ibid.
13. Charles Barnett would later wed Maggie Branson in December 1867.
14. Smith, *Between the Lines,* pp. 302, 303, 309, 310.
15. William E. Doster, *Lincoln and Episodes of the Civil War* (New York: G.E. Putnam's Sons, Knickerbocker Press, 1915) p. 257.

Chapter 15

1. "The Career of an Assassin: Payne Described by One Who Knows Him," *Louisville Union Press,* May 11, 1865.
2. George Alfred Townsend (GATH), "Portraits of the Accused," *New York World,* May 26, 1865.

A popular war-time journalist, noted for his colorful and melodramatic writings, Townsend incorporated his account of the assassination and subsequent trial into a paperback pamphlet, *The Life, Crime and Capture of John Wilkes Booth and the Pursuit, Trial and Execution of His Accomplices.* Twenty-one years later, in 1886, he composed a novel, *Katy of Catoctin,* which revolved around the actions of Booth and the conspirators.

3. Ibid.
4. Unidentified and undated clipping, *New York Times,* 1865, Lincoln Obsequies File, Rare Book Room, Library of Congress.
5. "Appearance of the Prisoners Payne and Atzerodt," *Washington Star,* May 15, 1865.
6. Shelton, *Mask for Treason,* p. 75.
7. "The Conspiracy Trial. The Proceedings this Afternoon. Third Edition Half-past Five, P.M.," *National Daily Republican,* June 6, 1865.
8. *New York Times,* May 17, 1865.
9. Undated clipping, *Pittsburgh Chronicle,* Lincoln Obsequies File, Rare Book Room, Library of Congress.
10. *Washington Star,* May 20, 1865.
11. Barclay, *Trial of the Assassins,* p. 34.
12. "The Trial of the Assassins," *New York Times,* May 20, 1865.
13. "The Trial on Wednesday," *New York World,* May 31, 1865.

Chapter 16

1. "A Remarkable Lecture: John H. Surratt Tells His Story," *Lincoln Herald,* December 1949, p. 28.

Wallace's so-called portrait of Mrs. Surratt is falsely labeled. The sketch, appearing in Helen Jones Campbell's historical novel, *Confederate Courier,* and in Leroy Hayman's book, *O Captain! The Death of Abraham Lincoln,* is identified as "Mrs. Surratt." However, scrutiny of the features reveals the portrait to be that of Powell. Although the expression is wistful, the face is masculine. The unkempt hair is also suggestive of Powell. Wallace had little chance to see Mrs. Surratt's face; she kept herself closely veiled throughout the trial and only lifted the veil once for identification purposes.

2. "The Conspiracy Trials, Third Edition," *Philadelphia Inquirer,* undated clipping, Lincoln Obsequies File, Rare Book Room, Library of Congress.
3. Ward Thoron, ed., *The Letters of Mrs. Henry Adams—1865–1883,* pp. 10, 470.
4. Doster, *Lincoln and Episodes,* p. 264.
5. *Hartranft Letterbooks,* p. 35.
6. Letter, William E. Doster to the Rev. George C. Powell, June 23, 1865, General Ethan Allan Hitchcock papers, Library of Congress.
7. Doster, *Lincoln and Episodes,* pp. 265–66.
8. "Last Days of Payne," *New York World,* April 3, 1892.
9. Provost Marshall's Records, LAS File, Fold3, http://www.fold3.com/.
10. Pitman, p. 160, Testimony of Miss Margaret Branson.
11. "The Trial of the Assassins ... Evidence Touching on the Insanity of Payne," *New York Times,* June 3, 1865.
12. *Hartranft Letterbooks,* p. 49.
13. Peterson, p. 128, Testimony of John B. Hubbard.
14. John A. Gray, "The Fate of the Lincoln Conspirators," *McCall's Magazine,* 1911, p. 627.
15. Ibid.
16. "Hangman of President Lincoln's Assassins Tells His Story," *New York Press,* September 4, 1898. Courtesy of Michael W. Kauffman.
17. *Hartranft Letterbooks,* p. 53.
18. "Trial of the Conspirators: The Mystery of Payne," *Baltimore Clipper,* June 5, 1865.
19. "Payne the Mysterious," *Boston Sunday Herald,* June 11, 1865; also, "Who is Payne? The Mystery Still Unsolved," *Evening Express,* June 10, 1865.
20. "The Great Conspiracy—Proceedings This Morning," *Washington Chronicle,* May 17, 1865.
21. "The Conspiracy Trials," *Washington Star,* Undated clipping, Lincoln Obsequies File, Rare Book Room, Library of Congress. James O. Hall Research.
22 Henry Kyd Douglas, *I Rode with Stonewall* (Chapel Hill: University of North Carolina Press, 1940), p. 328.
23. Pitman, pp. 167–68, Testimony in Rebuttal Concerning Lewis Payne.

Chapter 17

1. Letter, William E. Doster to the Rev. George C. Powell, June 23, 1865, General Ethan Allan Hitchcock Papers, Library of Congress.
2. Peterson, pp. 167–69, Argument by W. E. Doster in Defense of Payne.
3. "The Conspiracy Trials . ... Argument of Mr. Doster," *Washington Star,* June 22, 1865.
4. Doster, *Lincoln and Episodes,* pp. 259–60.
5. "The Conspirators: Last Days of the Doomed," *Washington Star,* July 10, 1865.
6. "Execution of the Conspirators—How the Conspirators Received their Sentence," *Massachusetts Spy,* July 14, 1865.
7. William Wilkins Glenn, Bayly Ellen Marks and Mark Norton Schatz, eds., *Between North and South: A Journalist Views the Civil War* (Cranbury, N.J.: Fairleigh Dickinson University Press. 1976), p. 242.

In his diary, journalist Glenn gives a brief account of Stryker's association with Powell:

> Last year he noticed a man plainly dressed who was a stranger and who attended St. Barnabas quite regularly, morning and evening. After some weeks, he spoke to him one day, after church and asked him if he had not been in the Confederate Army. Payne told him he had. Afterwards, they became more intimate, and Payne came frequently to see him. Mr. Stryker found him to be gentlemanly, intelligent and earnest. When he saw in the papers that Payne had asked to have Mr. Stryker come to see him, he thought it was the same man, and went to Washington, where after long effort, he obtained a pass....

He [Payne] was induced to join with Booth in the assassination of men whom he considered most wicked with the conviction that he was benefitting his Cause and doing a deed for which his country would hereafter thank him .... It is quite evident that no promise of gain influenced him.

Augustus P. Stryker (1833–1891), along with many other Maryland Episcopalians, refused to pray for Union victories, going so far as to defy the orders of the Bishop. When Maggie Branson wed boarder Charles Barnett in December of 1867, Stryker officiated at the ceremony.

8. "The Hanging of Mrs. Surratt," *New York Herald,* Undated clipping, Gettysburg College Library, Hartranft Collection. (The author wishes to thank Mrs. Nancy Scott, archivist, for her help in locating and obtaining this material.)

9. "Visit to the Prisoners: Preparations for the Executions," *Albany Evening Journal,* July 7, 1865.

10. "Sixteen Hours in the Cells," *Daily Morning Chronicle,* July 10, 1865.

11. "Last Days of Payne," *New York World,* April 3, 1892. Daniel Gillette, son of the Rev. Dr. Abram Dunn Gillette, wrote that his father had ministered to young Powell for "three or four days" before the execution, but this allegation is not substantiated by either the Reverend Doctor himself, or Hartranft.

12. "Local Matters: The Weather," *Baltimore Sun,* February 13, 1865.

13. "The Execution," *Boston Post,* July 8, 1865.

14. "The Last Days of Payne," *New York World,* April 3, 1892

15. "The Execution," *Boston Post,* July 8, 1865.

16. "The Last Moments on the Scaffold," *Albany Evening Journal,* July 8, 1865.

17. "The Conspirators: Payne's Farewell to His Counsel," *Washington Evening Star,* July 10, 1865.

18. "The Assassins Convicted," *Boston Daily Advertiser,* July 7, 1865.

19. *Hartranft Letterbooks,* p. 88.

20. "Lewis Powell's Exploits: Reminiscences of the Remarkable Youth Who Stabbed Secretary Seward," *Philadelphia Weekly Times,* June 3, 1882.

21. "The Conspirators: Payne's Farewell to His Counsel," *Washington Evening Star,* July 10, 1865.

22. "Sixteen Hours in the Cells," *Daily Morning Chronicle,* July 10, 1865.

23. "Drummer at Mrs. Surratt's Hanging," *Boston Daily Globe,* February 18, 1911.

24. G. A. Townsend, *Life, Crime and Capture of John Wilkes Booth* (New York: Dick and Fitzgerald, 1865), pp. 71, 72.

25. "The Solemn Procession," *Philadelphia Inquirer,* July 8, 1865.

26. "Execution," *Washington Evening Star,* July 7, 1865.

27. Ibid.

28. "Judgement: The Assassins and Their Doom," *Washington Daily Morning Chronical,* July 8, 1865.

29. "The Last Moments on the Scaffold," *Albany Evening Journal,* July 8, 1865.

30. Ibid.

31. "The Assassins Executed," *Boston Daily Advertiser,* July 8, 1865.

32. Ibid.

33. "Last Days of Payne," *New York World,* April 3, 1892.

Chapter 18

1. Letter, Shyrl Littleton to the author, June 9, 1979.

2. "Booth's Conspiracy: The Desperado of the Party," *Washington Star,* December 3, 1887.

3. Ibid.; also Fillmon interview, October 1992.

4. Both letters in General Ethan Allan Hitchcock Papers, Library of Congress Manuscript Room.

5. Shelton, *Mask for Treason,* p. 390.

6. "In Ancient Graves: Strange Discoveries at Holmead Cemetery," *National Republican,* September 25, 1884; "Sold for a Trifle: Graveyard Held Remains of One of the Lincoln Conspirators," Unidentified, undated clipping.

7. Ibid.

8. Found on January 27, 1992, by archaeologist Stuart Speaker at the Smithsonian in the Anthropology Department. Identified by the old Army Medical Museum number 2244, it is now listed as specimen number 244046. Identification from a historic perspective was made by James O. Hall, Michael W. Kauffman and the author. See also, *Surratt Courier,* p. 2, Vol. 17 No. 3, March 1992, published by the Surratt Society.

9. Conversation with Jewell Powell Fillmon, grand-niece of Lewis Powell.

Appendix C

1. Powell was in reality the youngest of three surviving sons. His next-to-youngest brother, Oliver, had died after receiving wounds at the battle of Murfreesboro in January 1863. The surviving brother, George W., was severely wounded at the siege of Petersburg in April 1865 but survived the war to go home to Florida, become an esteemed judge and preacher and raise a large family. Lewis obviously thought that George had also perished. His father was in fact a Georgian, but of Virginia ancestry.

2. Powell had turned 21 years old on April 22, 1865, shortly after his capture. He was 21 when he died.

3. Powell did not desert from the infantry. According to General William H. Payne, Powell was introduced to Mosby and he was allowed to join the 43rd Battalion, Company B in October of 1863; more or less because of his family affiliations in that he was second cousin to General John Brown Gordon.

4. *Partisan Life with Col. John S. Mosby* by John Scott was published by Harper & Brothers, 1867. Since this was published after the assassination, trial and Powell's hanging, it is my impression that Scott was just reiterating what the public at the time thought of Powell. He was not considered in this light by anyone else who knew him in Mosby's Rangers.

5. That Powell had "killed a great many men" is incorrect in that before he died, the boy told Dr. Abram Dunn Gillette, his spiritual advisor, that before attacking Seward, that "he had never shed human blood before." "The Last Days of Payne," *New York World,* April 3, 1892.

6. This would be 2nd Sergeant Tom Benton Shipley, Company E, 43rd Battalion Virginia Cavalry.

7. The prisoner whose life young Powell saved was

Private Augustus Lockner, Company H, 21st NY Calvary.

8. According to the research of the late Dr. James O. Hall, as late as 1906, Powell's diary and photograph were still in the hands of his former girlfriend, Bettie D. Winter Meredith. The name "Lily Bowie" was used to disguise her identity. An accomplished Fauquier belle, she married Robert Hooe of Prince William County about 1869 and had three sons. Their descendants are still located in the Fauquier and Prince William areas.

9. This man was incarcerated in Western State Lunatic Hospital on August 17, 1865—after Powell left Mosby and long after Powell was dead. He apparently was in the jail for most of the period. He is registered in the record book (VA State Library, Vol 1, #247, Vol Index #266) as a Laborer, 48 years old, tall, fair complexion, brown hair and blue eyes. Reason for his incarceration: "Sexual Misconduct/Deviation." He is listed as having died September 11, 1885, of Phthisis, a "wasting disease." His brother was also declared "insane." Medical Register No. 1, Western Lunatic Asylum of Virginia Record Book, VA State Library, accessed September 7, 2012.

10. This particular "John Pratt" matches the identity of a John Pratt, a 28-year-old man who enlisted on March 28, 1864, in New York City as a private. He was a member of F Company, 25th NY Cavalry, promoted to sergeant and mustered out at Hart's Island, New York, June 27, 1865. His unit participated at the battle of Duffield's Depot in 1864.

11. The "romantic" elements of this story are suspect. There is nowhere on record that Powell was ever "shot through the lungs"; the only recorded wound he ever received was a gunshot through the right wrist received at Gettysburg on July 2, 1863.

12. Powell never earned any rank higher than private. It is surmised that the "lieutenant's uniform" that he wore when he first joined Mosby's command was one that he had taken from a fellow soldier when he deserted from Harry S. Gilmore's command; Powell claiming that the Gilmore company were composed of too "rough a group" for him. Powell prided himself on being a gentleman and supposedly, Gilmore's men were considered ruffians.

13. Powell during January and February boarded, except upon his arrival in Baltimore when he boarded at Miller's Hotel for two weeks, at the Branson House, corner of NW Eutaw and Fayette Streets. He was still residing there when he was arresting as a spy on March 13, 1865. Thenceforth, he journeyed to Washington and stayed for three days during the kidnap venture, leaving for New York with Booth and then returning to Washington about the first of April when he boarded at the Herndon House.

14. I think that this illustrates the exact opposite. Powell was extremely young. At 20 years of age, a youth, even if he has been through four years of war, is still not perceptive enough to be able to define certain things as can a more experienced 26-year-old. The facts that he did tell the truth to Smith and his going back to Mrs. Surratt's house only prove that he was attempting to go to the only place he knew in order to get a change of clothing, rest and a meal before he attempted to make his way to Baltimore and obviously, the Branson house. He could think pretty fast on his feet in extreme circumstances as indicated by what he told Smith and the arresting officers at the Surratt House.

15. Payne errs in his recitation of these events. Powell drew a Whitney revolver and when the weapon misfired, he pistol-whipped young Seward over the head with it, fracturing his skull and injuring him severely. Powell never touched Bell, who ran downstairs and out the front door screaming for help.

16. Hansell, a State Department messenger, was wounded as Powell was fleeing down the stairs, not in Seward's room.

17. No "colored man" held Powell's horse. His mount was tied to a tree in front of Seward's house.

18. Powell claimed that he had bought those boots in Baltimore. It is now thought that the supposition of JWB's name in Powell's boots were just a canard to identify Powell's affiliation with Booth.

19. Frederick Seward never testified at the trial as he was too incapacitated by his wounds.

20. Powell did die boldly, but also extremely contrite and upset over the damage he had wrought. He did not "slap Herold on the back." Powell had no real liking for Herold; besides the arms of the condemned were all secured before the walk to the gallows by Lilly Irons.

Appendix F

1. "A Brave Fight for Life" and "A Soldier's Christmas—How August Lockwood Spent the Merry Holiday in 1864," *Columbus Journal*, Columbus, Nebraska, January 14, 1902.

2. The same article appears in the *Chicago Inter-Ocean* for January 1902.

3. Letter from General William H. Payne to General Bradley C. Johnson, September 6, 1894, Eppa Hunton Papers, Virginia Historical Society.

4. "A Brave Fight for Life," *Columbia Journal*, Columbia, Nebraska, 1902.

5. Ibid.

6. "A Soldier's Christmas—How August Lockwood Spent the Merry Holiday in 1864," *Columbus Journal*, Columbus, Nebraska, January 14, 1902.

Appendix K

1. Brigham, William T., *Baltimore Hats Past and Present, An Historical Sketch of the Hat Industry of Baltimore from it's Earliest Days to the Present Time*, privately published by the Author, Baltimore, MD 1890, pp. 50–51

2. Smith, H. B., *Between the Lines—Secret Service Stories Told Fifty Years Afterwards*, Booz Brothers Press, New York, New York, 1911, pp. 255–311.

3. National Archives, Records Department—Rebel Archives, The vouchers show goods furnished or services rendered by private citizens and firms to the Confederate government, establishing the disloyalty of Southern claimants. War Department NARA M 346.

4. "A Surprise Party," *Philadelphia News*, May 4, 1865.

5. Statement of Mary Branson, LAS File, M-599, R3, National Archives.

6. E.F. Conklin, *Women of Gettysburg* (Gettysburg, PA: Thomas Publications, 1993), pp. 350–420; also E.F. Conklin, *Exile to Sweet Dixie, The Story of Euphemia Goldsborough, Confederate Nurse and Smuggler*, Gettysburg, PA: Thomas Publications, 1998), pp. 144–146.

7. Conklin, *Exile to Sweet Dixie*, p. 46.

8. Deposition of Mary Branson, May 1, 1865, LAS, "B" 428, (JAO) 1865; William Edwards and Edward Steers, *The Lincoln Assassination: The Evidence* (Urbana: University of Illinois Press, 2009), pp. 198–200.

9. Letter of Samuel Bond, June 5, 1865, LAS, "B" 462 (JAO) 1865, pp. 141–142.

10. Ibid, p. 46.

11. *The Conspiracy Trial for the Murder of the President, and the Attempt to Overthrow the Government by the Assassination of it's Principal Officers*, edited with an introduction by Ben. Perley Poore, Vol. III (Boston: J. E. Tilton and Company, 1866), pp. 74–75.

12. "Lewis Payne: Seward's Would-Be Assassin," *Saundersville Herald*, February 24, 1887.

13. Deposition of Mary Branson, May 1, 1865, LAS, "B" 428, (JAO) 1865; Edwards and Steers, *The Lincoln Assassination: The Evidence*, pp. 198–200.

14. Ibid.

15. Ibid.

16. Ibid.

17. "A Tragedy Recalled—Death of Witness in the Trial of Payne the Assassin," *Boston Herald*, March 27, 1883; also, "The Assassin Payne—Death of His Old Landlady," *National Republican*, March 27, 1883.

18. Ibid.

19. Ibid.

20. "The Assassin Payne—Death of His Old Landlady," *National Republican*, March 27, 1883; "A Tragedy Recalled—Death of a Witness in the Trial of Payne, the Assassin," *Boston Herald*, March 27, 1883.

21. *New York Tribune*, April 29, 1865; Deposition of James G. Stevens, April 27, 1865, LAS, "R" 428, (JAO) 1865; Edwards and Steers, *The Lincoln Assassination: The Evidence*, pp. 1196–1197.

22. "Local Matters: The Weather," *Baltimore Sun*, February 13, 1865; also "The Last Days of Payne," *New York World*, April 3, 1892.

23. "The Assassin Payne—Death of His Old Landlady," *National Republican*, March 27, 1883; also "A Tragedy Recalled—Death of a Witness in the Trial of Payne, the Assassin," *Boston Herald*, March 27, 1883.

24. Deposition of Mary Branson, May 1, 1865, LAS, "B" 428, (JAO) 1865; Edwards and Steers, *The Lincoln Assassination: The Evidence*, pp. 198–200.

25. Ladley Manuscript Collection, Manuscript Number 138, Wright State University, Dayton, Ohio.

26. Letter, H.B. Smith to Major W. H. Wiegel, April 21, 1865, National Archives.

27. "Witnesses for Payne," LAS file, Letters and Documents, NARA, Fold3.com.

28. Deposition of Mary Branson, May 1, 1865, LAS, "B" 428, (JAO) 1865; Edwards and Steers, *The Lincoln Assassination: The Evidence*, pp. 198–200.

29. Ibid.

30. "Local Matters—Military Arrests," *Baltimore Sun*, May 2, 1865. The actual arrest date was "on Friday Last," making it April 28, 1865.

31. Ibid.

32. NARA—LAS File—Letters and Documents, Fold3.com.

33. *Washington Evening Star*, June 9, 1865.

34. "The Assassin Payne—Death of His Old Landlady," *National Republican*, March 27, 1883; "A Tragedy Recalled—Death of a Witness in the Trial of Payne, the Assassin," *Boston Herald*, March 27, 1883.

35. Undated and unidentified newspaper clipping—"A Curious Bit of News," March 1883.

36. "The Assassin Payne—Death of His Old Landlady," *National Republican*, March 27, 1883.

37. Stockett, J. Shaaff, State Reporter, *Reports of Cases Argued and Determined in the Court of Appeals of Maryland*, Vol. XXXI, containing cases in April and October Terms, 1869, pp. 181–191.

38. NARA—LAS File—Letters and Pension Records, Joseph Branson, Fold3.com.

39. Webpage, *Green-Wood—A National Historic Landmark*, Burial Search—Branson, Joseph, Burial Date, November 1, 1872, Lot 12475, Section 170, www.green-wood.com/burial_results/index.php.

40. "The Assassin Payne—Death of His Old Landlady," *National Republican*, March 27, 1883; "A Tragedy Recalled—Death of a Witness in the Trial of Payne, the Assassin," *Boston Herald*, March 27, 1883.

Appendix O

1. The writer errs in that Powell was from a deeply religious background and retained his religious convictions up until his death.

Appendix S

1. "Bodies of the Conspirators Disinterred," *Daily Evening Telegraph*, Philadelphia, PA, October 4, 1867.

2. Ibid.

3. "John Wilkes Booth's Body," *Brooklyn Daily Eagle*, March 18, 1901.

4. "The Assassination Conspirators—More Pardons Expected—Reinterment of Remains," *Jersey Journal*, February 16, 1869; David Taylor, *BoothieBarn: Discovering the Conspiracy*, http://boothiebarn.com/2012/08/25/finding-george-atzerodt/#comment-466, accessed August 26, 2012. Atzerodt was buried in secret in St Paul's Lutheran Cemetery, Druid Hill, Baltimore. He was never interred in Glenwood.

5. "From Washington," *Sunbury (PA) American*, February 20, 1869.

6. "Lewis A. Payne," *New Orleans Times*, February 26, 1870.

7. "The Remains of Payne," *National Daily Republican*, February 23, 1870.

8. "Congressional Cemetary [sic] of 1825," *Duluth News Tribune*, August 11, 1912.

Bibliography

Books

Arnold, Samuel Bland. *Defense and Prison Experiences of a Lincoln Conspirator.* Hattiesburg, MS: The Book Farm, 1943.

Bates, David Homer. *Lincoln in the Telegraph Office.* New York: Century, 1907.

Becker, Carl M., and Ritchie Thomas. *Hearth and Knapsack: The Ladley Letters, 1857–1880.* Athens: Ohio University Press, 1988.

Boyd, Andrew. *Boyd's Washington and Georgetown Directory.* Washington D.C.: Hudson Taylor, 1864.

Burrows, J. Lansing, ed. *American Baptist Register for 1852.* Philadelphia: American Baptist Publication Society, 1853.

Cauchon, Barry, and John Elliott. *A Peek Inside the Walls: The Final Days of the Lincoln Conspirators. 13 Days Aboard the Monitors: The Early Incarceration of the Conspirators, the Mug Shot Photo Sessions and the Truth about the Hoods.* Surratt Society Conference, 2012.

Chamlee, Roy Z. *Lincoln's Assassins: A Complete Account of Their Capture, Trial and Punishment.* Jefferson, N. C.: McFarland, 1990.

Chappelear, B. Curtis, Esq. *Maps and Notes Pertaining to the Upper Section of Fauquier County, Virginia.* Warrenton, Va.: Warrenton Antiquarian Society, Publishers, 1954.

Clarke, Asia Booth. *The Unlocked Book: A Memoir of John Wilkes Booth by His Sister, Asia Booth Clarke.* New York: G. P. Putnam's Sons, 1938.

Conklin, Eileen F. *Exile to Sweet Dixie: The Story of Euphemia Goldsborough, Confederate Nurse and Smuggler.* Gettysburg, PA: Thomas Publications, 1999.

Davis, Michael. *The Image of Lincoln in the South.* Knoxville: University of Tennessee Press, 1971.

Doster, William E. *Lincoln and Episodes of the Civil War.* New York: G. P. Putnam's Sons, Knickerbocker Press, 1914.

Douglas, Henry Kyd. *I Rode with Stonewall.* Chapel Hill: University of North Carolina University Press, 1940.

Edwards, William C., and Edward Steers. *The Lincoln Assassination: The Evidence.* Urbana: University of Illinois Press, 2009.

Fanning's Illustrated Gazetteer of the United States. New York: Phelps, Fanning and Company, 1853.

Flack, Annice, and Shyrl Littleton. *Powell Family Genealogy.* Privately published. Glenn, William Wilkins. *Between North and South: A Journalist Views The Civil War.* Edited by Bayly Ellen Marks and Mark Norton Schatz. Cranbury, N. J.: Fairleigh Dickinson University Press, 1976.

Hanchett, William. *The Lincoln Murder Conspiracies.* Urbana: University of Illinois Press, 1983.

Janvier, Meredith. *Baltimore in the Eighties and Nineties.* Baltimore: H.G. Roebuck and Son, 1933.

Jones, John B. *A Rebel War Clerk's Diary.* Philadelphia: J. B. Lippincott, 1866. Vol. 1 and 2.

Judiciary House Committee, House of Representatives: The Impeachment Committee Investigation—President Andrew Johnson. Washington, D.C.: Government Printing Office, 1867. Vol. 1 and 2.

Kunhardt, Dorothy Meserve and Philip B. *Twenty Days.* New York: Harper and Row, 1965.

Lattimer, Dr. John K. *Kennedy and Lincoln: Medical and Ballistic Comparisons.* New York: Harcourt Brace Jovanovich, 1980.

Munson, John W. *Reminiscences of a Mosby Guerrilla.* New York: Moffat, Yard, 1906. Oldroyd, Osborn H. *The Assassination of Abraham Lincoln.* Washington, D.C., privately printed, 1901.

Olszewski, George J. *The Restoration of Ford's Theatre.* Washington, D.C.: National Park Service Publication, 1963.

Peterson, T. B., and Brothers. *The Trial of the Assassins and Conspirators for the Murder of President Lincoln.* Philadelphia, 1865.

Petz, Weldon. *In the Presence of Abraham Lincoln.* Harrogate, Tenn.: Lincoln Memorial University Press, 1973.

Pitman, Benn. *The Assassination of President Lincoln and the Trial of the Conspirators.* Cincinnati: Moore, Wilstach and Baldwin, 1865.

Poore, Ben Perly. *The Conspiracy Trial for the Murder of the President.* Boston: J. E. Tildon and Company, 1866. Vol. 1–3.

Roscoe, Theodore. *The Web of Conspiracy.* Englewood Cliffs, N. J.: Prentice Hall, 1959.

Shelton, Vaughn. *Mask for Treason.* Harrisburg, Pa.: Stackpole Books, 1965.

Shepherd, Henry Elliot. *Narrative of Prison Life in*

Baltimore and Johnson's Island, Ohio. Baltimore, MD: Commercial Printing and Stationary Company, 1917.

Smith, H. B. *Between the Lines: Secret Service Stories Told Fifty Years Afterwards.* New York: Booze Brothers, 1911.

Surratt Trial. Washington, D.C.: Government Printing Office, 1867. Vol. 1 and 2. Tidwell, William A., James 0. Hall and David Winfred Gaddy. *Come Retribution.* Jackson: University of Mississippi Press, 1988.

Thoron, Ward, ed. *The Letters of Mrs. Henry Adams 1865–1883.* Boston: Little, Brown and Company, 1936.

Townsend, G. A. (GATH). *The Life, Crime and Capture of John Wilkes Booth.* New York: Dick and Fitzgerald, 1865.

Trial of the Assassins and Conspirators for the Murder of Abraham Lincoln. Philadelphia: Barclay and Company, 1865. Reissued by James L. Barbour, Port Tobacco, Md., 1981.

Turner, Thomas Reed. *Beware the People Weeping: Public Opinion and the Assassination of Abraham Lincoln.* Baton Rouge: Louisiana State University Press, 1982. Weichmann, Louis J. *A True History of the Assassination and of the Conspiracy of 1865.* Edited by Floyd A. Risvold. New York: Alfred A. Knopf, 1975.

Whiteman, Maxwell. *While Lincoln Lay Dying.* Philadelphia: Union League of Philadelphia Press, 1968.

Woods, John W. *1865 Woods Baltimore City Directory.* Baltimore, MD, 1865.

Manuscripts and Records

Amy Gillette Bassett Papers, Manuscript Room, Library of Congress.

David Rankin Barbee Papers, Georgetown University, Georgetown, District of Columbia.

Department of Vital Statistics, Brooklyn, New York.

Department of Vital Statistics, State of Maryland.

Eighth Army Corps Papers, RG 93, Register 125, National Archives.

Fold3.com, Lincoln Assassination Papers, http://www.fold3.com.

Fold3.com, Provost Marshal's Records, LAS File, http://www.fold3.com.

General Ethan Allan Hitchcock Papers, Manuscript Room, Library of Congress. General Services Administration, National Archives, Confederate Army Records, Company Muster Rolls, Florida.

General William Henry Payne Letterbooks, 1894. In possession of the family of Eppa Hunton, V.

The Hartranft Letterbooks Logs kept pertaining to imprisonment of the conspirators at the Old Arsenal—April through July 1865, John F. Hartranft Papers, Collection of Gettysburg College, Gettysburg, Pa.

Houston Letter Collection, Leyburn Library, Washington and Lee University.

Investigation and Trial Papers Relating to the Assassination of President Lincoln (LAS File), Microcopy 599, National Archives, Washington, D.C.

Lincoln Obsequies Files, Rare Book Room, Library of Congress, Washington, D.C. Marriage Licenses, 1865–1869, Record of Marriage of Charles Barnett and Margaret Branson, Baltimore City, December 17, 1867, Maryland Hall of Records, Annapolis, Md.

Papers Relating to Suspects in the Lincoln Assassination, Records of the Provost Marshall's Office, Record Group 110, National Archives.

Prints and Photographs, Map Division, Library of Congress.

Raymond, Col. Julian. *History of Fort Leslie J. McNair.* Unpublished manuscript, Washington, D.C., 1901.

Records of County Clerk, Talbot County Courthouse, Talbot County, Ga., Marriage Book "A."

Reports of Cases Argued and Determined in the Court of Appeals of Maryland, Vol XXXI, Containing Cases in April and October Terms 1869. Baltimore: John Murphy and Company, 1870.

Rock Creek Cemetery, Interment Book, 1822–1893, Listing # 1737–1740.

U.S. Census of 1850, Stewart County, Ga., House # 193.

Newspapers and Periodicals

Albany Evening Journal, "The Conspiracy Trial." June 6, 1865.

_____, "A Visit to the Prisoners: Preparations for the Executions." July 7, 1865.

_____, "The Last Moments on the Scaffold." July 8, 1865.

American Heritage, "I Have Supped Full on Horrors: The Diary of Fanny Seward," by Patricia Carley Johnson. October 1959.

Baltimore Clipper, "Trial of the Conspirators: The Mystery of Payne." June 5, 1865.

Baltimore Sun, "Local Matters: The Weather." February 13, 1865.

_____, "Local Matters: Arrested as a Spy." March 15, 1865.

_____, "Death of Miss Seward," October 31, 1866.

Blue and Gray Magazine, special issue, "Assassination," by Michael W. Kauffman. April 1990.

_____, special issue, "Assassin on the Run: John Wilkes Booth's Escape Route," by Michael W. Kauffman. June 1990.

Boston Daily Advertiser, "The Trial of the Conspirators: Proof Against the Prisoners." May 31, 1865.

_____, "The Assassins Convicted." July 7, 1865.

_____, "The Assassins Executed." July 8, 1865.

Boston Daily Globe, "Drummer at Mrs. Surratt's Hanging." February 18, 1911.

Boston Herald, "A Tragedy Recalled." March 27, 1883.

Boston Post, "The Execution." July 8, 1865.
Boston Sunday Herald, "Payne the Mysterious." June 11, 1865.
Civil War Times Illustrated, special issue, "The Guerrilla War." October 1974.
_____, "In One Deadly Encounter," by Jeffry D. Wirt. November 1980.
Columbus Journal, "A Brave Fight for Life." December 31, 1902.
_____, "A Soldier's Christmas." January 28, 1903.
Critical Record, "Remains of the Conspirators." December 29, 1884.
Daily Courier, "The Conspiracy Trial." May 20, 1865.
Daily Evening Telegraph, "The Bodies of the Conspirators Disinterred." October 4, 1867.
Deseret Weekly, "Booth's Detective Friend." July 2, 1898.
Evening Express, "Who is Payne? The Mystery Still Unsolved." June 10, 1865.
Florida Historical Quarterly, "Lewis Payne: Pawn of John Wilkes Booth," by Leon Pryor. June 1965.
Lincoln Herald, "A Remarkable Lecture: John H. Surratt Tells His Story." December 1949.
_____, "Fort Leslie McNair and the Lincoln Conspirators," by Michael W. Kauffman. Winter issue, 1978.
Louisville Union Press, "The Career of an Assassin: Payne Described by One Who Knows Him." May 11, 1865.
Macon Telegraph, "Payne's Skeleton Exhumed." December 20, 1884.
Massachusetts Spy, "Execution of the Conspirators: How the Conspirators Received Their Sentence." July 14, 1865.
McCall's Magazine, "The Fate of the Lincoln Conspirators," by John A. Gray. 1911. *National Republican,* "In Ancient Graves: Strange Discoveries at Holmead Cemetery." September 25, 1884.
Morning World Herald, "August Lockner, 73, Pioneer of Nebraska" (Obituary). January 30, 1920.
National Daily Republican, "The Trial." May 15, 1865.
_____, "The Conspiracy Trial—Third Edition, Proceedings This Evening." June 6, 1865.
_____, "The Execution." July 8, 1865.
_____, "The Remains of Payne." February 23, 1870.
New Plain Dealer, "A Curious Bit of News." March 30, 1883.
New York Herald, "The Assassins." April 19, 1865.
New York Herald Tribune, "The Assassination." May 19, 1865.
New York Press, "Hangman of President Lincoln's Assassins Tells His Story." September 4, 1898.
New York Times. May 17, 1865.
_____, "The Trial of the Assassins. May 20, 1865.
_____, "The Trial of the Assassins: Evidence Touching on the Insanity of Payne." June 3, 1865.
_____, "Seward at 82 Talks of April 14, 1865." July 8, 1912.
New York Tribune, "How the Game Was Bagged." April 19, 1865.

New York World, "Portraits of the Accused," by George Alfred Townsend (GATH). May 26, 1865.
_____, "The Trial on Wednesday." May 31, 1865.
_____, "The Last Days of Payne." Daniel Gillette, April 3, 1892.
Newport Mercury, "Payne and Seward." December 28, 1872.
North American Review, "The Trial of Mrs. Surratt," by J. W. Clampitt. September 1880.
Philadelphia Inquirer, "The Plot: Counsel of the Assassins." May 3, 1865. *Philadelphia Press,* "Attempted Suicide of Payne." April 26, 1865.
_____, "The Solemn Procession." July 8, 1865.
Philadelphia Weekly Times, "Lewis Powell's Exploits: Reminiscences of the Remarkable Youth Who Stabbed Secretary Seward...," by Lewis Edmonds Payne. June 3, 1882.
Portsmouth Journal of Literature and Politics, "Sketch of the Convicts." July 15, 1865.
Richmond Times Dispatch, "They Knew Payne." December 11, 1902.
Roanoke Evening News, "About John Wilkes Booth," by John Peddicord. June 6, 1903. *Saundersville Herald,* "Lewis Payne: Seward's Would-Be Assassin." February 24, 1887. *Surratt Society News,* "The Confederate Plan to Abduct President Lincoln," by John C. Brennan. March 1981.
St. Paul Daily Globe, "Capturing Lincoln's Assassins." July 14, 1881.
Saline County Journal, "The Assassination." July 14, 1881.
Saundersville Herald, "Lewis Payne—Seward's Would-Be Assassin." February 24, 1887.
Washington Constitutional Union. July 10, 1865.
Washington Daily Morning Chronicle, "Judgement: The Assassins and Their Doom." July 8, 1865.
_____, "Interesting Facts About the Late Assassins: Sixteen Hours in the Cells." July 10, 1865.
Washington Evening Star, "The Execution." July 7, 1865.
_____, "The Conspirators: Powell's Farewell to His Counsel." July 10, 1865.
Washington Morning Chronicle, "Judgement," July 8, 1865.
Washington Star, "Classified Section." November 30, December 7, and December 27, 1864.
_____, "Appearance of the Prisoners Payne and Atzerodt." May 15, 1865.
_____, May 20, 1865.
_____, "The Conspiracy Trials: Argument of Mr. Doster. June 22, 1865.
_____, "The Conspirators: Last Days of the Doomed." July 10, 1865.
_____, "Booth's Conspiracy: The Desperado of the Party, Lewis T. Powell Alias Payne." December 3, 1887.
Weekly Rocky Mountain News, "Payne the Assassin—a Strange Character." August 9, 1865.

Index

abduction plans 3, 25, 26, 31, 33, 34, 38, 44, 45, 46, 47, 48, 49, 50, 52, 53, 54, 56, 60, 86, 107, 113, 114, 115, 135, 141, 142, 145, 163, 176, 194, 200, 204
abolitionism 10, 60, 149, 155
Alexander, Sam (member, 43rd Battalion, Co. B) 24
Alexandria, Virginia 28, 49, 89, 130, 136, 145, 153, 197
Anderson, Gen. R.H. 14
Andersonville, Georgia 124, 149, 188
Antietam, Battle of 150
Apopka, Florida 10
Army Medical Museum 126, 189, 199
Army of Northern Virginia 14
Army of the Potomac 14
Army of the Shenandoah 24
Arnold, Samuel Bland 25, 44, 45, 47, 48, 49, 50, 51, 58, 82, 86, 88, 93, 112, 139, 195, 197, 202
Arsenal Penitentiary 79, 86, 87, 88, 89, 90, 91, 105, 114, 115, 118, 124, 126, 139, 162, 182, 187, 188, 197, 203
Ashby, Gen. Turner 131, 133
Atzerodt, Andrew 45
Atzerodt, George A. 25, 45, 47, 49, 50, 51, 54, 57, 58, 60, 61, 62, 63, 82, 98, 100, 105, 111, 112, 115, 116, 121, 125, 139, 142, 173, 184, 187, 188, 198, 201, 204
Atzerodt, John 95
Augur, Christopher C. 65, 74, 77, 80, 81

Baker, Lafayette C. 73, 80, 85, 118, 151
Baltimore, Maryland 1, 14, 15, 16, 17, 18, 19, 21, 25, 26, 30, 31, 32, 33, 34, 35, 36, 38, 39, 40, 41, 42, 43, 44, 51, 52, 60, 61, 69, 70, 80, 84, 86, 90, 93, 95, 102, 106, 107, 110, 112, 113, 114, 116, 124, 125, 130, 132, 135, 136, 145, 151, 153, 154, 155, 163, 167, 168, 169, 170, 171, 172, 173, 174, 178, 179, 180, 182, 188, 194, 197, 200, 201, 202, 203
Barnes, Surgeon Gen. J.K. 110, 138

Barnett, Charles E. 107, 178, 179, 180, 182, 197, 199, 203
Barnum Hotel 44, 155, 156
Bassett, Amy Gillette 193, 203
Bates, David Homer 56, 194, 195, 197, 202
Bell, William H. 62, 63, 64, 65, 70, 73, 80, 81, 82, 84, 102, 138, 196, 197, 200
Belleville, Florida 6, 10
Benjamin, Judah P. 58
Beulah Baptist Church 7
Bingham, John H. 39, 92, 93, 107, 112, 176
Bishop, Jim 64, 93
Blackwell, Joe (member, 43rd Battalion) 40
Blair, E.W. 30, 32
Blazer, Capt. Richard "Dick" 24, 25, 131
Boiseau, R.F. 119, 186
Bond, Samuel S. 17, 170, 194, 201
Booth, Asia 33, 194, 202
Booth, Edwin 33
Booth, John Wilkes 3, 12, 23, 25, 26, 29, 32, 33, 37, 38, 40, 44, 45, 46, 47, 48, 49, 50, 51, 52, 53, 55, 56, 57, 58, 60, 61, 62, 63, 68, 69, 73, 74, 85, 86, 87, 90, 97, 100, 101, 102, 109, 111, 114, 116, 124, 126, 129, 135, 136, 137, 138, 141, 142, 155, 156, 157, 176, 183, 184, 188, 189, 192, 193, 194, 197, 198, 199, 200, 201, 202, 203, 204
Booth, Junius Brutus 188
Bowie, Lily see Meredith, Bettie
Branson, Joseph 26, 30, 31, 95, 107, 168, 179, 201
Branson, Margaret L. 14, 15, 18, 32, 34, 39, 40, 42, 95, 96, 107, 116, 168, 169, 170, 171, 173, 175, 176, 178, 179, 182, 196, 197, 199, 203
Branson, Mrs. Mary A. 30, 31, 38, 39, 95, 107, 153, 154, 175, 176, 179, 168, 182
Branson, Mary E. 18, 20, 21, 26, 30, 31, 32, 34, 37, 38, 39, 40, 42, 41, 51, 52, 69, 78, 95, 96, 116, 125, 168, 169, 171, 172, 173, 174, 175, 176, 178, 179, 180, 182, 193, 194, 195, 201

Branson Boarding House (Branson family) 14, 15, 17, 18, 20, 21, 26, 30, 31, 32, 34, 37, 38, 39, 40, 51, 52, 54, 57, 69, 78, 93, 95, 96, 113, 116, 125, 145, 167, 168, 169, 170, 171, 172, 173, 174, 175, 176, 178, 179, 180, 182, 188, 193, 194, 195, 196, 197, 198, 199, 200, 201, 203
Breckenridge, J.C. 13
Brooklyn, New York 107, 178, 179, 180, 188, 201, 203
Brown, John 10, 33
Bryant, G.W. 6
Burnette, Col. H.L. 16, 92, 93, 95

Camp Barry 80
Camp Chase 168
Campbell, Helen Jones 198
Campbell, Mason 93, 95
Campbell Hospital 48, 50
Canterbury Music Hall 61
Carauran, A.H. 186
Cartter, David 70
Chancellorsville, Battle of 12, 129, 150
Chapman, Elizabeth Barnett 182
Charles Town, Virginia 33
Chester, Samuel Knapp 38
Clampitt, J.W. 69, 70, 196, 204
Clay, Clement C. 52, 53
Cloughley, Alford 70
Coleman, Margaret 58
College Park, Georgia 4
Confederate Cabinet 52
Confederate Secret Service 26, 32, 33, 46
Congressional Cemetery 71, 201
Congressional Medal of Honor 69, 109
Coolidge, Mrs. 25
copperheads 52
Corbett, Boston 85
Corder, Elias 133, 134, 200
Cornwall, John 133
Cox, Chappel 4
Cox, Ichabod 4
Cox College 4
Coxe, John H. 26, 135
Coxhall, William 115
Croffuth, W.A. 186
Croggon, James 186

Culpeper, Virginia 144
Custer, George Armstrong 21

Dana, Charles 83
Davenport, E.L. 50
Davis, Jefferson 101, 104, 105, 145, 146, 147, 153
Dean, Apollonia 47
DeVoe, Ely 74, 77, 197
Dodd, Col. L.A. 89
Doster, William E. 4, 6, 11, 14, 26, 27, 28, 32, 39, 95, 96, 100, 101, 103, 105, 106, 107, 108, 110, 111, 112, 116, 117, 122, 123, 138, 139, 147, 167, 176, 193, 194, 197, 198, 202, 204
Douglas, Maj. Henry Kyd 109, 110, 198, 202
Druid Hill Cemetery 201
Duffield's Depot, Virginia 134, 136, 200
Dukehart, Mary Ann 168
Dukehart, Thomas 31

Early, Jubal W. 25
Eckert, Maj. Thomas T. 15, 56, 58, 60, 83, 86, 90, 91, 111, 113, 114, 115, 123, 165, 197
Egerton, Mrs. Adelaide DuBois 14, 168, 178
Egerton, John P. 31
Elmira, New York 168, 197

Fairfax Court House 21, 28, 131
Fauquier County, Virginia 20, 21, 22, 26, 40, 76, 132, 133, 136, 139, 140, 141, 153, 194, 200, 202
"Ferguson" (alias) 30, 173
Ferguson, Syd (member, 43rd Battalion, Company B) 24, 131
First Baptist Church of Washington DC 3, 6, 114, 118, 193
Fitzpatrick, Honora 47, 56, 74, 113
Florida Hospital, Richmond, VA 12
Ford's Theatre 63, 137, 195, 202
Fort Bunker Hill 71
Fort Early Baptist Church 7
Fort McHenry 168
Fort Sumter 60
Fortress Monroe 44, 146
Foster, Col. John A. 34, 71, 92, 194
Fourth Florida Infantry 10, 12
Frayser's Farm, Battle of 12
Frederick, Lt. Col. G.W. 89
Frederick County, Maryland 30
Fredericksburg, Battle of 12
Frier, Joshua Hoyet 8, 9, 193
Front Royal, Virginia 21, 131
Fuller, Dr. Richard 93, 114, 163, 174

Gaines Mill, Battle of 12
Gardiner, Mary E. 196

Gardner, Alexander 38, 126, 83, 167
Gardner, Mary J. 61, 62, 71, 93
Gardner, Gen. W.M. 196
Gardner Sisters 61, 62, 71
Garrett, Richard 85
GATH *see* Townsend, George Alfred
Gautier's Restaurant 47
Gawler, Joseph 126, 189, 191
Geishinger, Lt. G.W. 89
Geneva, Florida 124
Gettysburg, Battle of 14, 15, 16, 17, 18, 19, 90, 107, 110, 122, 124, 129, 130, 150, 153, 168, 169, 170, 171, 197, 199, 200, 201, 202, 203
Gillette, Dr. Abram Dunn 1, 3, 6, 25, 26, 31, 58, 70, 71, 93, 114, 115, 117, 118, 119, 120, 121, 122, 161, 162, 163, 164, 165, 168, 174, 193, 196, 199
Gillette, Daniel 161, 166, 194, 199, 204
Gilmore, Harry S. 20, 21, 200
Gleason, Capt. D.H.E. 74
Glenwood Cemetery 188, 189, 201
Gobright, L.A. 186
Goldsborough, Maj. W.W. 25
Goldsborough, Euphemia "Effie" 194, 201, 202
Gordon, Gen. John Brown 4, 5, 20, 70, 101, 144, 199
Gordon, Melinda 4
Gordon, the Rev. Zachariah 4
Graceland Cemetery 125, 189
Grant, John 28, 107, 132, 143
Grant, Lucy Ann 27, 28, 107, 132, 143, 153
Grant, Gen. Ulysses S. 33, 60, 62
Green Hill, Georgia 7
Green Hill Farm 7
Green Mount Cemetery 170, 188
Green-Wood Cemetery 107, 179, 201
Grover, Sergeant 118

Hagerstown, Maryland 19
Hale, Sen. John P. 38
Hale, Lizzie 38
Hale, Lucy 38
Hall, Dr. James C. 110, 138
Halleck, Maj. Gen. Henry H. 140
Hamilton, Blues 10, 128
Hamilton County, Florida 6, 10, 11, 127
Hancock, Maj. Gen. W.S. 89, 112, 162
Hansell, Emerick 68, 138, 200
Hardee, William J. 3
Hartranft, Gen. John F. 89, 91, 92, 93, 100, 102, 108, 109, 110, 112, 113, 115, 116, 117, 118, 119, 121, 162, 191, 197, 198, 199, 203
Haslett, F.B. 115, 118
Heim, Charles G. 30, 32, 34

Heim, Mrs. Charles G. 32
Heim, Jacob B. 32
Henry Ward Children's Aid Society 179
Herndon House 54, 55, 56, 57, 60, 61, 63, 99, 102, 113, 116, 136, 200
Herold, David E. 45, 46, 47, 49, 51, 58, 60, 61, 62, 63, 68, 85, 86, 90, 98, 112, 115, 116, 117, 118, 121, 125, 139, 187, 188, 195, 200
Hill, Gen. A.P. 14, 150, 151
Hitchcock, Gen. Ethan Allen 111, 123, 198, 199, 203
Holmead Cemetery 125, 126, 189, 191, 199, 204
Holohan, Eliza 44
Holohan, John T. 74
Holt, Joseph 92, 93
Hooe, Robert H. 194, 200
Hooper, Sarah Ann 7
Houston, Thomas P. 170, 171, 203
Hubbard, John B. 108, 198
Hunter, Gen. David 21, 92, 131
Hutchins, Lt. Col. 25

Jackson, Gen. Thomas E. "Stonewall" 109, 129, 150, 151
Jacksonville, Florida 10, 12, 122, 123, 124, 129, 134, 147
Jasper Blues 10, 127
Jenkins, Olivia 56, 74
Jenkins, Zadock 57
Johnson, Pres. Andrew 62, 63, 73, 89, 91, 92, 112, 113, 115, 139, 147, 202
Johnson, Brig. Gen. Bradley T. 1, 25, 140, 194
Johnson's Island 14, 168, 170, 171, 194, 203
Jones, Virgil Carrington 24
Jones County, Georgia 4, 5
Judge Advocate General 16, 28, 39, 64, 84, 92, 93, 95, 107, 112, 142

Kaighn, Margaret 38, 39, 175, 195
Keene, Laura 60
Keith, Isham 27, 132, 142, 143
"Kincheloe" (alias) 55, 61, 173

Ladley, Oscar E. 39, 175, 195, 197, 201, 202
Lafayette Square 58, 59, 62, 63, 70
Lake City, Florida 123
Lake Jessup, Florida 124
Lakeland, Florida 12
Lee, Dan Murray 111
Libby Prison, Richmond, Virginia 25
Liberty Baptist Church 5
Lichau House 61, 62
Lincoln, Abraham 1, 3, 87, 135; abduction plot 3, 25, 33, 45, 45, 47, 48, 50, 51, 145, 163, 189;

assassination of 56, 60, 63, 74, 79, 86, 92, 133, 136, 137, 144, 151, 162, 166, 167, 183, 193; cabinet 62; enemies 31, policies 141, 153, 155; second inauguration 37, 38, 192; speeches 3, 58
Lincoln Memorial University, Harrogate, Tennessee 55
Live Oak Station, Florida 10, 106, 111, 122, 123, 124, 147, 148, 164
Lloyd, John M. 45
Lockner, Augustus 28, 143, 144, 145, 200, 204
"Longfellow" (alias) 31, 173
Longstreet's Corps 19

Maddox, Cab (member, 43rd Battalion, Company B) 24, 131
Maryland Court of Appeals 178
McCall, Lt. Col. W.H. 89, 108
McCrea, Henrietta 170
Meredith, Bettie D. 22, 23, 28, 116, 133, 135, 136, 141, 142, 144, 194, 200
Metropolitan Music Hall 61
Metropolitan Police Force 74
Miller's Hotel 30, 34, 171, 172, 173, 200
Mitchell, Samuel A. 10, 18
Moffit, Daniel (member, 43rd Battalion, Company B) 40
Monroe, Frank 84
Monroe, Sgt. Seaton 126, 194
Montauk 82, 84, 85, 126, 166, 194
Montgomery, Richard 52, 53, 85, 195, 197
Montreal, Canada 32, 45, 53, 58
Morgan, R.C. 74, 75, 76, 95, 196, 197
"Mosby" (alias) 47
Mosby, Col. John Singleton 1, 19, 20, 21, 22, 23, 24, 25, 28, 30, 40, 46, 47, 49, 52, 55, 86, 126, 129, 130, 131, 133, 140, 142, 143, 144, 145, 166, 171, 173, 194, 199, 200, 202
Mudd, Dr. Samuel A. 33, 49, 86, 88, 139
Munson, John W. (member, 43rd Battalion, Company B) 21, 194, 202
Murfreesboro, Tennessee 12, 13, 123, 150, 199
Murray, Martha 54, 56, 61, 102, 195, 196
Murray, Patrick 54

Nelson, Robert 70, 138, 196
Nelson, Jr. (slave) 6
Nelson, Sr. (slave) 6
Newman, James O. 6, 128
Newman, Mary Ann Caroline Powell 128
Nicholes, Dr. Charles H. 108
Noakesville, Virginia 136

Norfolk, Virginia 4, 26, 135
Norris, Dr. Basil 110, 138
Nutt, Capt. Adam C. 123, 124

Oath of Allegiance 3, 14, 20, 24, 28, 39, 41, 42, 43, 76, 77, 79, 136, 142, 145, 153, 166, 176
O'Laughlen, Michael 25, 44, 45, 47, 51, 58, 82, 139
Olcott, Col. H.S. 74, 76
Old Capitol Prison 88, 107, 176
Old St Paul's Cemetery 178, 179, 180, 182
Orange County, Florida 124
Orlean, Virginia 40, 112, 132, 201

"Paine" (alias) 3, 20, 24, 25, 29, 39, 40, 42, 43, 44, 46, 47, 51, 52, 54, 76, 77, 81, 85, 95, 98, 101, 102, 104, 111, 114, 119, 142, 166, 167, 173, 187, 189, 192, 197
Palmer, W. Ben (member, 43rd Battalion, Company B) 25, 145
Paris, Virginia 22, 23, 133
Parr, David Preston 1, 33, 34, 36, 37, 42, 194, 195
Partisan Ranger Act 19
Payne, Dr. Albin S. 21, 22, 107, 129, 166
Payne, John Scott 19, 129, 199
Payne, Lewis Edmonds 1, 21, 24, 116, 126, 129, 166, 204
Payne, Naomi 22
Payne, Gen. William H. 140, 143, 144, 145, 173, 194, 199, 200
Peddicord, Sgt. John 84, 85, 197, 204
Pennsylvania College 14, 150
Pensacola, Florida 123
Petersburg, Virginia 13, 199
Philadelphia, Pennsylvania 39, 41, 42, 85
Pickett, Gen. George E. 14
Pope, M.P. 60, 196
Port Tobacco, Maryland 45, 47
Porter, George L., M.D. 89, 90, 110, 138
Powell, Angeline "Annie" 6, 8, 9, 128
Powell, Ann 128
Powell, Benjamin F. 7, 128
Powell, the Rev. George Cader 4, 5, 6, 7, 8, 9, 10, 11, 49, 106, 111, 116, 122, 123, 124, 130, 144, 147, 148, 149, 162, 164, 175, 198, 199
Powell, George W. 13, 123, 125, 193, 199
Powell, John 4
Powell, Lewis Thornton: abduction plot 3, 25, 26, 31, 33, 34, 38, 44, 45, 46, 47, 48, 49, 50, 52, 53, 54, 56, 60, 86, 107, 113, 114, 115, 135, 141, 142, 145, 163, 176, 194, 200, 204; adolescence 5, 6, 7, 8, 9, 10, 11, 12; aliases 3, 29, 30, 31, 40, 55, 61, 73, 173; alleged suicide attempt 85, 86, 90, 108, 197, 204; Anna Surratt and 35, 36, 144; army life 10, 11, 12, 13, 14, 15, 16, 17, 18, 19, 20, 21, 22, 23, 24, 25, 26, 27, 28, 29, 114, 129, 130, 131, 132, 133, 134, 135, 136, 137, 138, 139, 140, 162, 163; arrests 38, 39, 40, 41, 42, 43, 74, 75, 80, 102, 106; assaults by 38, 39, 40, 41, 42, 65, 66, 67, 68, 69, 70; assisted father on farm and in blacksmith shop 10; battles participated in 12, 13, 14; Bettie D. Meredith and 23, 28, 116, 141, 144, 194, 206; birth 4, 5; burial 124, 125, 179, 188, 189, 190, 191; Capt. Christian Rath and 108, 109, 112, 114, 119, 121; Capt. Richard "Dick" Blazer, assists in capture 24, 25, 131; capture at Gettysburg 14, 15; characteristics 6, 7, 8, 9, 12, 17, 22, 23, 26, 27, 30, 31, 38, 44, 54, 70, 71, 78, 84, 85, 93, 98, 99, 100, 101, 104, 106, 108, 109, 113, 114, 115, 118, 124, 144, 145, 162, 163, 164, 165, 166, 173, 182, 183, 184, 185; childhood 4, 5, 6, 7, 8, 9, 10, 11; Col. John H. Mosby and 19, 20, 23, 24, 25, 40, 49, 52, 86, 129, 131, 133, 145, 199; Confederate Secret Service 25, 26, 30, 32, 46, 51, 60, 78, 163, 175; confessions 56, 114, 115, 141, 142, 147, 161, 165; confinement 81, 82, 83, 84, 85, 86, 87, 88, 89, 91, 93, 108, 109, 112; David Edgar Herold and 58, 60, 61, 62, 63, 68, 90, 91, 200; David Preston Parr and 1, 33, 34, 36, 37, 42; death 1, 3, 6, 25, 58, 100, 101, 113, 114, 116, 117, 118, 119, 121, 124, 125, 126; defense of by Doster 39, 40, 96, 105, 106, 111, 112, 147, 148, 149, 150, 151, 152, 153, 154, 155, 156, 157, 158, 159, 160, 161, 176; "Doc" or "Doctor" nickname of 7, 8, 14, 15, 171; Dr. Abram Dunn Gillette and 1, 3, 6, 25, 58, 70, 71, 93, 114, 115, 117, 118, 119, 121, 161, 162, 163, 164, 165, 166; Dr. Albin H. Payne and 21, 22, 107, 166; education 5, 6, 30, 105, 106, 124, 133, 147, 175; engaged to be married 167, 168, 169, 170, 171, 172, 173, 174, 175, 176, 177, 178, 179, 180, 181, 182; enlistment 10, 11, 128, 182; escape from Baltimore Wests Buildings Hospital 16, 17, 18, 19, 30, 171; family life 5, 6, 7, 123, 124; Gen. John F. Hartranft and 102, 108, 109, 110, 112, 113, 115, 116, 117, 191; George A. Atze-

rodt and 45, 49, 50, 54, 57, 58, 60, 61, 62, 116, 173; hospitalization while in service 12, 14, 15; identification as Seward assailant 64, 81, 82, 83, 95, 142; imprisonment 106, 119; insanity plea 107, 108, 110, 158; investigation 75, 76, 77, 78, 79, 80, 81, 82, 83, 84; John H. Surratt, Jr., and 1, 34, 36, 37, 44, 47, 50, 61, 75, 90, 114; John Wilkes Booth and 12, 25, 26, 44, 46, 47, 49, 50, 51, 52, 53, 55, 56, 57, 58, 60, 61, 62, 86, 90, 102, 114, 116, 135, 136, 137, 141, 142, 155, 156, 157, 176, 184, 192, 200; Louis Weichmann and 34, 35, 36, 43, 44, 46, 47, 49, 51, 52, 54, 55, 56, 57, 99; Margaret Branson and 14, 15, 16, 17, 18, 30, 32, 170, 171, 173, 175, 176, 178, 179, 182; Mary Branson and 18, 20, 21, 30, 31, 32, 38, 39, 40, 42, 51, 52, 69, 78, 96, 116, 125, 168, 169, 171, 173, 174, 175, 176, 178, 179, 182; Mary Surratt and 3, 6, 41, 43, 44, 46, 47, 50, 51, 54, 55, 56, 57, 63, 69, 70, 72, 74, 75, 76, 77, 79; medical problems while incarcerated 108, 146; military records 12, 13, 14, 21, 140, 141, 142, 193; *Montauk* 82, 84, 85, 126, 166, 194; Mosby's Rangers and 1, 20, 21, 23, 24, 25, 30, 40, 46, 47, 52, 55, 86, 130, 131, 133, 140, 142, 143, 144, 145, 166, 173; Mrs. Surratt, exoneration of 50, 113, 114, 115, 117, 118, 160, 161, 162, 163; "Paine," assumes name 28, 29, 140, 141, 142; parents 4, 5, 6, 7, 8, 9, 10, 11, 12, 122, 123, 124, 125; personality 6, 7, 8, 9, 12, 7, 22, 23, 26, 27, 30, 31, 38, 44, 54, 70, 71, 78, 84, 85, 93, 98, 99, 100, 101, 104, 106, 108, 109, 113, 114, 115, 118, 124, 144, 145, 162, 163, 164, 165, 166, 173, 182, 183, 184, 185; physical appearance 10, 19, 29, 59, 60, 73, 75, 80, 82, 97, 98, 99, 100, 101, 102, 104, 105, 106, 107, 109, 118, 119, 129; prison experiences 85, 86, 88, 92, 93, 105, 106, 108, 109, 136, 137; religious beliefs 7, 8, 9, 115, 148, 165, 174, 201; romantic relationships 15, 16, 17, 18, 22, 23, 28, 30, 31, 32, 39, 51, 52, 58, 69, 78, 96, 116, 134, 135, 136; sisters' reminiscences 7, 8; statements made by 26, 27, 28, 40, 70, 71, 76, 77, 79, 80, 83, 84, 85, 86, 90, 93, 105, 106, 108, 109, 111, 113, 114, 115; William E. Doster and 4, 6, 11, 14, 26, 27, 28, 32, 39, 95,

96, 100, 101, 103, 105, 106, 107, 108, 110, 111, 112, 116, 117, 122, 123, 138, 139, 167, 176; William H. Seward and household, assassination attempt 3, 25, 58, 59, 60, 62, 63, 64, 65, 66, 67, 68, 69, 70, 71, 72, 82, 83, 84, 85, 102; wounds 14, 17, 19, 129
Powell, Lydia 7, 128
Powell, Mary Ann Caroline 6
Powell, Mary Polly Cox 4
Powell, Minerva 124
Powell, Oliver H. 7, 10, 12, 13, 128, 199
Powell, Patience Caroline 4, 5, 6, 7, 9, 11, 12, 70, 79, 110, 112, 114, 122, 123, 124, 137, 148, 149, 153, 182, 183
Powell, Richard 4
Powell, William 4
Powell, William L. (William Levy) 5
Pratt, John 134, 200
Prentiss, S.S. 23
Preston's Brigade 13
Price, Thomas 71, 102

Queen, Andrew Forest 60
Queen, Benjamin F. 60
Queen's Hotel 52

Randolph County, Alabama 5, 128
Rath, Capt. Christian 108, 109, 112, 114, 119, 121
Revere House 52, 176
Richards, Maj. A.C. 74
Richards, Capt. Adolphus (member, 43rd Battalion, Company B) 24
Richmond, Virginia 1, 12, 24, 25, 26, 30, 32, 33, 44, 58, 60, 90, 124, 130, 135, 145, 148, 150, 153, 156, 163, 204
Richmond Grays 33
Richter, Hartman 82
Roberts, John F. 108
Robinson, Sgt. George F. 59, 65, 66, 67, 68, 69, 82, 102, 138, 170, 196
Rock Creek Cemetery 126, 189, 190, 191, 203
Rosch, C.H. 74, 77, 78, 80, 102
Roscoe, Theodore 78
Ross, Julia 61
Rushin, Polly 4
Rushin, William 4
Russell County, Alabama 5

St. Albans Raid, St. Albans, Vermont 97, 197
St. Barnabas Episcopal Church 93, 95, 113, 174, 178, 179, 198
Salem, Virginia 71, 132
Sampson, Thomas 74, 76, 77, 79, 80, 81

Saugus 82, 83, 84, 182
Secession of Florida 10, 11
Second Florida Infantry 10, 14, 19, 109, 128, 148
Seven Pines, Battle of 12
Seventh Baptist Church 93, 174
Seward, Augustus 68, 82, 138, 197
Seward, Fanny 64, 66, 67, 82
Seward, Frederick 5, 64, 65, 66, 68, 138, 200
Seward, William Henry 3, 26, 56, 58, 59, 60, 62, 63, 64, 65, 66, 67, 69, 70, 73, 80, 82, 84, 90, 92, 102, 111, 114, 123, 126, 129, 137, 138, 144, 145, 147, 152, 154, 160, 162, 163, 166, 183, 196
Shepherd, Henry P. 202
Shipley, Tom Benton (member, 43rd Battalion, Company B) 21, 199
Shoupe, D.F. 115, 118
Shriver, C.S. 95
Shriver, Henry 40, 95
Sickles, Daniel 63
Smith, Maj. H.B. 17, 30, 31, 39, 40, 41, 42, 95, 106, 107, 168, 175, 176
Smith, Maj. H.W. 74, 75, 76, 80, 95, 133, 137, 200
Sowers, William H. (member, 43rd Battalion, Company B) 26, 135
Spangler, Edman 82, 112, 113, 139
Speed, James 91, 92, 131, 158
Stanton, Edwin M. 15, 31, 56, 73, 83, 85, 89, 92, 112, 113, 114, 116, 122, 123, 124, 136, 139, 165, 176, 188
Stewart, Judge H.J. 11
Stewart County, Georgia 127, 128, 147, 193, 203
Stone, Frederick 86
Stone River Campaign 12
Stryker, the Rev. August P. 93, 95, 113, 116, 118, 120, 174, 178, 186, 198, 199
Stuart, Captain 148
Stuart, Gen. J.E.B. 19
Surratt, Anna 35, 36, 45, 56, 74, 113, 144
Surratt, John, Jr. 1, 24, 25, 32, 33, 34, 35, 36, 37, 38, 42, 43, 44, 45, 46, 47, 50, 51, 52, 54, 56, 58, 61, 70, 74, 75, 76, 85, 90, 112, 114, 125, 184, 192
Surratt, Mary E. 34, 35, 36, 41, 43, 45, 46, 47, 50, 51, 54, 55, 56, 57, 63, 69, 72, 74, 75, 76, 77, 78, 79, 86, 88, 98, 104, 105, 109, 112, 113, 114, 115, 116, 117, 118, 119, 121, 133, 137, 138, 139, 141, 162, 163, 184, 187, 188, 192, 197, 198
Surratt Boarding House 30, 35, 41, 42, 44, 45, 47, 50, 57, 63, 70, 72, 74, 75, 78, 99, 138, 141, 144, 173, 176, 197

Index

Surrattsville, Maryland 33, 46, 49, 70
Swannee County, Florida 123
Swisshelm, Jane 101

Talbot County, Georgia 4, 193, 203
Tallahassee, Florida 10, 124, 147, 148
Tanner, Cpl. James 70
Tayloe, Ogle 62, 63
Taylor, G.F. 115, 118
TB, Maryland 49
Tenth Florida Infantry 10
Thomas, Joseph 174
Thompson, Lt. Edward (member, 43rd Battalion, Company B) 21, 22, 52, 131, 132
Thornton, Dr. Reuben 5, 9
Toffey, John J. 80, 105
Toronto, Canada 52
Townsend, George Alfred (GATH) 97, 98, 99, 162, 196, 198, 199, 203, 204
Towson, Maryland 180, 182
Tung, Willie (member, 43rd Battalion, Company B) 40
Twelfth Army Corps Field Hospital 14

Vanderpoel, Benjamin W. 61, 196
Van Doren Stern, Philip 64
Verdi, Dr. Tullio S., M.D. 59, 64, 82, 83, 138
Vogdes, Brig. Gen. I. 123, 124

Walker, Dr. Mary 109, 118
Walker, Capt. Robert S. (member, 43rd Battalion, Company B) 25, 145
Wallace, Gen. Lewis 92, 104, 191, 192, 198
Walter, Father Jacob Ambrose 113
Ward, Anna 54, 195
Ward, Annie (Branson servant) 38, 39, 95, 107, 175, 176
Warrenton, Virginia 19, 21, 22, 23, 26, 27, 40, 106, 107, 129, 130, 131, 132, 134, 140, 141, 142, 143, 194
Washington, Pres. George 70
Washington, D.C. 1, 3, 4, 17, 25, 29, 30, 31, 33, 34, 35, 37, 40, 42, 45, 53, 54, 55, 60, 61, 63, 69, 72, 73, 74, 81, 85, 89, 91, 92, 95, 96, 104, 109, 111, 114, 115, 116, 118, 122, 124, 125, 126, 130, 131, 133, 135, 136, 137, 138, 139, 140, 142, 146, 148, 151, 152, 157, 162, 163, 165, 167, 170, 171, 173, 176, 185, 193, 194
Waynesboro, Virginia 19
Weichmann, Louis J. 34, 35, 36, 38, 43, 44, 46, 47, 49, 51, 52, 54, 55, 56, 57, 74, 99, 113
Wells, Col. H.H. 52, 79, 83, 84, 102, 193
Wermerskirch, Capt. W.M. 74, 80
Wests Buildings Hospital, Baltimore, Maryland 15, 41, 110, 168
Wheeler, William E. 53
Wiget, Father Bernadin F. 113
Williams, Isabel Branson 31
Williams, Capt. William 183
Williamsburg, Virginia 12
Winchester, Virginia 21, 24, 131, 134, 153
Windsor, A.H. 24
Winter Garden Theater 26
Wirz, Henry 188
"Wood" (alias) 35, 36, 44, 47, 52, 58, 167, 173
Woodlawn Cemetery 182
Woolsey, Col. Charles 176
Worth County, Georgia 6, 7, 193

Yorktown, Virginia 12